D0842342

DATE LOANED

FEB. 2 8 1972			
MAY 19 '78			
DEC 2 '81			
DEC 19 '82			
MAY 1 7 2008			
GAYLORD 3563			PRINTED IN U.S.A.

EVOLUTIONARY PHILOSOPHIES
AND CONTEMPORARY THEOLOGY

EVOLUTIONARY PHILOSOPHIES AND CONTEMPORARY THEOLOGY

BY

Eric C. Rust

THE WESTMINSTER PRESS

PHILADELPHIA

ST. THOMAS SEMINARY LIBRARY
DENVER 10, COLO.

Copyright © MCMLXIX The Westminster Press

All rights reserved — no part of this book may be reproduced
in any form without permission in writing from the publisher,
except by a reviewer who wishes to quote brief passages
in connection with a review in magazine or newspaper.

STANDARD BOOK No. 644–20845–2

LIBRARY OF CONGRESS CATALOG CARD No. 69–10419

Published by The Westminster Press
Philadelphia, Pennsylvania

PRINTED IN THE UNITED STATES OF AMERICA

TO
THE DEAN AND FACULTY
OF THE
SCHOOL OF THEOLOGY
SOUTHERN BAPTIST THEOLOGICAL SEMINARY
κοινωνία τῆς παιδείας ἐν Χριστῷ

PREFACE

THE CURRENT revival of interest in Alfred North Whitehead and in process philosophy and the popularity of the evolutionary ideas of Pierre Teilhard de Chardin lie behind the writing of this book. In many ways we are now moving, in the Anglo-Saxon world, beyond the preoccupation with the critical investigation of and justification for, if any, metaphysical and theological language. Those of us who believe that such justification is possible need to take up again the issue of the nature of Christian philosophy.

The rehabilitation of Christian philosophy must take place within the consideration of the nature of philosophical thought in general. In the opening chapter I have endeavored to do this, emphasizing the significance of absolute presuppositions or faith principles in all rational processes. It is clear that, in this post-critical period, the insights of linguistic investigations must be taken account of. In particular, I have emphasized the place of analogues or models in metaphysical language. Furthermore, the contemporary secular atmosphere and the success of the scientific method require a realistic and empirical approach. I have endeavored to show that idealism is not to be discounted — the panpsychism of process philosophy is a reminder of this. Even so, our approach must take account of this world and its processes. Time and becoming have to be taken seriously. Human "existence," in the sense that the existentialist philosophers use this term, is tied up with our temporal and this-worldly structures. All such concerns and emphases must be taken into account by any Christian who is speaking to his contemporary world. In par-

ticular, the widespread acceptance of evolutionary development
and the concern with man's historical existence require that the
Christian faith come to terms with what is increasingly being
substantiated about man's historical origins and his place in the
process of nature. It is to this task that I have set myself.

This book seeks to examine the various process and evolutionary philosophies, Christian and non-Christian, from Hegel to
Hartshorne. It examines their insights critically in the light of the
prerequisites for Christian philosophizing which are set forth in
the opening chapter. The closing chapter seeks to incorporate
such insights into a Christian approach to the world process.

The author is indebted to many friends who have aided him in
the course of the preparation of this volume. Dean Penrose St.
Amant and Dr. Glenn Hinson of the faculty of theology of the
Southern Baptist Theological Seminary have read the manuscript
thoroughly and helped in the removal of some blemishes. For
what remains, I accept sole responsibility. Mrs. Glenn Hinson has
painstakenly typed the manuscript from my somewhat illegible
script. My teaching fellow, Manfred Grellert, B.D., has undertaken the preparation of the index. My appreciation for this ardu-
ous task is gladly recorded. My wife, as with my previous books,
has patiently borne with an absentee or else an absentminded
husband while the book has been in process. Her companionship
and sanity of judgment have kept me on course. The volume is
dedicated to my colleagues on the faculty of theology of Southern
Seminary, especially Dean St. Amant whose friendship means
much to me. Their Christian fellowship and encouragement have
meant much across the past fifteen years. This is a very inadequate acknowledgment of my indebtedness.

                                                        E. C. R.

Southern Baptist Theological Seminary

CONTENTS

Part Two: PROCESS IN CHRISTIAN PHILOSOPHIZING

Contents   11

I

The Problem of a Christian Philosophy

THE CHRISTIAN CHURCH is bearing its witness in a pluralistic age.
There is no one dominant philosophy to which it has specifically
to address itself. Rather, the dominant force is not any philosophy
but science itself. Yet the impact of science has influenced our
culture so profoundly that certain philosophical trends have been
spawned. On the one hand, the dehumanizing and depersonal-
izing aspects of contemporary secular society have been largely a
result of the tremendous success of modern science and technology. The latter have tended to minimize the individual and
the personal, to downgrade man's inner freedom, and in neurology
and certain forms of psychology — depth psychology and be-
haviorism, for instance — they have stormed the central citadel
of man's dignity and spiritual claims. In consequence we have
seen a rebellion against the various forms of tyranny of the external and an effort to affirm man's freedom and the place of human decision in secular depersonalized society. So there has
arisen existentialism — in Christian, theistic, and atheistic forms —

from Kierkegaard through Jaspers and Heidegger to Camus and Sartre. Here is one trend of which Christian thinking and witness have had to take account.

On the other hand, science has also produced "scientism," a brand of naturalism that regards scientific knowledge as the sole knowledge and that explains man's moral experience and spiritual claims in purely naturalistic terms. Its emphasis on the empirical as the only way of knowing has in the present century taken the form of logical positivism. Philosophical speculation is spurned and the thinker becomes preoccupied with language and its meaning. The position is already pre-opted by the commitment of such thinkers to a purely empirical verification of meaning. Any sentence is meaningful only when it can be tested, verified, even falsified, at the empirical level. Here, too, the Church has to take a stand, to analyze the significance of religious and theological language, to determine what basic meaning it is seeking to convey in sentences like " God is love," which in form appear to be as factual as statements made about observable objects.

More recently the later Wittgenstein switched gears sufficiently to put the challenge in a new form and to emphasize the " use " meaning of language. We may play many language games, but we must determine what function any particular language game is serving. It is not our purpose to look at this issue, for it has been dealt with competently in many books.[1] It is sufficient here to note that the whole movement has tended to put both metaphysics and theological speculation into some measure of disrepute. There are, however, signs that both are tending to reassert themselves in a postcritical form, seeking to base their discussion upon a reassessment of the nature of metaphysical language and thinking and upon the significance of theological statements.[2] We must note that this linguistic movement has exercised much more influence in the Anglo-Saxon world than on the Continent of Europe, where Heidegger and Pannenberg respectively are reminders that neither metaphysics nor theological thought is obliterated.

Now there is yet a third factor that Christian thinkers must take seriously, and this is the influence of evolutionary and process categories upon contemporary thinking. The revolution in biological thought brought about by Darwin has had wide repercussions. As evolution has become increasingly established as the regnant model of development at the biological level, thinkers have sought to take this category out of its original reference and employ it as a basic model for the understanding of the universe. Herbert Spencer marks the beginning of a line of thought that is still with us. Once the Christian Church had, somewhat belatedly, made its peace with " evolution " as a creative process, the category entered theological thought at the levels of Biblical study and systematic theological thinking. No intelligent man, whether Christian or non-Christian, can avoid this current way of thought. The issue for the Church is how far evolutionary categories may be taken from the biological level in which they originated and applied to the understanding of the whole creative process of the universe, of the movement of human history, and of the nature of the God whom Christians worship. One thing is certain: the emphasis in our time falls on process, on a dynamic understanding of our world. Static categories are finished with. Our task as Christians is to seek what light evolutionary and process models may throw upon our theological understanding.

To do this, certain issues will have to be dealt with in this opening chapter. To use evolutionary and process categories in this way means that we have to indulge in constructive philosophy, metaphysics, even while we listen to the critical philosophy of the linguistic analysts. Hence we must inquire into the nature of metaphysical thinking and be clear about what we are doing. A further question then arises: Is a specifically Christian philosophy possible? If so, what are the distinguishing marks that should identify any philosophy that claims to be Christian? Furthermore, how far may a Christian philosophy, if such there be, borrow categories and models from other non-Christian philosophical systems, and to what degree may it employ them? The present century has seen many philosophies that have " evolution " and " process " as key ideas, most of them moving toward some religious interpretation of the universe. We must look at these and see their significance. This will be developed in the first half of the book. The second and final half will be concerned with philosophies that could claim to be apologetic for the Christian faith and that employ in various ways the same models of " evolution " and " process." In the light of this we must assess critically the significance of such ideas for Christian philosophizing and theologizing.

Metaphysics as an " Analogical Art "

Philosophy may be defined as the attempt, by rational reflection upon human experience in its totality, to arrive at some integrative insight in which the nature of man, the nature of the universe, and the relation of the two may become intelligible. Thus the raw material of such constructive philosophy is the data afforded by science, the material provided by the historian, the insights of the poet and the artist, the moral imperatives by which men are beset, the intuitions of the religious man and the mystic, and the everyday personal experiences of the philosopher himself. The goal is some integrating wholeness in which all these experiences will be drawn into a reasonable unity. Here we move beyond the search for specific reasons for individual entities in our world by relating them to other entities, that is to say, by intramundane relations such as causation and personal activity. This is the business of science.

This search for an integrative system of the totality of experience has, ever since the time of Aristotle, been styled " metaphysics," originally because the volume in which the Greek philosopher attempted such a venture was written after his volume on nature, the science of his time. The term came to mean, however, not " after physics " in this chronological sense, but " beyond physics " in the sense of probing deeper into the underlying principles of the universe. Here we do not concern ourselves with the explanation of the " being " of a certain thing in terms of its relation to other existent things. Rather, we probe deeper and ask what it means " to be " at all.

In this sense metaphysics becomes ontology, the inquiry into "being itself," ultimate reality. For it is not sufficient to ask what it means for anything "to be" but what it means for the totality of man and the universe "to be." Here man moves beyond intramundane phenomena and seeks for the unconditioned ground of all being, the ultimate reality which explains all individual beings but is itself self-explanatory, that final principle which carries its meaning in itself while giving meaning to all the entities involved in the totality of human experience. Thus metaphysics is finally concerned to discover the dimension of depth in the universe, if such depth there be.

Now in such philosophical reflection, the instrument of rational dialectic and logical argumentation occupies a central place. But the issue has to be settled whether "reason," defined in such a narrow sense, is the key to such thinking. In the past two centuries rationalism has become closely identified with empiricism, that is to say, with the idea that only those entities which can be sensibly perceived should form the basis for any rational procedure and, indeed, can have any intelligible meaning. Thereby the term "the world" has come to mean the world of the sensibly observable, and other aspects of human experience are barred from the basic data with which philosophical reflection must deal. The result is the current atmosphere of naturalism. In this it is taken for granted that the fundamental and reliable data are those provided by the sciences and that all other human experiences are to be explained or to be explained away in the light of these. Yet such thinkers do not recognize that, in thus selecting the data provided by sensible observation, they are exercising a judgment as to what they believe to be most significant in human experience. In other words, prior to their dialectical processes there has been a faith commitment. It is this stance of faith which has determined the movement of their logic.

But "the world" embraces for all of us more than the sensibly observable. It embraces the realm of religious response to reality to which all the religions of mankind bear witness, the realm of moral obligations in which we are related to other persons and to the totality of things in higher ways than the purely physical and natural, the inner world of decision in which, by exercise of our freedom, we choose our own existence. All such areas of human experience testify to something more than is superficially indicated by perceptual observation and the analytical processes of science. The religious response involves an intuitive awareness of the unconditioned mystery behind the universe. Man's universal sense of obligation and unconditioned demand points to a moral background of the totality of things. Man's inner sense of freedom and the right to determine his own existence offers a key in its experience of self-transcendence to a transcendent depth in the universe. Now men may narrow their view of " the world " and try to explain away such dimensions of experience. They must, however, recognize that in so doing they are exercising a judgment which may not be shared by the religious man, the moralist, the existentialist with his emphasis on inner freedom and decision.

This emphasis on prior judgment and the above reference to intuitive insights are guides to the nature of philosophical thought. For it is not simply reason operating upon the data of human experience, but reason operating with a prior selection of those data which are regarded as significant. At this level of prior selection we are concerned, not with rational argumentation, but with the intuitive aspect of our rational capacities, our ability to grasp the significant and to make a judgment of value, our feelingful insight into the nature of things. Thus we begin our philosophical speculation with absolute presuppositions which result from a direct insight into reality and are not the end result of some process of discursive reasoning. According to Dorothy Emmet:

Like religious judgments, the basic metaphysical judgments are of the nature of total assertions. If you ask from whence are these basic judgments derived, I would suggest that they are derived predominantly from some particular type of experience — e.g. intellectual, aesthetic or moral, which has seemed to provide a clue in terms of which a *Weltanschauung* or philosophical attitude could be developed. . . . The basic impetus to the creation of that particular interpretative theory comes from a particular kind of experience which gives rise to a certain judgment of importance.[8]

It is within such faith principles that discursive reason operates. A man thinks as he does because he believes as he does. Consciously or unconsciously there is not one of us who is free from his metaphysical bias. The rationalistic idea that reason, freely operating upon the evidence, can demonstrate the nature of ultimate reality is held by few nowadays. Karl Marx and Sigmund Freud, each in his own way, have pointed to the inner forces that make men think as they do. We may not agree with Freud's rejection of thought as rationalization, but we do have to recognize the presence in the human mind of a prior attitude toward the world before reasoning takes over.

Wilhelm Dilthey spent much time investigating this business of a prior *Weltanschauung*. Such a world view is rooted for him, not in the intellect, but in life itself. Despite his concern with historical understanding, he held that such world views were beyond history, for they were behind the application of reason to the understanding of history. Hence no reason could be given for them. He proceeds to analyze the types of such world view and finds that they fall broadly into three classes. The naturalistic type is exemplified in materialists and positivists from Democritus to Hume, Comte, and their contemporaries. The type that Dilthey styles the idealism of freedom takes personality as the highest value and is found as theism in its various forms, Christian in root and finding philosophical expression in Kant and Fichte. Bergson and William James are also examples of this type of thinking. Finally we have objective idealism, a type that emphasizes the wholeness of the universe, tends to pantheism, finds religious expression in the Oriental religions, and is given philosophical form in thinkers as various as Spinoza, Leibnitz, Schleiermacher, Schelling, and Hegel.

Dilthey might seem at this point to leave us in complete relativism, and yet he tries to avoid this. He declares that "the last word of the mind which has run through all the world-views is not the relativity of them all, but the sovereignty of the mind in the face of each one of them, and at the same time the positive consciousness of the way in which, in the various attitudes of the mind, the one reality of the world exists for us." [4] Holding that there is something unknowable, ineffable, in all reality, he can also argue that it is irrational. So he can write, " All *Weltanschauungen* arise from the objectification of the ways in which living man, perceiving and thinking, feeling and desiring, seeking to have his way with things, experiences the world." [5] Reality has depths that reason cannot finally plumb.

We must add the influence of Collingwood, whose thought runs strangely parallel to that of Dilthey, though in a more idealistic strain. With him we arrive at complete relativism. He can describe metaphysics, not as the search for ultimate reality, but as " the attempt to find out what absolute presuppositions have been made by this or that person or group of persons, on this or that occasion or group of occasions in the course of this or that piece of thinking." [6] Thus metaphysics is turned into a historical science. This is consonant with Collingwood's view of history, but it leaves us with a real problem. Since all is relative, we have no way of validating any metaphysical system.

This problem of validation is heightened by the fact that our absolute presuppositions spring from existential or life situations and have an intuitive base, for intuition always raises questions with the skeptical. If we hold with Dilthey that reality has unfathomable depths, is ineffable and irrational, we may dismiss any attempt to move farther. If, on the other hand, we believe that ultimate reality is to some extent understandable by man, we must examine this issue of existential decision and intuitive awareness more closely. In doing so, we have to admit our own metaphysical bias. We cannot escape our prior faith principles, and the reasons we give for them are formulated within them. Our knowledge is inevitably personal knowledge. It involves decision and commitment.

Michael Polanyi, in a sustained and penetrating investigation,[7] has shown the presence of such a tacit component of vision and commitment in all knowledge. He holds, as a result of his discussion, that personal expectation and commitment have a primal place in every act of knowing, including the area covered by scientific investigation. Thereby even empirical investigation belongs also to the area of personal commitment. As a consequence, the attack of logical positivists and linguistic protagonists upon religious and metaphysical language is countered. The theological thinker and the speculative metaphysician can turn the table upon their critics by pointing out that the modes of verification of meaning demanded by the latter are determined by their own tacit commitment. Polanyi thus insists that, in all knowing, imagination and intellect are both involved and that every act of knowing involves the person as a whole. We can no longer bifurcate the scientific sphere from that of religion and metaphysics.

This imaginative aspect in all intellectual comprehension has already found expression, at the level of metaphysics, in the description of metaphysics as an analogical art rather than a demonstrative science. The faith principle or absolute presupposition from which metaphysical thinking takes its rise involves the selection of certain fundamental models in terms of which the universe as a whole is to be understood. Thus the philosopher takes an analogy from the particular type of intellectual or spiritual relationship which he regards as significant for the understanding of reality. For Hegel, committed to the rational wholeness of the universe, human thinking became the key analogy to interpret the processes of the whole. For Plato, beauty of form in mathematics provided the model for the idea of the Good. Aristotle found the basic analogy for his commitment to a teleological universe in biological development. For Marx, the model was provided by the economic struggle which he was convinced is the significant fact in experience. So one could continue. The various types have their basic models or analogies.

Dorothy Emmet can affirm that a metaphysical system is the " creation of aesthetic imagination, or an attempt to dominate the world in theory from a standpoint of merely personal impression governed, as William James would say, by whether we are temperamentally ' tough ' or ' tender ' minded." [8] Again she suggests that " it takes concepts derived from some kind of experience or some relation within experience, and extends them either so as to say something about the nature of ' reality,' or so as to suggest a possible mode of coordinating other experiences of different types from that which the concept was originally derived." [9] Likewise Tillich suggests that " one could say that in each system an experienced fragment of life and vision is drawn out constructively even to cover areas where life and vision are missing." [10] Perhaps Emmet's general discussion does not bring out sufficiently the large element of personal involvement within which such selection of analogies or models takes place. If what we have said be correct, a man's philosophy discloses the man himself. As Casserley says: " Each philosopher will draw his analogies from that realm of experience which his character prompts him to regard as the most significant in life. By their analogies, we may say, ye shall know them." [11]

Thus intuition, commitment, and imagination are all involved in metaphysical thinking. It is interesting to note that John Macquarrie seeks to express this imaginative and intuitive aspect in what he terms the " architectonic reason." Although he is discussing the theological discipline and is shunning too evident a use of rational speculation, he suggests that there is a function of reason that is akin to its speculative use and yet in some respects distinct from it. He writes of

a constructive use of reason in which we build up rational wholes, theories, or interlocking systems of ideas, but do so not by deductive argument but rather by imaginative leaps which, so to speak, integrate the fragmentary elements in inclusive wholes. Of course, such imaginative leaps need to be immediately tested and subjected to scrutiny, yet something of this kind goes on in most intellectual disciplines, including the natural sciences.[12]

He suggests that such a functioning of reason has something in common with aesthetic sensibility. It is certainly true that the great advances of the natural sciences have arisen when intuitive hunches and imaginative restructuring of models and concepts have supervened upon rational procedures. The same holds of metaphysical speculation, for here, too, imaginative flights often lead the way and speculative reason then seeks to substantiate the structure which results.

It is at this point that differentiation between *Weltanschauungen* becomes possible. The coherence test can at least be employed to justify our metaphysical faith. Our commitment must be evaluated by the degree of illumination that it offers to our human experience. The comprehensiveness of the intuitive vision to which we have primarily committed ourselves must be demonstrated as coherent by the processes of reflective reason. We seek to understand the various aspects of human experience in all their multiplicity, and thus metaphysics moves on its way to develop a rational system.

Since, however, the primal vision involves the total person, more is involved than speculative reason and even the exercise of imagination to which we have just referred. Commitment is not easily shaken and there is a psychological aspect here as well as the rational one. A judgment of significance or an axiological decision is not easily changed, and no transition from a primal commitment can be forced by rational argument. Polanyi points out that in the adjudication between two rival *Weltanschauungen* no explicit rules can be formulated. The more unlike they are, the less common ground they have, the less will rational argument help. He suggests that " the process of choosing between positions based on different sets of premises is . . . a matter of intuition and finally conscience." [13] Here he believes that the ultimate decision of conscience is aided by the fairness and tolerance which a free society makes possible. By fairness he means the effort to lay our whole position open to the opponent and frankly to acknowledge limitations in our own knowledge and our personal bias. By tolerance he points to a readiness to see the sound points even in a hostile attack and to appraise the reasons for the other's errors. Thereby a man may move to a point of view with a richer perspective.

The Issue of a Christian Philosophy

At this point we come upon the issue of a religious *Weltanschauung* and specifically of a Christian philosophy. Since all metaphysics begins with the conviction that a specific relationship in human experience is the key to the comprehension of all experience, and since personal knowledge and commitment are central, there seems on the surface to be no ground for denying that a Christian philosophy is possible. At the same time, metaphysics begins with what is regarded as significant in experience and seeks to show, by reflective argument, that a model for reality borrowed from this explains or explains away every other aspect of experience. In this sense, it is tied to some universal structure of experience which all thinking men might acknowledge to be present but to which all of them would by no means attribute a like significance, e.g., mind, matter, personal being, to name three obvious instances. But Christian thought begins with what it claims to be a unique divine disclosure and is thus bound up with the historical and the singular. This has led many to argue that there can be no Christian philosophy as such. Christian theology is the attempt to start with such a disclosure and build up a coherent structure centering in it. Christian philosophy is a misnomer, since it would attempt to start with general experience and show that this points to the disclosure. There can be a Christian philosophizing but not a Christian philosophy.

Now it is true that the old natural theology did attempt to start with such general experience and argue for the existence and the general nature of deity. As this was formulated in the medieval period by Aquinas and his followers, it made use basically of the cosmological and teleological arguments, was grounded in the philosophy of Aristotle, and made much of the argument from analogy. Yet its absolute presupposition was Christian, and really its evaluation of the data from which it commenced was dictated by the insights of the Christian faith. Once Hume and Kant had dismissed the rational arguments of such natural theology (which had by then become the accepted apologetic in Protestant circles), the idea of a natural theology which, by its rational dialectic, should appeal to all reasonable creatures was outmoded. It has been in disrepute ever since. Refuge was found in the moral experience and judgment by Kant and his followers, while Schleiermacher took refuge in feeling for the defense of religion.

Already, in Ritschl, the severance of revealed theology from metaphysics and thus from natural theology was very evident.

Ever since Ritschl, there has been a tendency for Continental theologians to shun metaphysics and to confine themselves solely to revelation. Barth disowned the influence of Kierkegaard and proceeded to develop a system which Bonhoeffer acutely defined as a "positivism of revelation." Yet his interest in Anselm and the speculative moments in his vast dogmatic are reminders that he has not escaped from involvement in ontology. Indeed, can a theologian ever really do so? Bonhoeffer himself attacked "religion," one phase of which he could describe as "the temporally influenced presuppositions of metaphysics." [14] But some of his self-styled disciples are not averse to metaphysical speculation, as witness T. J. J. Altizer,[15] who includes aspects of Hegel's thought in the "witches' brew" with which he replaces the Christian Gospel. Furthermore, the influence of Heidegger on Bultmann, the post-Bultmannians, and Heinrich Ott [16] is an indication that theology and philosophical speculation cannot finally be separated. Indeed, Bultmann's use of Heidegger has an avowedly apologetic aim and is an attempt to meet modern man on the level of existentialism.

The same motif lies behind the thought of Paul Tillich,[17] who would use philosophical speculation to ask questions which he believes that revelation alone can answer. This "method of correlation" attempts to lead man to the point where the Christian disclosure may be heard. Tillich carefully differentiates reason into two aspects, the ontological and the technical. He reserves for the former those intuitive insights into reality with which we have already associated absolute presuppositions. He indicates by the latter the discursive and dialectical use of reason by which systems of philosophy are built. He argues, as we have already seen, that the technical reason gets nowhere unless the ontological reason be grounded in "being itself," that is to say, unless it have access to the Unconditioned, to God. Such rapport between the human logos and the Logos of the universe makes reason theonomous. Without it, reason becomes autonomous, depending upon man's own structures of being, or heteronomous, depending upon authoritative direction from external social structures. The autonomous reason produces the naturalistic philosophy. It fails because the answers to the questions raised by man's existence have to come from " beyond."

Hence Tillich can define the theological treatment of the arguments of traditional natural theology as follows: In order " to develop the question of God which they express and to expose the impotency of the ' arguments,' their inability to answer the question of God, . . . they drive reason to the quest for revelation." [18] Finally it is out of the awareness of his own finitude that man begins to ask questions about God. According to Tillich, " Natural theology was meaningful to the extent that it gave an analysis of the human situation and the question of God implied in it." [19]

This negative evaluation of natural theology is at least an attempt to rehabilitate it to some degree. It is very evident that, in its old rationalistic form, it can never be restored, but one can hope that some more positive philosophical bridge might be provided to the Christian revelation. We would agree with Tillich that the Christian man depends for his certainty and authority upon the divine disclosure in the Incarnation. We certainly cannot establish the Creation and the Incarnation by rational argument from the generalized field of human experience. Yet, as Howard Root reminds us:

If we continue to say that there are reasons for accepting one set of beliefs rather than another, we are that far committed to something which I should call metaphysics. But it will have to be a metaphysics which can somehow do justice not only to our desire for a Natural Theology but also to our religiously inspired distrust of Natural Theology. [20]

Roger Mehl objects to the term " Christian philosophy," but holds that a Christian may be a philosopher. [21] He finds the key in Christian motivation and speaks of " a philosophy of Christian intention." [22] Standing in the Reformed tradition, he attacks any claim of autonomous reason to judge revelation, but he equally objects to any idea of incorporating Christian revelation into a philosophy as a principle of intelligibility.[23] This would imply annexing revelation to philosophy and depriving it of some of its judging power. For the Christian philosopher claims the right to submit his findings to the final judgment of the revelation. How far, then, can the content of his philosophy be made intelligible by the Biblical revelation? Mehl writes:

It is a question of knowing whether for a philosophy which is fully rational in other respects, its reference to Christianity becomes a source of greater light or intelligibility: does the solution which I propose as a philosopher about the relation of time to eternity become enlightened by what Revelation teaches me about the relationship between the Kingdom of God and the Church?[24]

Thus philosophy can lay no claim to have founded a rational theology of its own, and metaphysical experience cannot serve as a basis for a Christian dogmatics. Because the Christian is a rational being and because he is involved in the world, he cannot be denied a philosophical activity. But equally he must grasp the "fundamental discontinuity between the metaphysical quest for God and the Scriptural revelation of God."[25]

Mehl, however, finds a valuable dialogue between the theologian and the philosopher, and he cites existentialism and personalism as "signs of the Church's presence in the realm of rational thought."[26] The Christian philosopher must have sufficient knowledge of revealed truth to receive insights which will shed new light on the problems that philosophy studies. He should be motivated by his commitment to the person of Jesus Christ and the Biblical revelation.

Mehl's attitude toward reason must be called in question. He follows Calvin and regards it as sadly dislocated by sin, whereas Augustine would see reason in need of proper direction. Tillich's emphasis on theonomous reason fits in with Augustine's *credo ut intelligam* at this point. Yet Mehl does emphasize the presence of Christian intention, motivation, commitment in Christian philosophizing, and he also indicates that the Christian revelation may provide greater insight and intelligibility where philosophical positions have been adumbrated. Here he points in a limited way toward our analysis of the nature of metaphysical thinking.

If all philosophical knowing is personal and involves the total man, his commitment and his passion, this will also hold of the Christian philosopher. If logic is directed by belief, we may believe that a Christian's faith commitment will have something to say to his thinking. His rational reflection and its starting point, what he regards as significant in the general structures of human experience, will be influenced by his Christian motivation. He is thinking as a committed Christian. The danger here is that we should begin to transform philosophy into revealed theology. As Christians we are looking for a natural theology that is Christian in intention and that may lead men to appraise the Christian revelation and seek to understand its systematic theological expression. Yet such natural theology or Christian philosophy must begin with the world of our common experience rather than overtly, as does revealed theology, with a special and singular divine disclosure. It must start at the level where men are. But it will have its faith commitment, its absolute presupposition, and it will select the beginning point of its rational development from those aspects of human experience which it regards as most significant and as best offering analogies by which its understanding of the whole may be approached.

Let us at once note that the old natural theology, with its demonstrative approach, was both too narrowly based and too rationalistic and abstract. First of all, it concentrated upon the natural order, and the word "world" largely described the physical realm. When the logical fallacies and practical deficiencies of the cosmological and teleological arguments were exposed by Hume, Kant, and Darwin, the old system of rationalistic theology collapsed. In the last century and a half, man's "world" has been expanded to embrace aspects of experience far beyond those with which science deals. The earlier dismissal of the ontological argument had diverted attention from man's inner self-consciousness with which Augustine had been concerned in his own apologetic work. Kant recovered this concern with the analysis of man's inner life and his moral emphasis. Yet he treated it so abstractly and rationally that it became a foundation for what he regarded as a demonstrative metaphysic. Actually it could much better be described as an attempt to comprehend reality on the basis of a moral analogy. The employment of the moral dimension of man's nature in the " theistic " philosophies of the past century points to a significant dimension of man's experienced " world."

Side by side with this must be placed the existentialist concern with man's inner being and his self-transcendent personhood. Kierkegaard's influence has grown into the widespread existentialist emphasis of our own time, with its challenge to turn the philosophic inquiry upon man, his purpose and freedom, his destiny and will. Once again a new dimension of man's " world " has been opened. No longer can the philosopher be concerned just with the physical world and its abstract categories; no longer must he be concerned, like Plato, Aristotle, and Descartes, with mathematical analogies. Fear, guilt, responsibility, freedom, decision, are also a part of that experience which may be significant in man's quest for meaning.

Again, since the time of Hume, concern with man's religions has grown. The inquiry has again been turned to the religious consciousness with attempts to investigate it phenomenologically, stripping it of all extraneous elements. From Schleiermacher's emphasis on the feeling of absolute dependence as central in all religious experience through Otto's concern with the numinous feeling before the mysterious and transcendent Other, men have sought to analyze the religious phenomena present throughout our world. The religious factor has been added to experience, and men have become aware of a dimension of divine disclosure in their world.

Moreover, in the eighteenth century, man began to discover the significance of history in a new way, and in the last two centuries his historical consciousness has developed. Vico's emphasis on the sympathetic and imaginative aspects of historical knowledge brought to the center the realization that there was an inner side of history which man could penetrate because it was the inner side of man. Man could unveil in history the movement of human self-consciousness, and he could understand it because it was like unto his own. Without our agreeing with the differing metaphysical attitudes of Dilthey, Croce, and Collingwood, they have all emphasized that true historical understanding involves the reliving of the inner life of past generations in the historian's own mind. Dilthey would emphasize intentions, motives, and feeling where Collingwood would emphasize the intuitive grasping of thoughts alone, but both approaches are reminders that man's own existential self-awareness and his existential decisions need to be enriched by the dimension of the historical. For in history we can expand, beyond our own individual self-consciousness, our understanding of what it is to be responsible, self-transcendent man exercising his freedom. Casserley cogently expresses this:

A rich and diverse cultural tradition may evoke and require freedom and personal responsibility in those whom it nourishes, by setting alternatives before them, and insisting upon sober, life-determining acts of choice as part of the ordeal by which personal maturity is manifested and recognized.[27]

To sum up this first point: Man's " world " needs to be enlarged to include his own inner self-transcendence and self-consciousness, the responsibility to decide his own " existence." It also has the moral dimension in which all men experience the pressure of moral demand, however rudimentary may be its expression. Again, it has a religious dimension in which men feel and intuit the presence of the awesome and mysterious Other in disclosing activity. Finally, it has a historical dimension as man has enriched his own self-awareness through the experience of self-transcendent personal being down the story of time.

This brings us to our second stricture – that the older natural theology was too rationalistic and abstract. By beginning with the structures of nature, it tended to be abstract rather than dealing with the concrete facts of human life, personal being, moral demand, and historical existence. Furthermore, it tended to view its task as demonstrative rather than analogical and descriptive. But if Christian philosophy is truly to function, it must start where man is and with man himself rather than with the realm of nature. As history becomes more central and even nature is understood historically, the emphasis has begun to change. Indeed the seemingly objective, rationalistic, and reductive structures which science has claimed to possess have so depersonalized and dehumanized man that man has become concerned with his own personal being and existence. Thus modern man has come to agonize about himself, his existence and his behavior, and any attempt of Christian philosophy to build a bridge that shall point to faith requires a central concern with modern man in his loneliness, frustration, and alienation. But here we require, not abstract rational structures, but a descriptive and phenomenological attempt to delineate the structures of human existence. Imagination and intuitive insight must march side by side with rational reflection. Even at the secular level we might guess that man, in his self-transcendence and agonizing freedom, might provide the key analogy with which to understand the whole of man's "world." As John Macquarrie contends:

There is a broader understanding than that which belongs to the purely theoretical reason, and it is this broader understanding, arising out of the whole range of our existence in the world, that can alone help us to penetrate into the meaning of religious faith.[28]

In this sense, he advocates what we have referred to earlier, "architectonic reason."

If Christian philosophy is to be characterized by Christian motivation and by basic insights derived from the Christian revelation, this is not inconsonant with what has just been said. For the Biblical revelation is marked by just this concern for man in his moral, religious, existential, and historical dimensions. Furthermore, it is rich in analogies and images that are shaped within the give-and-take of the divine-human disclosure, the central ones being the personal nature of God, the emphasis on the divine will and activity, the analogy of creation as one indication of God's relation to his world, the picture of God's involvement with his world, brought to a focus in the Incarnation but present throughout Israel's history. As Casserley puts it:

For the Christian, the Bible is a mirror of both personality and history, and it is to history and self-conscious personal existence, as he discovers them revealed with unparalleled clarity in biblical religion, that he turns for the analogies most requisite and necessary to his metaphysical needs, with the maximum of expectation and the minimum of disappointment.[29]

It is no accident that Mehl points to personalism and existentialism as two philosophical attitudes that have been profoundly influenced by the insights of the Church. But we need to go beyond this. Although it is true that throughout its history, Christianity has been a religion in search of a metaphysic, it is also true that there are certain metaphysical implications in the Biblical testimony.

Christian Philosophy and the Metaphysical Implications of the Christian Revelation

The Biblical understanding of man, in contrast with the Greek, emphasizes the will and not the reason. Man is viewed in his concrete psychosomatic wholeness. The emphasis falls upon his personal totality, and in his knowing that the whole personal being is involved. Hence, when man is described as in the image of God, the concern is with him as an existential being, able freely to decide his destiny in the light of the claims of God and of his fellows. His freedom is set within his relationships. His knowledge of other persons is born out of his personal involvement with them, and not in any abstract reflective process. He becomes a real person in such relationships and most of all in his relationship to God. For the moral claims of his fellows are understood always within the setting of the divine disclosure. Man is fundamentally related to God. Augustine was essentially Christian and Biblical when he saw man's self-consciousness as rooted in his awareness of the divine.

God, too, is known in his disclosures, and not by discursive reasoning from nature. He is known in what he does, in his involvement with man in history. And so the historical dimension becomes central in man's existential decisions. The God who meets him in life is the God of his fathers. Behind the disclosure situations in which he knows himself to be confronted by divine claim, in mercy and in judgment, there is the historical memory of God's past disclosures to Israel and to Christ's Church. Man himself becomes a real person in his own historical encounter with God, historical in the sense that it is itself temporally extended across his own life and historical because his understanding of God is enriched and deepened by the historical confessions of old Israel and of the Christian community.

Furthermore, the God who so discloses himself gives himself to be known in personal form. The revelation, when it is expressed in language, is rich in personal analogies and models. Men speak of God's will and purpose, of his love and his mercy, of his righteousness and his claims, of his fatherhood and his grace, of his judgment and his wrath. The whole is brought to a focus in the Incarnation when God comes in human form and becomes supremely involved in the historical life of his creatures.

This disclosure of God as merciful and forgiving, even when man in rebellion or alienation chooses his own path, points to the disclosure of God as Creator. Once more the emphasis must fall on disclosure. This was an insight granted to Israel and the Christian Church within the disclosure of God's Saviorhood. In its developed and New Testament form it is formulated as *creatio ex nihilo* — creation out of nothing. It is the attempt to safeguard the absolute dependence of man and his world upon God. Man is not divine or semidivine. He is a created being utterly dependent upon his Creator, with no element of deity in his structure. The world is no emanation from the divine substance, no expansion of the divine being into an objective form, no temporal extension of deity whereby the latter attains self-realization. Yet, although creaturely, both man and his world can be pronounced " good." They are still more declared to be of value in God's eyes by the Incarnation itself. There is no suggestion, however, that God creates the world because of any deficiency in his own being. Creation is a free act of his grace. He wills to share his bliss with his creatures, and hence he rejoices over his creation because it may share in his love.

Again, in the Incarnation, God becomes involved in his world at all levels. Its historical movement is lifted up into his eternal life. Time is shown to be meaningful to God in terms of purpose. Man's bodily existence and therefore his physical and natural order are lifted up into the divine life and made sacramental of God's saving love. In the Lord's Supper, the physical creatures of bread and wine become signs and symbols of God's presence. The physical and the natural are not spurned in the Biblical revelation, and there is a basic " realism " in the Hebrew and early Christian approach to God and his world.

Finally, the creation of the world and man is regarded as a continuing and historical act. The creation stories are prehistory and mythical in form, yet they point to God's creative act as a continuing process that underlies all time and is continued in that new creation which is made possible through the Incarnation.

All this has repercussions upon the understanding of God. God's " otherness " or transcendence is matched by his " presence " or immanence. Although expressed often in spatial imagery, the thought is always of a God who in his remoteness is also near, in his hiddenness is also revealed, in his absence is also present. Such an understanding of God is brought to a focus once more in the Incarnation. There we understand that the secret of God's transcendence and immanence lies in his personal being, that his transcendence is not to be found beyond the limits of his world but in the midst of it, and that such transcendence is consonant with an immanence in which he identifies himself with his creatures. Even the Cross has to be lifted up into the heart of God, and his transcendence is such that time matters in his eternity.

All these insights say much about the nature of any Christian philosophical theology. They rule out any philosophy that does not take seriously this world and man, time and human history.

Their implied realism will have nothing to do with attempts to treat the physical as evanescent or unreal, for it, too, is to be redeemed in God's ultimate consummated cosmos (Rom. 8:22 f. and Revelation). They demand a broader empiricism than naturalism would permit. Many forms of idealism are thereby eliminated. A Christian philosophy will not be at home with any scheme of thought that ignores or eliminates aspects of man's total personal being. Man must be seen as a religious, moral, existential being, whose destiny turns upon his own free decision. Mind or reason is not the key analogy. Equally, Christian philosophy will not be at home with thought that ignores the reality and significance of the temporal and historical dimension of man's world, both natural and social. The world is real, but it is an unfinished world. Man is alienated and is in process of being saved.

Furthermore, such philosophical theology can have no sympathy with any system that emphasizes God's transcendence and minimizes his immanence and vice versa. It rules out deism and pantheism in their many forms. Nor can it be happy with any understanding of God that makes him less than perfect in his innermost being or regards creation as the means of realizing a divine deficiency. The doctrine of absolute and free creation is very evidently a part of Christian insight, and it must be embodied in any philosophical approach that claims the name Christian. Furthermore, creation and redemption must in some sense be understood in historical terms. God is acting creatively and redemptively within the process of time. The historicomythical form of the creation story and the historical basis of the divine disclosure to Israel and in the Incarnation demand this.

In such philosophical thinking, reflective thought needs to be accompanied by imagination and intuitive insight. Abstract speculation can do little justice to man's concreteness and his unique singularity expressed in his freedom. Least of all can it do justice to the reality of a personal God in his unique " otherness." Universalistic thinking that deals with general concepts can never finally embrace the personal. Here the best language is that of myth which retains the singular by employing a narrative form.

Nor should this dismay us, for the father of all philosophy, Plato, was familiar with such a need, especially when he moved into the understanding of man's own predicament and destiny and when he sought to express the Ultimate, the Good. Again, Bergson emphasizes intuitive insight and uses vivid descriptive imagery, while the existentialists bid us turn from the abstract categories of the older philosophers to the personal concepts of anxiety and dread, responsibility and guilt, decision and love. This again points to Macquarrie's useful identification of "architectonic reason."

To say all this does not mean that secular and other philosophies may not make and have not made real contributions to Christian thinking. We have only to remember the way in which Aquinas and Catholic scholasticism have adopted Aristotelian categories. Yet we note how radically the Aristotelian system had to be transformed to find place for the Christian insight of creation and the Christian understanding of God. Again, we find Augustine's acceptance and incorporation of Neoplatonic ideas, the influence of Kantian metaphysics on much modern theological thought, the employing of the existentialist categories of Kierkegaard by many twentieth-century Christian thinkers, the adaptation of Heidegger's insights by thinkers as diverse as Rudolf Bultmann and Paul Tillich. In the light of the involvement of the Christian God in the creative and historical process and the concern with divine immanence expressed theologically in the doctrine of the Holy Spirit, we must ask how far systems grounded in the biological categories of "evolution" and "organic process" can contribute to Christian thinking. We are not concerned here with evolution at the biological level. That we take to be scientifically established and accepted by intelligent people. Our concern is how far the categories involved may be used as analogical models to cover larger areas of human experience in a specifically Christian type of thinking.

One final word needs to be said before we launch into this kind of investigation. We are concerned in Christian philosophizing to defend the Christian position and make it intelligible to thinking men. To do so we have to embody insights from a specific divine disclosure which we regard as final, while seeking also to deal with aspects of experience which all men have in common but which we regard as peculiarly significant. Our thought will at times cross the lines of Christian theology. It is by no means clear that a firm line can be drawn here between philosophy and theology on our definition of Christian philosophy. After all, both are concerned with the world we live in, although the Christian philosopher begins with the world and uses the divine disclosure a little more obliquely. As Ninian Smart reminds us:

Christian metaphysics is not an essay in the exercise of pure reason (which happens to be on the side of the angels), but a defence of a position which cannot be worked out by reason alone. Moreover, this is (in a broad, very broad, sense) an empirical approach, since we consider what is given rather than legislate for reality.[30]

Part One: *TAKING PROCESS AND TIME SERIOUSLY*

II

The Absolute Spirit and Process — From Being to Becoming

WE SHALL BEGIN our investigation with the emergence of a real historical consciousness in the eighteenth century. Until then the Greek preoccupation with nature had dominated philosophical thought. As we have already noted, natural theology was fundamentally cosmological and demonstrative, seeking to argue for the existence of God by the cosmological and teleological arguments. Starting in the former argument from the conviction that finite things were bound together by a chain of causal relationships, never sufficient in themselves, it sought for the ground of all such contingent and secondary causes in an original uncaused cause, Necessary Being, and identified this with God. Commencing in the latter argument with the evidence for design and teleology in the cosmos, it tried to demonstrate the existence of a Supreme Designer. Hume and Kant both contributed to the eclipse of such arguments, the logical fallacies of which have long since made them unacceptable at the demonstrative level. These arguments and philosophy generally employed static categories and borrowed most of their key concepts from mathematics and physics. Only the Cambridge Platonists, More, Cudworth, and Ray attempted a more organic approach to reality.

Yet, paradoxically, the tremendous success of physical science awoke men to a new look at history. The advances at the level of technology and social improvement awoke in many the conviction that history was marching on to a glorious future. What Becker has termed " the heavenly city of the eighteenth century philosophers " became the accepted outlook of many. Man's scientific achievement betokened a glorious future. Mankind was on the march and historical movement began to enter the human consciousness. Early in the next century, Auguste Comte could declare that mankind was leaving behind the successive eras when theological concepts and metaphysical ideas had respectively dominated human society. It was moving into the final age of positivism when the scientific approach to all areas of life, individual and social, would reign supreme.

This, however, was not the only aspect of the historical awakening. For science had produced so deterministic a universe that human freedom could find little place within its scheme of things. Hume sought to demolish causation with his skeptical empiricism, thereby fathering positivism, and Kant relegated science to the phenomenal world, finding a justification for freedom at the noumenal level of moral obligation. But another thinker was seeking the way of the historical consciousness. Vico described history as " the new science " and sought to delineate the nature of the historical consciousness. For him, the inner side of history is open to man as that of nature is not. Man possesses, in his own self-consciousness, a capacity to understand history from within. He knows man from within and history is the story of men. So historical knowledge came into the picture as distinct from scientific knowledge, as the " new science."

Science was also contributing to a new concern for the historical in yet another way. As the eighteenth century closed and a new century dawned, geology and paleontology were coming to birth as sciences in their own right. The geological strata and the prehistoric fossils found in them raised questions in men's minds about the past of nature. Hitherto, believing men had thought of creation as a far-off temporal event when the structure of all things had been fixed, once for all. From Aristotle to Linnaeus, the fixity of the species had been tacitly accepted. Now doubts began to develop. Buffon, Erasmus Darwin, and Lamarck began to speculate about an evolutionary process. It might be that nature, too, must be understood historically and that "life" in its many organic forms up to man had been through a developmental process.

Thus at the turn of the eighteenth century the time was ripe for a concern with the historical and for the introduction of more dynamic categories into philosophical thought. In the center of this new concern with "process" we must place Hegel. In his thinking, strictly evolutionary ideas have little place, for he came before the major scientific breakthrough of Darwin and Wallace. Hegel did, however, make a move in emphasis from being to becoming and envisaged the universe as a process of rational dialectic. Nature and history were alike pictured in this way. Along with Vico he stands as a philosopher of history, while, as a typical child of the Enlightenment, he sought to enthrone reason as the sovereign key to historical experience.

Rational Spirit as the Basic Analogy

Hume and Kant between them had dismissed the possibility of any metaphysical speculation based on nature and its scientific study. Kant had, however, sought to find an answer in man's moral experience and had taken refuge in the practical reason operating upon the universal experience of moral obligation. Vico had likewise pointed to man's inner experience in his "new science." Hegel was, in some sense, the child of the Enlightenment because of his emphasis on reason, but he also began with man, while rejecting Kant's dichotomy between the phenomenal and the noumenal. Whereas Kant had found man's moral experience to be the core of man's self-revelation, Hegel found it in the rational aspect of man's inner life. The idealistic philosophy that he formulated came to dominate the last century.

Starting with man's rational life, Hegel found his key analogy in the concept of " spirit." His philosophy is a good paradigm of what we meant when we described metaphysics as an analogical art, for the human " spirit " becomes the model for the understanding of the whole universe. We have to understand, however, what Hegel meant by " spirit." Like Augustine, he begins his philosophizing with man's self-consciousness, but for him the core of this is rationality, thought. Man's " spirit " is his rational activity. Man is a " Self," an " I ," a center of thinking. Hence Hegel can define " spirit " as " subject," not merely " substance," implying thereby that it is essentially discursive thought and is set over against an object. Hegel contends that our self-consciousness has its background in our consciousness of objects. Consciousness lies in the relationship of a subject to an object, and it reaches its fullest expression in our own self-consciousness. Spirit is continually seeking to disengage the universal from the mass of particulars, objects, in human experience. Findlay describes it as " the activity which disengages universality and unity from particularity and plurality, and which interprets the latter through the former." [1]

Hegel himself could write: " In my view . . . everything depends upon grasping the ultimate truth not as substance but as subject as well." [2] Here he is moving beyond " spirit " as individual to " spirit " as universal. For although " spirit " is the individual " I," the ego, yet for Hegel every individual " I " must be seen as not merely personal and finite. In interpersonal relationships, where categories and standards of reflective judgment are shared, the " I " is seen to be essentially public. At the level of discursive logic, moral judgment, and aesthetic taste our standards are shared with our fellows and intelligent communication is possible. This is so because the individual " I " is also universal " spirit." As Findlay expresses it: " In all these norms there is an attempt to reach a position which takes account of *everyone's* experience or attitude, and which therefore accords no special privileges to *anyone*. Such norms are for Hegel fit expressions of the 'universal in action.'" [8] Thus "spirit" is infinite and universal, although finding individual expression. It is suprapersonal, and the presence of the norms points to the freedom of the universal "spirit," the true self. So Hegel can move from individual self-consciousness to universal "spirit," regarding the former as both an analogy of the ultimate reality and also as a manifestation of it.

In its activity as conscious subject, spirit requires objects upon which to operate. Indeed consciousness, for Hegel, means fundamentally the capacity to master objects and other persons theoretically and practically. It does this by processes in which their essential content is disengaged and fitted by reason into some universal meaning or unifying pattern. Consciousness is in some sense spirit positing itself in an object, for the object is also a manifestation of spirit. Thus individual persons and the realm of nature must all be regarded as manifestations of spirit. In rational thought the individual subject or self is spirit seeking to control practically, in moral activity, and theoretically, in reflective thought, objects, both other persons and the entities of nature, and to bring them under rational control and understanding. Indeed, everything in nature and history is an expression of the one Spirit which is also the core of every individual being.

So Hegel arrives at a vision of the universe in its totality as a rational whole in which the final reality is the Absolute Spirit or Idea. The universe is a unity of thought, indwelt by the universal Spirit. Reason holds the key to the process in which individual human spirits are involved, and reason is activity and energy. Hegel can contend that, in philosophy, it is

proved by speculative cognition, that Reason . . . is *Substance,* as well as *Infinite Power;* its own *Infinite Material* underlying all the natural and spiritual life which it originates, as also the *Infinite Form* that which sets this Material in motion. On the one hand, Reason is the *substance* of the Universe; viz. that by which and in which all reality has its being and subsistence. On the other hand it is the *Infinite Energy* of the Universe; since Reason is not so powerless as to be incapable of producing anything but a mere ideal, a mere intention —

having its place outside reality, nobody knows where; something separate and abstract in the heads of certain human beings.[4]

As energy, Reason has to posit itself in individual rational subjects and in individual objects, be the latter persons or natural entities. It requires the particularity that sense experience and impulse make possible in order to exercise its power and organize and control. Findlay notes that

it is *as* essential . . . for Spirit to be wedded to particular finite contents and to determinate places in the world, as it is for it to be freely ranging and "infinite," since it is only by being the former that it can be the latter.[5]

Hence Spirit requires "otherness," "over-againstness," if it is to be other than abstraction. Absolute Spirit needs a world, if it is to function as rational energy. "God as an abstraction is not the true God: only as the living process of positing His other, the World (which conceived in divine terms is His Son), and first in the Union with His other, as Spirit, can He be subject."[6]

The Absolute Spirit and Process

Hegel can be called an objective idealist, because he did hold to the necessity of objects as distinct from subjects. He was no subjective idealist like Berkeley, taking refuge in ideas present to the mind. For him, the truth lay in the relationship of subject to object, and the subject was essentially a rational activity, spirit disengaging the rational universal from the particularity of the object. Equally he rejected the critical idealism of Kant which relegated the objective world to the phenomenal. The objects of thought had an objective existence even though they were essentially mind, manifestations of that one Absolute Spirit which constituted the reality of the subject and posited itself in the object. What was illusory in the object was not the object itself but its over-againstness, which the subject must overcome by appropriating its essence to itself. Thus the object was alien to the subject only in an illusory way, for the subject was not imposing some foreign pattern upon the object in the movement of thought but disengaging the implicit meaning of the object. Findlay notes that

the opposition between self-conscious Spirit and its objects may also be regarded as illusory in that it is essential to self-conscious Spirit that there *should* be such others opposed to it, on which it can exert, and in exerting enjoy, its various unifying and universalizing activities.[7]

This objective idealism can thus regard the processes of nature and history as objectively real while, at the same time, seeing them as manifestations of the one Absolute Spirit. Hegel states that " God has two revelations, as Nature and Spirit. Both these divine formations are temples of God that He fills by His presence." [8] In Nature the Absolute Spirit posits itself as object; in history it becomes many subjective centers in relationship, each individual center treating other persons as objects. The whole is a necessary process in which the Absolute Spirit moves to self-consciousness. Thus history and nature are to be understood in rational terms as objects of that dialectical process in which the Absolute spells itself out in time and without which the Absolute would be " lifeless, solitary, and alone." [9]

Now the paradigm for this process is found in the individual consciousness. Hegel begins with his basic model, the human mind, and in his logic he adumbrates what he regards as the fundamental movement of dialectical thought. Hence there emerges his famous triad — Thesis, Antithesis, Synthesis. In his analysis of human thought, he sees the positing of a thesis which, on examination, so shows its inadequacy and one-sidedness that its antithesis or contradiction is set up. This too, however, shows itself to be inadequate, and so thought moves on to a synthesis in which the tension between the two opposite ideas is overcome. Hegel describes this last step as the *Aufhebung* or annulment of the preceding steps. He means that the final stage resolves the tension between the two preceding stages and posits a new idea which, while annulling them, yet preserves the truth in both of them and expresses it in a richer and more comprehensive idea.

This synthesis soon shows its own inadequacy, and so the dialectical movement is repeated again.

Now Hegel, by identifying the finite spirit as a manifestation
of the Infinite Spirit and by further identifying Spirit with Reason, could describe this movement of human thought as a paradigm of Reality. The processes of the human mind provide clues
to the processes in Reality itself. The movement of thought is a
movement of being. The universe itself becomes a dialectical
process in which each successive stage preserves the truth of the
previous one and moves on to a more comprehensive expression
of truth. So, in reality, the universe becomes a rational movement in which truth already expressed is both preserved and
superseded in later stages of development. The key to nature and
history is to see them as the rational dialectic of the Absolute
Spirit as it moves to self-realization.

Hegel's logic becomes a logic of being, for being itself is rational spirit. Logic becomes ontology. In the process of the universe, ideas that contradict one another find expression and their
tension is resolved in a higher synthesis, in which the truths they
express are preserved and united in a more adequate way, even
though their one-sided forms of expression are annulled or superseded. Here we understand the Absolute Spirit as rational energy
and activity.

Because the logical dialectic is a dialectic of being, Hegel sees
the fundamental triad as that of Being, Nothingness, and Becoming. He regards pure or absolute being as indeterminateness, to
intuit which is to intuit nothing. So pure being moves to nothingness. But nothingness has no content and so it cannot remain
within itself and come to being. The tension is resolved in becoming, in which the indeterminate becomes determinate. An
inexorable ontological necessity drives being into the process of
becoming. The Absolute Spirit thus expresses its ontological logic
by subjectivizing itself in personal subjects and objectivizing itself
in Nature and History.

Nature is what is not the " self," what is other than the subject.
It is the object of spirit and as such is only implicitly spirit. It

appears to be other than spirit and waits to be worked upon and molded that it may move beyond itself to Spirit. It is, indeed, the raw material on which Spirit works, and thus its appearance is the antithesis of Spirit. Because of this, Hegel regards Nature as incomplete in itself, as unfinished. It cannot exist without Spirit, for it is only in Spirit that it attains its true meaning. Equally, Hegel thinks of Spirit as not merely something abstract beyond nature but as really existing and showing itself to be Spirit only " when it involves Nature as absorbed in itself." [10] Indeed, nature is chronologically prior to the emergence of Spirit as individualized subjective centers. It is the presupposition of Spirit, which realizes itself in the conscious embracing of the object by the subject. The Spirit moves to realization as its externalization is done away with and the idea comes back out of nature to identity with the knowing self. [11] Findlay has expressed Hegel's viewpoint concisely:

Spirit is the only reality, but it must confront itself with something seemingly alien, in order to see through its own self-deception, to become aware that it is the only reality. And the creation and setting aside of this strange deception is moreover *necessary* to Spirit, which could have no being without it: Spirit is in fact not merely the goal of its own game, but is indistinguishable from that game itself. [12]

In history and society we have a higher manifestation or revelation of Spirit. The history of the world constitutes " the rational, necessary course of the World Spirit — that Spirit whose nature is always one and the same, but which unfolds this its one nature in the phenomena of the World's existence." [13] History is indeed God's justification, his theodicy, for in history all that has happened and that is happening every day is not " without God " but is actually God's work. [14] In history we have the Spirit in its subjective form, as individual subject, seeking in encounter with natural objects and other persons to move toward self-realization.

In this process the Spirit is manifested not only as " subjective spirit " but also as " objective spirit," for in various human groupings, such as family, city, civil society, and state, it expresses itself in the laws and customs by which man's institutions maintain order. Thus in social ethics the truth of subjective and objective spirit is realized for man, when, as a real person, he accepts his obligations and fulfills his duties according to his station in society. The final form of " objective spirit " is the State. This is an objective reality, in fulfilling their obligations to which persons as " subjective spirit " move to a fuller realization of Spirit. In no actual State is this ideal state realized, although Hegel becomes arrogant in his contention that the German state comes nearest to the ideal. Such realization will be the culmination of universal history. To quote Findlay:

Each more developed State will arise *historically* out of less developed ones, until the fully developed State is achieved. The reason for this historical development of States lies, of course, in the fact that it is only in States, the " Second Nature," that Spirit can achieve full self-consciousness, that it is only by detaching itself from finite individuality through the rules of an established State-order, that it can be aware of itself as universal and " infinite." [15]

Hegel sees history, therefore, as a series of eras, each era characterized by the manifestation of objective spirit for that time. As Boas suggests: " Thus all history can be called spiritual history; it is really the history of the manifestations of the *Geist*." [16]

We have pointed to history as theodicy. Hegel is aware of the tragedy and suffering, frustration and evil, of history, but he regards these as necessary steps in the self-realization of the Spirit. His rational dialectic provides a rationalized form of the doctrine of providence. Since universal history " is the exhibition of Spirit in the process of working out the knowledge of that which it is potentially," [17] all such aspects of history must be necessary aspects in the attaining of the end of Spirit, its self-fulfillment, its full self-consciousness. Thus Hegel declares:

Our intellectual striving aims at recognizing that what eternal wisdom *intended* it has actually *accomplished*, dynamically active in the world, both in the realm of nature and that of the spirit. In this respect our method is a theodicy, a justification of God.[18]

Here Hegel criticizes Leibnitz, and Collins points out that, for Hegel, "Leibnitz ultimately failed because he kept the being of God distinct from the historical process, from the finitude, evil and error in history." [19] There is a "cunning of reason" operative in history, whereby the Spirit inherently completes itself in the process. All history, even its contradictions, serves this grand design. "The struggles and decisions, victories and defeats of moral persons are really only appearances, manifestations of the inner dialectic of the Absolute as it determines itself in time. They are tools in the hands of God and are subject to the power and cunning of reason." [20] Again, the great figures of world history, the conquerors and dictators, have sought their own glory and power, yet they have made possible movements to new realizations of self-consciousness and generally destroyed themselves in the process. [21]

From "objective spirit," Spirit returns to the subjective aspect. The interaction of "subjective" and "objective" spirit in history leads beyond morality to the roots of reality in the deeper levels of religion and philosophy. It is here that the Spirit attains maturity as "Absolute Spirit." "Spirit must now not merely shape the world to its will: it must also see the world as having no other function but to be so shaped, it must see itself, in short, as the 'truth' of everything." [22] The well-ordered State provides, as Findlay points out, the background for such a movement.

Hegel sees, at this point, more fundamental activities of "subjective spirit" — art, religion, and philosophy. He regards art as the synthesis which emerges out of the conflicting claims of our sensible experience and the realm of pure thought. [23] Spirit produces fine art as the first way of reconciling the external and sensuous with the realm of pure thought, expressing its self-consciousness in sensuous form. Art detaches Spirit from the objective by the creation of sensuous forms that, while copying actual things, yet imaginatively distort the objective to express deeper meanings. There is an apparent reference to the objective, for art finds its forms in the external, and yet what is thus imaginatively created is more "true" than actual objects. Artistic creation is based on nature, but it so idealizes nature in its imaginatively created sensuous forms that more dominant ideas take over. The inner life of the Spirit becomes manifested throughout what is objective in its appearance.

The Christian Religion and Philosophy

It is in religion, however, that Spirit progressively moves nearer to self-realization. In religion, man's consciousness of God is central. Here the "subjective" spirit moves to a higher level by its union with the "Absolute Spirit." Hegel passes rapidly from natural religion to revealed religion, and holds that, at this level, there is accomplished through symbol and myth the movement of the finite spirit to union with the Absolute, which can only finally be attained in philosophy. It is significant that Hegel's system rests back upon his early preoccupation with a meditation upon the Christian faith. As Findlay puts it: "It was in the course of his wanderings in the neighbourhood of Golgotha and Gethsemane, rather than in his sojourn in Athenian gardens and colonnades, that Hegel first met 'the Idea.'" [24]

He has, of course, his own peculiar slant upon the religious consciousness. Since his emphasis falls on reason and the universal, he is bound to do two things. First, he will concern himself with the cognitive aspect of religion. He is interested in knowledge, and thus he thinks of religion as a form of knowledge. It expresses such knowledge in metaphorical form. Its language is the language of symbol and myth. It offers a pictorial presentation of truth, and universality is given a semipictorial form. In the religious consciousness we have an imaginative presentation of universal truth. For Hegel, in contrast to Schleiermacher, religion can never be identified with feeling. Feeling cannot be communicated, and to seek to justify faith at this emotional level is impossible. "If one person says you ought to have such feelings, another may reply, I simply *have not* those feelings; as a matter of fact, I *am* not so constituted." [25] Hence Hegel looks for knowledge, even though it be portrayed in imaginative form.

This, in the second place, leads him always to find his idealism in the forms of religion. He is quite clear that faith needs reason to make its content intelligible. The meaning of the revelation that comes to men needs philosophical categories for its understanding. Hegel is convinced that God can be attained only by speculative knowledge. In philosophy alone does the Spirit realize self-consciousness through finite spirit. Hence, for Hegel, religion is wholly a symbolic and pictorial way of expressing the philosophical truth. It does not offer a distinctive truth that passes beyond that which speculation can attain. Its content is in every way identical with that which speculative thought can encompass. It does, however, make such truth available to the masses, who only in this lower way can grasp spiritual truth, i.e., the rational spirit.

Hegel does not deny revelation, therefore. For him, it is perfectly reasonable that the Absolute Spirit should reveal itself to itself as subjective spirit in its movement to self-consciousness. He can write: " Religion is a product of the Divine Spirit; it is not a discovery of man, but a work of divine operation and creation in him." [26] Since the finite spirit is itself a manifestation of the Absolute Spirit, it would be expected that the latter would be operative bringing back the finite spirit to itself. Thus " religion is not only man's consciousness of God but also God's consciousness of Himself in and through man's consciousness of Him." [27] But the Christian religion does not realize this. Hegel regards it as the final religion, but sees its deficiency in its theistic understanding of God. It retains the separation between finite spirit and Absolute Spirit which characterizes " subjective spirit." It does not fully understand that union with God which it describes in terms of love.

Indeed the transcendent God of religious theism must die if the Absolute Spirit is to attain its goal of self-realization in and through the finite spirit in which it is immanently operating. The concept of transcendence bars that basic identity of finite and infinite spirit and, therefore, the God of theism has to die. The movement from religion to philosophy is the transition by which such a "death of God" is accomplished. Only so can the consciousness return to its deep ground of being. There must be "the death of the divine Essence as something abstract and apart"; as Findlay puts it, "We must learn to sing, not despairingly but exultingly, that God Himself has died." [28] There is only one Absolute Spirit, one unified totality of finite and infinite spirit.

Thus, far from accepting the Christian revelation in its unique particularity and in its emphasis on both a personal God and a historical disclosure, Hegel seeks to universalize its insights and to include them in his system as characteristics of the whole process, which apply at every point of that totality. For him, a personal God is simply an inadequate portrayal of that Absolute Spirit which is moving to self-realization through the process of nature and history. The Christian understanding of the Trinity must be universalized to embrace the whole process, since the latter is at every point a manifestation of the Spirit. Hence the triune structure of the divine nature must be understood cosmically. The Father is the simple, eternal Idea, the one Essence, the Spirit in abstraction. But this Essence must present itself as object to something and so it begets of itself the Son. Thereby it returns to itself in self-realization.

At this point creation is given its own peculiar meaning by Hegel. For him, the Christian doctrine of Creation points to the eternal production of objective nature and subjective spirit whereby the Spirit fulfills its movement to self-determination. The Spirit begets the World, and in so doing becomes the World. Hence, for Hegel, the World is the Son. As the World in its centers as "subjective spirit" comes to know the Spirit in nature and in the historical expressions of "objective spirit," the Son comes to know the Father and so the Spirit turns to itself. The Biblical doctrine of the Son or Word as the creative principle through whom all things are created and sustained becomes universalized and conceived in pantheistic terms. The World is no order created out of nothing, but itself an expression of the divine Being. The abstract Essence which is Spirit and indeterminate seeks determination as Son. The World comes into being as Son, to whom the Father presents himself as object. Through the speculative knowledge of the subjective spirits in the world, the Spirit moves back to itself, full circle. Such knowledge is the Holy Spirit.[29]

We note that there is here no suggestion of a personal God creating out of grace, willing in love to share his bliss with his creatures. The world is no act of God's freedom in love. The World comes forth from Spirit as a matter of logical necessity. The Christian doctrine of Creation is an inadequate pictorial presentation of Hegel's conviction that the Eternal Idea or Absolute Spirit is moved by logical necessity to move out of itself into otherness. The Father moves to self-determination in the Son, and, in the World, the one Spirit becomes the many. The World is the alter ego of God, as, in Christian thought, the Son is the alter ego of the Father.

Furthermore, Hegel can now universalize and rationalize the estrangement that Christian insight describes as sin. In the doctrine of the Fall, Christianity represents it as an event, places its emphasis first on the human will. But Hegel emphasizes, first of all, reason. For him this estrangement is associated with the dialectic of the Absolute Spirit. He rightly sees that the Fall story is not just the story of Adam as the first man but the story of every man. Yet he also regards each man as subjective spirit, as a finite manifestation of the Absolute. And it is in man's finitude and particularity that he finds the root of estrangement. This latter is no result of man's free will, no consequence of human rebellion, but a logical necessity in the dialectic of the Spirit. As the Spirit directs itself into centers of subjective spirit, the latter are finite and conscious. As such they feel their independence from the Absolute Spirit, and their persistence in their particularity and finitude is the root of their sin. There arises in man's consciousness a contradiction between his universal nature as spirit and his particularity as a finite self. Sensuous and natural impulses move him to self-centeredness, but even this is within the dialectic. For the sense of estrangement engenders in man a pain and sorrow in which man yearns for reconciliation and atonement. Man of necessity must return to God, for as finite spirit his logical movement is back to the Absolute Spirit. His essential being is the universal Spirit, and he is not just a finite and particular being. The Spirit must return to self-realization out of its finite form.

The Christian religion expresses this reconciliation in the particularity of the Incarnation and in the doctrine of atonement. Hegel can declare that

> man can only know himself taken up, accepted in God in so far as God is to him not a strange being, his relation to whom is merely outward, but in so far as he knows that in God his own being as spirit, as freedom, as subjectivity, is affirmed. But this essential unity of the divine nature with human nature can only be brought home to the consciousness of man, can only become an immediate certainty to him, by God appearing as man and man as God.[30]

In the Incarnation the finite popular consciousness is made immediately aware of its oneness with Absolute Spirit at the level of sense experience. The Christian religion is right in seeing reconciliation as a divine act. God " humbles himself."

This religious presentation really means that the universal Spirit in its indeterminateness enters into particularity by necessity. Indeed the Absolute Spirit becomes particular and finite. Further, it moves to the extreme point and suffers death. As Stace puts it: " Negation, otherness, finitude, are part of the very substance of God, and this is a necessary element in the idea of God as Spirit." [31] In this way the estrangement is removed, and finite spirit is reunited with infinite spirit. For the Resurrection and Ascension of Christ, in which the Christian religion glories, are also a part of the movement. The Absolute Spirit has become a particular subjective spirit, and now it returns to itself. The Incarnation, Death, Resurrection, and Ascension become exemplifications of the pattern that the Absolute Spirit must *continually* fulfill as it moves from abstract loneliness to full self-realization. This is why Hegel can write that " the seriousness, the suffering, the patience, and the labour of the negative " are requisite for Spirit.[32]

The Incarnation both makes men certain of the unity of the finite spirit with the universal spirit and is paradigmatic of the whole movement of the Absolute to self-determination. "The descent of the abstract universal into sensuous embodiment is also, of course, the elevation of what is sensuous into what is abstract and notional: the death of God leads to His Resurrection and Ascension."[33]

In the same way, Hegel universalizes and rationalizes the Christian understanding of the Church and the Holy Spirit. The Holy Spirit is present in Christ's Church. Here the unity of God and men is made explicit. In the Incarnation, the self-consciousness of Jesus was actually a communal self-consciousness. His realized oneness with the Absolute Spirit waits to be shared by all men. In the Church that process is taking place. As the Divine Man, Christ's self-consciousness is incorporative. Other men may make it theirs. The return movement of spirit to the unity with the Absolute Spirit is not confined to the Incarnation, and the latter must not be regarded as merely an event in the past. The life, death, resurrection, and ascension of Christ must be moments in the life of the community of the Church. They must mark the continuing movement of the Spirit in the Christian community. The Spirit "dies there daily, and daily rises again."[34] Indeed, just as the Father is the Divine Essence alone and in the abstract and the Son is the World, so the Holy Spirit is the movement to self-realization of the Absolute Spirit. He is present in the Church.

In this community, the Incarnation loses its factuality and particularity. The death of the Mediator becomes universal. Just as, in the movement of his life, subjective spirit was united with the abstract Divine Essence and the process to self-realization of the Spirit attained, so with the communal life of men in the Church. His death loses its particularity and becomes universalized. His self-existence loses its particularity and factuality to become a universal self-consciousness.[35] Men must die to their particularity and rise to that self-consciousness in which they know their oneness with the Absolute.

That men feel this union with the Absolute Spirit in the form of love is only a pictorial presentation. In the Church man gives up his self-centered existence and enters into union with God. His retention in this of the picture of a transcendent God and his own over-againstness must finally be dissolved. To die to particularity means finally to die to all imaginative and pictorial presentation. Hence religious imagination, with its myths and symbols, must give place to philosophy. Theistic personal distinctness must be annulled or overcome. Hegel sees religion as the threshold of "the process, in which what is absolutely in opposition recognizes itself as the same as its opposite." [36] Here "Ego is nothing but bare identity with Ego, a darkness distinguishing and knowing nothing more outside it." [37] As the religious consciousness, to which the Absolute Spirit is disclosing itself, realizes this, it "does away with the distinction of its self from what it beholds." [38]

But this means also the death of the theistic God, the transcendent deity. The death of the pictorial idea of religion means the death of the abstraction of Divine Being. This happens as religion moves to the higher level of philosophy. As Collins has put it:

Since theism stands in the way of the essential identity between the consciousness and its highest object, philosophy must regard God as forever a dead God and must seek the living actuality only in the one absolute self or spiritual totality of finite and infinite being. Only then is the religious impulse toward self-transcendence given a thoroughly immanent interpretation and realization free from all illusion of theistic personal distinctness. [39]

Religion paints a picture of God's otherness, so that salvation is an act of his grace. But this imaginative presentation has to be annulled, for the Spirit is identified with man himself. This is what the Incarnation means when it is universalized. The theistic God and human particularity must alike die, be annulled, and universal self-conscious Spirit rise out of their grave. Man must cease stubbornly to assert his irreducible particularity and independence, and to do this he must affirm the death of the Christian God. The realm of the Holy Spirit marks this movement in the process, and Hegel can celebrate the "death of God," not in Nietzsche's sense, but in the sense of abstract transcendent deity.[40]

At the philosophical level, the Spirit moves to self-realization. Here man sees the whole as a rational system. Philosophy sees "truth," "ultimate truth," as the system of reality. The Absolute Spirit is sole Reality and it is rational. Hence it is the Truth. All that is finite is a moment in the life of the Spirit, and thus all finite entities must be understood in their relatedness to all other entities within the Whole that is Absolute Spirit. Thus Hegel would have us see Reality on the basis of an organic model. Yet the relatedness is not conceived in vital terms but in rational terms. The parts are moments in the evolution of the Absolute Idea. The Whole in its differentiation is a process moving to ever greater self-determination and self-enlightenment. This is the Truth.[41] Only as the philosopher knows himself rationally as one with that Whole can he build all the parts into a rational system and so attain the Truth. So Hegel can tell us that "truth is only realized in the form of a system." [42] Philosophy seeks for a comprehensive and rational Whole in which all the individual truths can alone be really true. Taken apart from their relationships within the Whole as the rational process of Absolute Spirit, they lose significance. Their particularity and independence must be overcome by the movement of reason to show their interrelatedness within a rational system.

Even temporal relations must be so understood. Hegel can tell us that "time is the pure self in external form, apprehended in intuition and not grasped and understood by the self, it is the notion apprehended only through intuition. When this notion grasps itself, it supersedes its time character, (conceptually) comprehends intuition, and is intuition comprehended and comprehending." [43] But let us note at once that time is here given objective reality, for it is "spirit's destiny and necessity, where spirit is not yet complete within itself." The Truth is process built into a system that culminates in the self-realization of the Absolute Spirit. As the philosopher attains this system, he is Spirit coming to such self-determination. When he attains it, time is annulled or overcome.[44]

Hegel's Significance

Hegel was undoubtedly one of the most influential philosophers down to the early decades of the present century. He shared with Kant the leading place in influencing and providing a framework for theological speculation, although by the 1920's he was being superseded by his great critic Kierkegaard and the existentialist emphasis. As the form of classical idealism which he represented fell into disrepute and a new empiricist emphasis began to take its place in the present century, his thought has fallen under a cloud. But there are signs that some aspects of his teaching are still actively present with us, and it is to such aspects that we must soon turn our attention.

It is not difficult to see that Christian thinkers might be attracted by Hegel in the last century, for he was profoundly influenced by Christian concepts in the early days of his thought, and he clothed his system in a Christian dress. As we have just seen, he attempted to universalize and immanentize the Christian revelation and thereby robbed it of its true content. He detached it from its historical roots, trying to remove the scandal that attached to the historical particularity of its revelation. He dethroned the transcendent Creator and elevated the finite creature, finishing with a system that is at root pantheistic or, at best, pan-entheistic.

In his attempt to find what was universal and rational in the Christian Gospel and to eliminate its particularity, he was a true child of the Age of Enlightenment. The rational deists of the eighteenth century had attempted just the same thing. We have only to remember a title like Anthony Collins' *Gospel as Old as Creation* to realize this. Reason operating upon the works of creation was sufficient to provide the enduring and significant content that Christianity claimed in its own specific divine revelation. Hegel's rationalism and its method were different from this. He leaned much more on the revelation itself and made no attempt to employ arguments, such as the cosmological and teleological, which the older rationalism had employed because of its empiricist base. Yet the net result was the same — the transformation of the Christian Gospel into universal truth that could be rationally apprehended and confirmed.

Hegel was evidently not a Christian philosopher in any sense, even though he attempted to give his system a Christian veneer. Fundamentally, he rejected Christian theism with its transcendence and its stance on the separation between God and man, Creator and creature. He began with man's universal experience, but his basic analogue was not personal being with its freedom of decision. He began with that reason which he believed all men to have in common and made it the model for understanding the universe. Furthermore, he identified the human logos with the divine Logos and defined " Spirit " in rational and universal terms. " Spirit " was not for Hegel personal being but the dynamic energy of thought. By identifying the human " spirit " with the divine " Spirit," the Absolute Idea, he moved away from theism to a near pantheism.

He himself frequently rejected such a description. In particular, he ridiculed the popular cosmic form of pantheism which identifies God with everything in the world as everything appears at the empirical level. It makes every entity divine without relating it to the One. The more sophisticated systems like those of Spinoza and Hinduism were attacked on the ground that they relate individual entities to the One in the wrong way. Such systems do not identify God with everything that is finite. Instead, they regard God, the One, as the sole reality, and all finite things as unreal. Their acosmic pantheism is as false as the popular cosmic pantheism.[45]

Their mistake, Hegel contends, is in not regarding the One as mind. In such a system, finite entities can have their own degree of reality. Hence Hegel's system can be styled objective idealism. The finite is real, but it is not ultimate reality. The latter must be understood as dynamic rational " Spirit," as mind, as Idea. Thus the unity in the universe is to be conceived in dynamic terms, and the universe becomes the dialectical movement of one rational Spirit. The finite entities of the world then have reality as moments in the divine life as it unfolds itself. Hegel sees pantheism as static. Its One is unchanging substance, an undialectic stuff. He therefore rejects the description " pantheism " for his system, claiming that his Absolute Monism does allow for the reality of the finite.

Yet the reality of the World is not that ascribed to it in the Biblical revelation or in Christian theism. Creation is not " out of nothing," for the World comes from God in the dialectical movement of his being. Finite spirits are identified with the One Spirit within this movement and have their own reality only within it. But the radical over-againstness of God and man is not maintained. Schmidt describes Hegel's system as " dialectical Panentheism." He writes: " All comes from God and all is in God; all is created by God and all remains as a moment in Him. God is the movement towards the world and the annulment (*Aufhebung*) of the world." [46]

Furthermore, the near pantheism or panentheism of Hegel denies transcendence. His is an immanentism, and he can celebrate joyfully the death of the transcendent deity as men move from the imaginative pictorial presentations of religion to the rational dialectic of philosophical thought. He even tries, as we have seen, to adapt the Trinity to his immanentist structure. The eternal generation of the Son or Word becomes identified with the dialectical movement of the Absolute Spirit from its lonely abstraction into the creation of the world. The Holy Spirit can be described as the return of the Absolute Spirit from this movement into self-realization.

We have defined Christian philosophy as Christian in intention. It seeks suitable analogues in the general human experience but applies to them insights which can be derived solely from the Christian revelation in its particularity. On this basis Hegel's philosophy can offer no satisfactory basis for a Christian natural theology or a Christian apologetic. It minimizes the individual and ignores the personal particular in its full range of relationships. It ignores also human freedom in any real sense and rationalizes human estrangement and alienation into a necessary stage in the logical dialectic of Spirit. Likewise, reconciliation becomes identification of the "subjective spirit" with the "Absolute Spirit" through rational process. The emphasis falls on the ontological rather than the ethical. It is not man's will or existential decision that matters but rational union with a rational Absolute. In thus ignoring personal being in all its dimensions, God, too, is denuded of personal being and becomes dynamic rational Energy. Thereby Hegel evades the issue of personal self-transcendence, which might be a model for divine transcendence, and finishes with an immanentism of rational Spirit.

Yet we can also be grateful to Hegel for his attempt to take time and history seriously and to emphasize the aspect of process and becoming in human experience. He helped to move men philosophically from static to dynamic categories. In the paradox of being and becoming, eternity and time, he sought to give becoming and time reality. Hegel gives "a magnificent recognition of the fundamental importance of history for man, of the place and necessity of the human sacrificial, self-giving element in the movement of history, and of the significant presence of the Spirit who gives history eternal meaning." [47] Except that we would interpret Spirit as personal will rather than rational Energy, there was here a genuinely Christian insight, for the Christian emphasis on Creation and Incarnation suggests that human history has meaning for God in terms of the divine will and purpose. God is involved in history, not in Hegel's sense of dialectical identification, but in the sense of personal relationship and love. Furthermore, temporal processes of nature and history are meaningful to God, again not in Hegel's sense of a divine movement to self-determination, but as the arena of God's grace, his self-giving, creative love. What this means we must yet seek to delineate.

Hegel's failure was due to his identification of the human spirit as an adjectival existence of the Absolute. As a consequence, he can hold that the essential aspects of man's personal and historical life are also necessary elements in the life of the Absolute. The "dying to live" which he finds in the life of the subjective spirit then becomes lifted to the Absolute Spirit. God also must die in his solitude and transcendence and live in the process of history. Altizer quickly seized on this idea and applied it illogically to his own mysterious amalgam.[48] History becomes logically essential to the life of the Absolute and not a manifestation of his free creating and gracious love — what Barth has called his "loving in freedom." Furthermore, "dying to live" becomes also a rational necessity for the Divine Essence.

Hegel did not resolve the paradox of being and becoming which might to some degree be resolved in more personal and theistic categories. He had launched idealistic thought on a movement from an emphasis on being to one on becoming. In doing so he had sounded the death knell of the old type of idealism. It could never return to concern with an unchanging Absolute. Indeed, in the end, the emphasis on time and process tended toward humanistic or naturalistic or even materialistic ways of thinking. Hegel's attempt to universalize the particulars of history and process is a reminder that, because of his rationalism, he never really escaped what William James called the "block universe." In some sense the Absolute Spirit was already there, and yet it was also becoming. Either Being or Becoming would appear to be superfluous. As Collins puts it:

Either eternal consciousness is sufficiently actual in itself and reduces the temporal process of nature and man to an illusory play of forms, or there is a total reduction of the absolute to the human spirit, which alone is truly actual in its natural setting. Upon this dilemma of an absolutism of infinite spirit versus an absolutism of man-in-nature, the Hegelian system founders and splits asunder.[49]

Hegel never really answered the question why the Absolute should have historical experiences.

The Emphasis on Process and Becoming

It is not our concern to trace in detail all the ramifications of Hegelian influence. It will be sufficient, for instance, to remind ourselves that the English Absolute Idealism of the turn of the nineteenth century went the way of " being " and denied any real significance to process and becoming. This is exemplified in the thought of F. H. Bradley, Bernard Bosanquet, and T. H. Green.

But idealism did also move into a more dynamic form and place its emphasis on process in the thought of Neo-Idealists like Croce and his English disciple R. G. Collingwood. Here the basic conviction is that the process of becoming is the sole reality, that it is to be understood from the idealistic standpoint, and that the fundamental model or analogy is thinking. To these philosophers we owe real insights into historical knowledge, especially R. G. Collingwood. For both him and Croce, the process of history took primacy over the evolution of man's natural environment.

Croce [50] was a complete immanentist for whom there was no transcendence. For him, as for Hegel, spirit is the sole reality, but the human spirit occupies a regnant position. The thought of any transcendent Spirit, such as theism claims, is vigorously denied. The sole reality is the process of history which is spirit itself, finding its supreme expression in the human spirit. Nature has no independence; it too must be understood as part of the process. Indeed, all that is real is this present moment in which the spirit is dynamic movement, active thinking. There is no transcendence in the sense that the past has any reality, for it too is only real as it is in the present thinking of some human mind. Even historical evidence, such as artifacts and documents, has to be taken into the human mind that it may evoke, in the self-knowledge of that mind, a living concern with the past. Only as the past lives again in the imagination of present thinking has it any reality. Historical evidences are instruments, " acts preparatory to that internal vital evocation in whose process they are resolved." [51] We are left with a creative, dynamic flux of events, the essence of which is thinking.

Indeed, philosophy is history. Its task is to describe the activities of the human mind as these are expressed in the historical process. Like Hegel, Croce places such philosophy in the center and relegates religion to a very subordinate place. It too is characterized by knowledge, for Croce is an idealist, but it is inferior knowledge, expressed in mythological form. "Philosophy," he writes, "removes from religion all reason for existing, because it substitutes itself for religion. As the science of the spirit, it looks upon religion as a phenomenon, a transitory historical fact, a psychic condition that can be surpassed." [52] Since the individual minds are Spirit thinking, history becomes philosophy. Philosophy is historical thinking, expressing in general and universal terms historical persons and events in their particularity. Science for Croce is purely pragmatic. It is concerned solely with universal relationships, whereas true and vital thinking, the true manifestation of spirit, historical thinking, weds the universal to the particular. As we shall see later, there are parallels here to the thought of Bergson.

Croce does, to some degree, give man a more significant place in history than Hegel. His immanentism makes man the focal manifestation of thinking Spirit. Yet he does this at the expense of transcendence and at the cost of denying any theistic God. Further, he denies to man true personhood and majors on the rational aspect of human experience. Yet he does give a larger place to man's freedom and creativity, as the title of one of his books indicates — *History as the Story of Liberty.* In doing this, however, he verges on a relativism. For if past history is real only in the mind of the thinker, its actualization is very much dependent upon the latter's outlook and values. The present concern and interest of the thinker is central.

To argue that all thinking is the Absolute Spirit, the expression of its total immanence, implies that true and false values and meanings in our review of the past cannot be really distinguished, since all are thinking and have their ground in the Spirit. We are left with complete relativism. [53]

This relativism becomes much more evident in R. G. Collingwood, although he was sufficiently under the influence of Dilthey to seek for objectivity in historical judgment and thinking. [54]

Very much more to the left of the Hegelian school and much earlier than Croce, we find Feuerbach, himself a pupil of Hegel.

With this philosopher, the movement from being to becoming is central, and with it the movement from the One to the Many. For the Absolute Spirit has no place in the thought of Feuerbach. Rather he is concerned with man in his natural setting, and the resultant might be labeled "naturalistic humanism." For him the true and actual is not the rational Absolute but man. Man is the measure of reason, and man's own nature is the absolute for man.[55]

Thus Absolute Spirit and theistic deity alike vanish from Feuerbach's understanding of what is actual. Indeed, God and religion are purely functional. Religion's apprehension of the infinite is really man's apprehension of the infinite depths of his own self-conscious being. God arises out of the situation in which man sees his own unlimited nature in objective terms and envisages it as separate from himself. His own actual nature is contemplated as another being, and he projects his own image on the backdrop of the universe. But actual man is the only true God to himself. The atheistic posture is the only true historical one, and when man adopts it, he is free to develop the inherent qualities of his own essential being. Faced by an environment that thwarts such realization, he tends to divide himself from the true deeps of his nature and project his essential being upon the universe as an independent infinite deity. His historical salvation consists in realizing this false dichotomy, and in giving his religion a humanistic and social expression in the service of his fellows.

Man in his temporal engagement and historical life thus becomes central. Historical process takes over as the sole reality, and man's interpersonal relationships, in which he realizes his own infinite depths, are the stuff of history. We must add to this anthropological reading of history its essential earthiness. There is a basic materialism in Feuerbach's understanding of man. Man is basically what he eats. At the practical level, the affirmation of God's existence makes no difference to man's historical life. No practical consequences flow from man's intellectual speculation about a supreme being. As an active being, man concerns himself with what he believes to be worth striving for. And for Feuerbach the dominant interests belong to the sensuous level.[56] Feuerbach sees historical man in his corporeality, his *Dasein*-ness. Man is a unity, but the unity of body and spirit is shot through by sensuousness. In interhuman relationships, man is an object of the senses to his fellows. " Only a sensuous being am I *I* (for myself) and likewise Thou (for others), for sensuousness includes outer and inner, spirit and flesh, thing and I. Thus truth, reality and sensuousness are all identical with human nature." [57] Here he gives emphasis to man's sexuality by which he is bound to a being different from himself, " a being which belongs to me and contributes to the determination of my own existence." [58] Man's historical existence is corporeal existence, and it is fundamentally bound up with the senses — empiricist and sensuous. For Feuerbach, history marches on man's stomach. Process has descended from the level of the self-determination by the rational Spirit to the level of determination by the natural. The way was prepared for Karl Marx.

III

From Process and Naturalism to Creative Evolution and Emergent Deity

WITH THE FULL ADVENT of evolutionary ideas at the biological level in consequence of the work of Darwin and Wallace, a new category entered philosophical thought. From being a useful concept for the understanding of biological development, "evolution" came to be regarded as a model in the light of which the universe might be comprehended. The ambitious attempt of Herbert Spencer [1] to construct a philosophical system in this way stands as an indication of how soon the "model" caught fire in philosophical circles. Hegel's understanding of "process" had made no use of such ideas, but some of those who were influenced by him soon took evolutionary ideas into their scheme of thinking, especially those who belonged to the left wing of the Hegelian movement.

It now became possible to take time seriously in a new way and to apply the idea of history to nature. Nature might no longer be regarded as a fixed and unchanging background against which the process of human history played out its drama. The species were no longer to be thought of as fixed. Static concepts were being replaced by dynamic ones in nature, just as such a change had already taken place at the human level under the impact of Hegelianism. Moreover, biological evolution, as developed by Darwin, had seemed to banish any idea of an extraneous intervention by a transcendent deity or even of any immanent directive presence. Darwin's emphasis upon small chance variations weeded out by natural selection had placed the emphasis upon randomness. It certainly demolished the old natural theology which had emphasized the presence of design in nature and had argued from biological evidence to the reality of a divine and transcendent designer. Darwin could write:

There seems to be no more design in the variability of organic beings and in the action of natural selection, than in the course which the wind blows. Everything in nature is the result of fixed laws.[2]

This last sentence might seem to suggest a return to the very position which he has just denied. But we must note that the fixed laws were no longer the cast-iron rails along which the universe had to travel as ordained by a beneficent creator. They were statistical in form. The law of natural selection is the declaration that the survival of the fittest operates universally and that nature moves forward by a process of trial and error. Even the idea of the fittest involves no transcendent value judgment, for the argument here is circular. The fittest is that which survives and only the fittest survive. There is no way within such a point of view to give any objective evaluation to the description "fittest." It is true, of course, that in their more optimistic moments the early Darwinists thought in terms of progress and celebrated the appearance of man in the process. This might seem to indicate some definition of "fittest." Yet such appearance was at best a happy concatenation of chance circumstances. In addition, the process by which man had been produced was so wasteful and full of suffering that it was difficult to reconcile it with a beneficent creator.

Thus Hegel's idealistic emphasis came to be challenged, on the basis of the new scientific data, by a growing naturalism. The latter took many forms, from Marx's dialectical materialism to Spencer's synthetic philosophy to the point of view advocated by the family line of the Huxleys. Implicit in some of these there was at least some indication of a directiveness which implied the presence of immanent Spirit. Furthermore, some religious people soon began, often with difficulty, to incorporate the movement of evolution into their theological understanding of the world. The idea of creation came to be associated with evolutionary development. There began to appear a new kind of dynamic natural theology or religious metaphysic in which phrases such as "creative evolution" and "emergent qualities" were used.

In this present century we have seen major philosophical attempts to use "evolution" as a key model for understanding the universe in teleological terms. We have also seen many philosophers who are convinced Neo-Darwinists, such as Dobzhansky [3] and Fisher,[4] advocating the description of the evolutionary process as "creative." Fisher can hold that the determinative factor in evolution is "the mutual reaction of each organism with the whole ecological situation in which it lives — the creative action of one species on another." [5] Biologists who are avowedly Christian, such as these and W. H. Thorpe,[6] thus have not the fears of nineteenth-century Christian thinkers in facing the scientific machinery postulated for evolutionary development.

It is our purpose to show how the combination of Feuerbach's naturalistic humanism with the evolutionary ideas of the last century produced in Marx, Engels, and their successors a form of naturalism, dialectical materialism, which has made and still makes extensive use of evolutionary categories. From this we shall pass to thinkers in the first decades of this century who recaptured the evolutionary model for, from the Christian point of view, a more creative approach to reality.

Dialectical Materialism — Naturalism Not Really Triumphant

We have just noted that Feuerbach stood Hegel's Absolute Idealism on its head. His saying, Man is what he eats, indicates his position. It is not mind but matter that is primary. Man's thought is determined by its material and natural context. The material conditions of man's life determine his nature in its totality. It is significant that Feuerbach holds that this position is not one of mechanical materialism, such as was advocated by Hobbes, La Mettrie, and Holbach. He does not elaborate the naturalism that he advocates, and it remained for Marx and Engels to elaborate it still more fully and to do so on a Hegelian basis.

Hegel had seen the universe as a process of becoming, which was fundamentally a dialectic of thought. Reality was rational. Marx and Engels, following Feuerbach, turned the process on its head and regarded it as a dialectical movement of matter. The world is not a projection of absolute mind into objective and subjective forms. It is grounded in the tension between opposing patterns of matter and their synthesis at a higher level. This holds alike of nature and history. Engels [7] was quick to indicate that the older mechanistic materialism could not account for the transformations in the process whereby the qualitatively new appeared. Because it concerned itself with quantity and mechanical relationship, it was inevitably cyclic. But the new approach to history and the evolutionary view of nature alike made it impossible to ignore the irreversible elements in the process. Mere rearrangements of quantity in a mechanical relationship could not account for or predict new qualities. Furthermore, science had by this time begun to be aware of the way in which energy could transform itself from mechanical to electrical and chemical forms. Nature itself had a dynamic quality at the physical level in the transformations of energy; at the vital level in the dynamics of the living cell; at the biological level with the process of evolution. Now these all seemed to require no nonmaterial intervention. Hence Marx and Engels looked for a materialist philosophy that was dynamic, not static.

They found it in a dialectical movement. In this movement there is a transformation of quantity into quality, as energy is transformed. Thus quantitative changes result in qualitative changes, and there is a leap from one level of organization of matter to another with new qualities. The Russian scientist

M. Shirokov, in describing how a living organism arose out of
inorganic matter, denies the presence of any "vital force" and
suggests that a purely external analysis of the organism into its
components would display nothing but physicochemical processes. He continues:

But this by no means denotes that life amounts to a simple aggregate
of these physico-chemical elements. The particular physico-chemical
processes are connected in the organism by a new form of movement,
and it is in this that the quality of the living thing lies. The new in a
living organism, not being attributable to physics and chemistry, arises
as the result of the new synthesis, of the new connection of physical
and chemical movements. This synthetic process whereby out of the
old we proceed to the emergence of the new was understood neither by
the mechanists nor the vitalists.[8]

Such a movement is characterized by two laws — the law of
the interpenetration or unity of opposites and the law of the
negation of negation. At every level in nature and every era in
history, the Marxist sees a tension of opposites, a struggle between elements in contradiction. Nature is full of apparently
irreconcilable antagonisms, and yet these are synthesized at a
higher level of organization. Stalin could write that these internal
contradictions are inherent in all natural phenomena and that
"the struggle between the old and the new, that which is dying
and that which is being born, constitutes the internal content of
the process of development."[9] He can describe nature as in a
"state of continuous movement and change, of continuous re-
newal and development, where something is always arising and
developing, and something always disintegrating and dying."[10]
Yet the negation of negation is also within a unity, for nature
is "a connected and integral whole, in which things, phenomena,
are organically connected with, dependent on, and determined
by each other."[11] Thus, we return to the issue of life. The opposites are the lower physicochemical movements of molecular
structures and the new aggregations which would make life possible. Out of their tension a new synthesis emerges, a living cell,

in which both contradictory elements play their part. Elements of both the warring movements are present at the higher integrated level, but the transformation to this level was possible only because new and contradictory movements of aggregation arose at the lower level. Here the transformation of quantity into quality, the unity of opposites, and the negation of negation are all illustrated.

Contemporary Russian Marxists make much of this dialectical movement whereby new forms of organization of matter appear. They are thus careful to differentiate between the laws operative at the physicochemical level and those at the biological level, while maintaining that the essential unity of the levels is material. Zavadovsky writes:

The true task of scientific research is not the violent identification of the biological and the physical, but the discovery of the qualitatively specific controlling principles which characterize the main features of every phenomenon, and the finding of methods of research appropriate to the phenomena studied. . . . It is necessary to renounce both the simplified reduction of some sciences to others, and also the sharp demarcations between the physical, biological and socio-historical sciences.[12]

Engels [13] was concerned with this dialectical movement in nature, but he and Marx threw a greater emphasis on its presence in history as the governing principle. Like nature, history was also dominated by the two laws. Engels can say that their presence in nature leads to the recognition of nature " as an historical process." [14] At the historical level proper, material forces operate as economic pressures. History is basically an economic movement. Political and ideological structures are simply rationalizations of economic processes. Here the Marxists are true to their thesis that the mental is determined by the material, and that thought arises out of and reflects its material matrix. Engels tells us that " the real unity of the world consists in its materiality, and this is proved not by a few juggling phrases but by a long and protracted development of philosophy and natural science." [15] Human thought simply reflects this material unity with its tension of opposites and its dialectical movement. The real difference between nature and history lies in just this presence of human consciousness. Engels writes:

The history of the growth of society appears, however, in one respect entirely different from that of nature. In nature are to be found as far as we leave the reaction of man upon nature out of sight — mere unconscious blind agents which act one upon another and in their interplay the universal law realizes itself. . . . On the contrary, in the history of society the mere actors are all endowed with consciousness; they are agents imbued with deliberation or passion, men working towards an appointed end; nothing appears without an intentional purpose, without an end desired.[16]

It might seem here as if Engels is denying the materialistic determinism which he claims to dominate both nature and history. He is careful, however, to safeguard his position at both levels. He acknowledges that at the level of nature, the element of contingency is present on the surface of things, but he points to a regularity that is inherent within the apparent randomness and accidental happenings. He then argues that the same holds of history. Here we find, on the surface, innumerable individual wills in conflict. The human actions are intended, directed to many opposing goals. Yet as with the contingency in nature, the overall " results which follow from the actions are not intended, or in so far as they appear to correspond with the end desired, in their final results are quite different from the conclusions wished." [17] Thus in the cases of both nature and history, the superficial impression of chance must be replaced by the understanding of inner, universal laws. And these laws are those associated with a materialistic dialectical movement. Engels can thus contend that history discloses the predominance of the unforeseen. He writes that " uncontrolled forces are far more powerful than those set into motion according to plan." [18]

Individual wills in history cannot, therefore, vitiate the inevitable movement of the dialectic, and the uncontrolled forces at this level take the form of economic pressures. Production is the governing factor in history for both Marx and Engels. The religious goals, moral ideals, cultural values, and political ideologies of any historical group are determined by economic needs. Men's intentions, however idealistic, basically reflect their economic conditions. Hence, for Marx as for Feuerbach, religion is a projection of man's material hungers. It is an opiate of the people, a drug by which the oppressed are kept in economic subjection by visions of a glorious afterlife. Or it and the call for some idealistic justice and freedom are the cries by which some rising economic group seeks to make a place for itself in the sun. What men really need is economic freedom and economic justice — the rest is appearance. Hence religion and philosophy alike have the quality of rationalizing procedures. Their real function is to protect the interests of a dominant economic group.

This is almost akin to Hegel's " cunning of reason." The materialistic dialectic attains its inevitable goal even in and through the human consciousness. Thus the economic " haves " will produce an opposing group from among the " have-nots," and out of the tension of the opposites, a new ruling economic group will emerge synthetically, only in its turn to be subject to the same dialectic with its negation of negation. Revolution becomes that step in the dialectic by which prevailing conditions are negated. Man's salvation consists solely in consciously controlling social production [19] and so hastening on the process by which the final leap of the dialectic will bring mankind to the abolition of social classes and the communist utopia. One might almost suggest that the dialectical process uses thought to achieve its goal, pointing thereby the human consciousness to ever higher social organizations. In this way, the antagonistic social structures will ultimately issue in a classless, economically satisfying society. Evolution will thus have attained its goal.

It is not our purpose in this book to subject the economic theories involved to criticism. But, because this naturalistic evolutionism is the dominant credo over large parts of the earth's surface, we should acknowledge its insights as well as its weaknesses.

Its emphasis on the economic factor, although utterly exclusive and deterministic, does remind us that economic conditions do play an important role in the processes of human history. While they do not determine man's ideals and religious goals, they certainly condition the way in which they are expressed. If we are concerned with man in his total personal being, we must take account of the economic factor in his *Sitz im Leben*. Even our religious institutions and the contemporary forms taken by our Christian faith reflect the shaping influence of such economic factors.

Again, Marx never forgot his Jewish origins. The system that he and Engels propounded could not have arisen except in a Judeo-Christian environment. Even though they claimed to invert the Hegelian system and put it the right way up, they were as much influenced by Christian ideas as Hegel himself. Their atheism is really a rejection of the institutional forms and fossilized structures of belief with which they themselves were familiar, in particular, the Lutheranism of Marx's Germany in the mid-nineteenth century. Yet what they offer is a linear movement of nature and history, on the model of the Judeo-Christian faith, but one that derives its directiveness from a purely materialistic base. They transform into economic terms the ideas of sin (capitalism), judgment (economic crisis and antagonism), salvation (economic freedom and the classless society). Theirs is a Messianism brought down to earth. Yet they can give no reason why once their end point is attained, the dialectical process should not itself continue.

Indeed, their atheism seems at times to deny itself, and there seems to be a kind of *deus ex machina* within their materialistic dialectic. R. C. Zaehner has pointed to passages in which Marx and Engels point to more than a purely materialistic dialectic. Thus Marx can describe the first and most important qualities of matter as motion. He goes on to define such motion as not only mechanical movement, " but still more impulse, vital spirit, tension." He continues: " The primary forms of matter are the living, individualizing forces of being inherent in it and producing the distinctions between the species." [20] Thus Engels' attack upon mechanistic materialism is confirmed, and matter is regarded in vital terms. This, indeed, would seem to be the only way in which it could be regarded, in the light of the emphasis on the dialectical movement and its universal laws. The same stricture would apply to the contemporary Communist emphasis on organizing relations and new integrative levels. These too indicate something akin to organizing purpose or spirit immanent in matter.

Zaehner points out that there is one passage in Engels' posthumously published *Dialectics of Nature* that even goes beyond such a position. For Engels can speak of death as

either the dissolution of the organic body, leaving nothing behind but the chemical constituents that formed its substance, or it leaves behind a vital principle, more or less the soul, that then survives *all* living organisms, and not only human beings.[21]

He evidently, by the context of this passage, is denying individual immortality. By associating this "vital principle, more or less the soul," with all living organisms, he may, however, be pointing to a World Soul as a live option of his dialectic and thus to a form of naturalistic pantheism. R. C. Zaehner comments on this passage and its context:

What he seems to mean is that since life and death are dialectical poles of the one substance, matter, life itself must survive the death of all individual living organisms, for in death too the free development of each is the condition for the free development of all. Whatever else may die, matter itself must live on forever.[22]

If this be true, then Hegel's emphasis on Absolute Spirit still endures in the left-wing camp despite the protestations of its protagonists. What the latter call matter also possesses inherent forms. This alone could account for its dialectical movement. And what is this but what idealists would call "Spirit"? Matter as motion is capable of producing heat, electricity, chemical action, life out of itself.[23] Its highest creation, the thinking mind, may be destroyed on this planet, but the inherent attributes of matter can never be destroyed, for "matter remains eternally the same in all its transformations . . . with the same iron necessity that it will exterminate on earth its highest creation, the thinking mind, it must somewhere else and at another time again produce it." [24]

This tacit acceptance of an inner nisus which gives inevitable directiveness to the dialectical process alone explains why, with their materialistic presupposition, Marx and Engels do not fall into a pure emphasis on chance and contingency. Even when they are dealing with the human consciousness, they are ambivalent. On the one hand, the human mind simply reflects the material processes that produce and determine it. Yet, on the other hand, it is the *highest* creation of the dialectical process. Indeed, the tremendous attraction of modern Marxism is that it does give men a this-worldly hope. It thus exalts that very aspect of human nature, thought and mind, which it is so anxious to treat in the stages of historical development as a mere reflection of the dialectical process of matter. The truth would appear to be that a process which produces mind in the end would demand an ontological base in mind.

Actually the attitude of Marx and Engels on religion is not true to the historical evidence. Far from supporting the *status quo,* Christianity has often opposed it. Although too often otherworldly, Christianity has also retained a this-worldly emphasis. Although economic factors have influenced theological thought and religious expression, prophets and martyrs have given the lie to any suggestion that economic pressures determine the thoughts and faith of a religious man. But the biggest refutation of their arguments is the presence of chinks in their armor where a more spiritual interpretation of process seems tacit under their dogmatic " materialism."

Emergent Evolution – From Naturalism and Empiricism to Pantheism and Evolving Deity

With the dawning of the twentieth century, the idea of using evolution as a controlling metaphysical model came to the fore. In the Anglo-Saxon world it found expression in the Gifford Lec-

tures of Lloyd Morgan and Samuel Alexander. Both these thinkers introduced into their interpretation of the universe the concept
of emergence. Lloyd Morgan [25] differentiated an emergent from
a resultant. A resultant is a new quality that is wholly explicable
in terms of its antecedents. An emergent is a novelty, a new appearance, which the previous level of the evolutionary process is
insufficient to account for. The antecedent arrangements of existent entities are not sufficient to account for the quality that
appears when a regrouping occurs. More evolves than was involved. Thus emergence indicates a new kind of relatedness to
the preceding levels of the evolutionary process, such that its
specific character could not be predicted by or explained in
terms of the lower levels from which it has emerged. As a simple
example of this, Morgan cites the coming together of carbon and
sulphur to form the compound carbon sulfide. The properties of
the latter are wholly different from those of the two elements and
could not be predicted in advance.

C. D. Broad [26] gives two alternative definitions of emergence at
the level of life. On the one hand, we may say that " the chemical
compounds which compose a living body have ' latent properties ' which are manifested only when they are parts of a whole
of this particular structure." On the other hand, we could argue
that " the properties of the constituents of a living body are the
same whether they are in it or out of it, but that the law according to which these separate effects are compounded with each
other is different in a living whole from what it is in any non-
living whole." He points out that it makes little difference which
point of view we take.

Morgan defines evolution in the broad sense as " the name we
give to the comprehensive plan of sequence in all natural
events." [27] He begins his philosophical investigation at an empiricist and realist level, accepting the evidence which, as a scientist, he himself finds. Thus he commences at the level of naturalism and applies his concept of emergence to the data supplied
by scientific investigation. In this way he deals squarely with
matter and space, as well as with life and time, whereas Bergson's vitalism, as we shall see subsequently, dealt only with the

latter. Evolution describes naturalistically the movement upward in historical sequence from one level to another, the three major levels being those of matter, of life or sentience, of mind or thought. Morgan finds subdivisions, intervening levels between these three major levels. Each level serves in its time as a basis for further advance to a new and higher level. It is here that the concept of emergence comes into play.

The process is not continuous, for it involves leaps to new levels. The presence of resultants ensures a measure of continuity, but the presence of emergents introduces a saltatory element. What emerges is genuine novelty. Morgan describes the emergent step as a " qualitative change of direction, or critical turning point, in the course of events." He continues: " In that sense there is not the discontinuous break of a gap or hiatus. It may be said, then, that through resultants there is continuity in progress; through emergence there is progress in continuity." [28] He discusses the situation with regard to the transition from the non-living to the living, where, since his time, increasing knowledge at the level of biochemistry and the investigation of the structure and coding of the DNA molecule have established continuity. His judgment still holds, however, when he writes: " One may still ask whether there is not at some stage of this process a new emergent character of life. . . . There does seem to be something genuinely new at some stage of the resultant continuity." [29]

Although his basic position is empiricist and naturalistic, Morgan's introduction of the idea of emergence enables him to reject mechanism and reductionism. The new emergents can neither be dismissed as products of what has gone before nor be explained in terms of it. Furthermore, they cannot in any way be reduced to the lower levels. Emergence " does not interpret life in terms of physics and chemistry. It does not interpret mind in terms of receptor-patterns and neurone-routes." [30] Each level has its own unique pattern of relatedness and manifests a new quality. Life and mind can therefore be described as " effective emergents " because, when they are present, some change in the existing flow of events occurs which does not occur if they are absent.[31]

Morgan is quick to suggest that such newly emergent qualities are not due to the ingression of a new factor into the situation, but rather to the release of a new tendency in the process which is now set free to control the process in its further development, regulating it and organizing it in a new way. He holds that the new emergent qualities cannot be explained but must be accepted with natural piety, and then he immediately suggests that they indicate a cosmic drive within the process.

Thereby his naturalistic stance moves over to a form of immanentism and pantheism. For he cannot rest with natural piety but must go on to construct a metaphysical scheme. Having refused to explain the higher in terms of the lower levels and accepted emergent qualities with natural piety, he then finds these qualities nascent within the lower by postulating a nisus or drive which directs the release of these new qualities at appropriate levels of development. Thereby he shows himself to be no positivist, but proceeds to metaphysical concerns.

He acknowledges God " as the Nisus through whose Activity emergents emerge and the whole course of emergent evolution is directed." [32] He further regards God as wholly immanent in the process. He sees the levels of evolution leading " upwards towards God as directive Activity within a scheme which aims at constructive consistency." [33] He does at times speak of a " beyondness " of God, but always falls back upon conceptions of immanence. Thus he speaks of an Ideal, which is independent of his own emergent ideals and really existent. He continues: " This Ideal within the human person but transcendent of his human level of deity is God — completing the scheme of relatedness from above. But in and through Activity, universal from base to apex of the whole emergent pyramid, God is no less Immanent." [34] The truth is that the higher cannot be explained in terms of the lower unless in some way the higher is already present in it, and this is actually the position that Morgan finally takes. For him, God is Spirit, and Spirit is not an emergent quality like life and mind. It is present throughout the whole process as creative power. Indeed, in some sense we have a pantheism in which the immanent deity or Spirit is itself evolving.

Morgan's system becomes highly intuitive and also shows inconsistency once he leaves his naturalistic base. He wants to retain his realism and yet also speak of God as Spirit. Thus the Cartesian dichotomy of mind and matter lifts its head, but he chooses its Spinozan and pantheistic form. He thereby falls into a position with regard to epistemology that is not consistent with his evolutionary and emergent ideas. He postulates a parallelism that is quite Spinozan. Mind and matter are correlates, neither being the cause or effect of the other. They never exist, however, apart from one another. A physical event will always have its parallel, mental counterpart. Indeed the world is dual throughout, with the physical and psychical as parallel attributes. But this is a denial of both Morgan's initial realism and his emphasis on emergence.

Alexander, a trained philosopher where Morgan was a scientist, offers a more consistent system and incidentally one that is much more speculative. Like Morgan, his model for understanding the whole of reality is an evolutionary one, and he too emphasizes "emergence." He is also a realist and a thoroughgoing empiricist, starting from a naturalistic base, from nature as science describes it. But, like Morgan, he is no positivist. He moves quickly to a constructive metaphysics on the basis of the analogical structures that he has chosen. Here he moves farther back ontologically than Morgan and also completes his scheme in a way that shows more clearly its evolutionary immanentism.

Being a realist and empiricist, he moves beyond positivism in the beginning and shows the influence of Einstein's relativistic linkage of space and time. Hence, Alexander postulates "Space-Time" as the primordial stuff out of which the universe evolves. Space and Time belong together. They are interdependent, so that there neither is Space without Time nor Time without Space.[35] More explicitly than in Morgan's thought, there is no suggestion of any transcendent principle beyond this primordial substance, and thus all later emergent qualities must be nascent within it, a position at which Morgan arrives later in his own characteristic way as a basis for metaphysical explanation. Since

Space-Time is all that is, it is the matrix of all existence. Out of it matter, life, mind, have evolved.

Alexander's interest in Spinoza doubtless lies behind his differentiation of two aspects in this primal stuff. He sees Space as representing the bodily or somatic component. Thus, although as in relativity theory, space and time are inseparable, Alexander does not envisage time spatially. Time is the active partner, the generator of all new qualities and of values. It is to Space what mind is to body. Space-Time is itself animated, so that there is nothing dead in the universe. In an almost Aristotelian style, Alexander writes:

The body or stuff of each new quality or new type of soul has itself already its own type of soul, and ultimately the body of everything is a piece of Space-Time, the time of which is the soul-constituent which is identical with the body-constituent.[36]

Like Morgan, Alexander defines different levels of existence, each possessing its own quality, but he finds the basis of such new qualities in the pattern that characterizes the emergent entity. The qualities of matter emerging from Space-Time are due to a certain pattern of the point-instants which constitute the primal stuff. Because of his realism, Alexander regards both the primary qualities, like extension, and the secondary qualities, like color and smell, as alike objective. Even the secondary qualities are not products of our sense organs, but belong to matter itself. They are properties associated with its structure. In the same way, living organisms are structures which are patterns of matter. The properties and qualities that distinguish them are associated with these particular patterns. Again, mind, which emerges in certain patterns of living organisms, manifests new qualities that are associated with these patterns. Within these three main divisions, Alexander finds subdivisions. There are, for example, higher and lower divisions within the order of life, the higher emerging from the lower and involving more complex patterns.

The process of evolution is thus one in which all the new emergents involve ever more complex convolutions of the primordial stuff which is itself neutral, neither material, vital, nor mental. Alexander suggests that the complexity thereby becomes a new simplicity. He writes:

Ascent takes place it would seem through complexity. But at each change of quality, the complexity as it were gathers itself together and is expressed in a new simplicity. The emergent quality is the summing together into a new totality of the component materials.[37]

Thus the realism of Alexander leads him to identify the quality with the pattern. As Errol Harris puts it:

New complexes of motion arise in space-time, which in virtue of their special pattern carry an emergent quality. But we must not imagine that the new quality is, in any sense, added to the space-time, *ab extra*. When the appropriate configuration arises it *is* the quality, just as radiation of a certain frequency is the quality of the colour.[38]

This model of evolution is described by C. D. Broad [39] as " emergent neutralism," since neither mentality nor materiality is the differentiating attribute of the primordial stuff — Space-Time. Both are emergent characteristics, emerging from its development. Yet we need to remember the influence of Spinoza on Alexander's thought. His emphasis on the conservative or somatic and the creative or qualitative aspects of the primal stuff is indicative of his whole approach. At every level, entities have both their somatic and their qualitative aspects, and these correspond at that level to the spatial and temporal aspects of Space-Time. Thus Alexander can say that " time is the mind of space and any quality the mind of its body." [40] We are back with the One Substance of Spinoza and its parallel attributes of mind and matter, except that Alexander views the one substance in dynamic terms and does not accept the epistemological viewpoint of Spinoza.

Alexander, like Morgan, offers us an empirical positivism in which the emergent qualities are, at first, described but not explained. He tells us that the real task of philosophy is to describe, observe, and correlate facts. He bids us accept emergent qualities with natural piety, but then moves beyond such a positivist position to an explanation in keeping with the speculative base of primal stuff from which he sees the whole process emerging. Thus, in the first part of *Space, Time and Deity,* he takes refuge in his doctrine of natural piety, but later reverts to his view of time as the dynamic component in primal Space-Time. At this point, it is clear that he would have us regard all future levels of quality as due to patterns of movement potential in the primordial substance. He suggests that "there is a nisus in Space-Time which, as it has borne its creatures forward through matter and life to mind, will bear them forward to some higher level of existence." [41] There is a forward-moving impulse in the evolutionary process which, at any stage, is seeking to attain the next highest.

Having so far issued in mind, the nisus is pushing on to its next and final stage when "deity" will be the emergent quality. "Deity," we are told, "is the next higher empirical quality to mind." [42] Actually this holds only for man, since it may also be said in general that "on each level a new quality looms ahead, awfully, which plays to it the part of deity." [43] For us, on the level of mind, deity *is* deity, but for creatures on the level of life, deity is the quality of mind that still lies ahead. Thus deity is not God. God is the being that possesses deity as its unique quality. Since deity in the real sense has not yet emerged, God is not actual. Alexander seeks, however, to give him some degree of actuality by identifying the universe with God on the ground of its nisus toward deity. He writes:

The infinite God is purely ideal or conceptual. The individual so sketched is not asserted to exist; the sketch merely gives body and shape, by a sort of anticipation for the actual infinite God whom, on the basis of experience, speculation declares to exist. As actual, God does not possess the quality of deity but is the universe as tending to that quality. This nisus in the universe, though not present to sense, is yet present to reflection on experience. Only in this sense of straining towards deity can there be an infinite actual God. [44]

Thus God as actual is the whole universe tending toward deity.

Alexander refuses to define deity. The infinite God will possess spirit, personality, mind, but these must not be identified with his deity. Rather, such qualities belong to his body.[45] " God's deity," Alexander states, " is not different from spirit in degree but in kind, as a novelty in the series of empirical qualities." [46] So the universe becomes God's body, outside which no lesser body exists. For God, all objects are internal, so that our minds and all other things in the world are " organic sensa " of God. " All we are the hunger and thirst, the heart-beats and sweat of God." [47] We have a form of evolutionary pantheism bearing strong marks of the influence of Spinoza. God, in the place of eternal Being, however, has become eternal Becoming. This is a naturalistic philosophy which issues in evolving deity.

Insofar as there is Deity in the universe in the normally accepted religious sense of the term, that is to say, as Creator, First Cause, and so on, that Deity is Space-Time itself. This neutral stuff would appear to contain all the potentialities for subsequent emergents. Out of it the nisus toward deity emerges, and Time is the generator of all qualities. Indeed, Time is creative. Alexander gets over this difficulty by arguing that, though the universe can be expressed in terms of Space-Time without remainder, yet it is not merely spatiotemporal. There are also the qualities of matter, life, and mind engendered in it. But then these are only potential in the original stuff. Strict empiricism can give no rational justification for this revolutionary viewpoint, and yet Alexander wants to retain a strictly realistic and empiricist viewpoint.

Alexander lacks the sense of wholeness pervading the process and manifesting itself at every level. This is where Jan Smuts [48] complements Alexander's viewpoint in his holistic theory, even though he lacks the specialized philosophical ability that Alexander possessed. This is very evident in the treatment of mind. On the basis of his strict empiricism, Alexander is concerned with parts rather than wholes, with analysis more than synthesis. His approach lacks the view of each subsequent stage of the process embracing, as a new whole, all the stages that have gone before it. We find no sense of mind as the whole process coming to self-consciousness and understanding itself. Limited by his empiricism, Alexander thinks of mind as finite, a small part of the universe as a whole, and a quality that emerges out of life at particular complexities of relationship. Certain variations in the fundamental pattern of Space-Time make it possible. Indeed, it is bound up with the neural processes of the cerebrum.

This is, of course, empirically true, and a purely realistic theory of knowledge offers Alexander no way of making mind an inclusive whole. He defines the characteristic behavior of mind as knowing, but there is no sense of the knowing mind as bringing subject and object together comprehensively into wholeness and unity. The object is nonmental. It has no kinship with mind. All that the mind possesses is the enjoyment of an experience. As Errol Harris puts it: " The contemplation of the object . . . is no more than the occasion for the mind's enjoyment of itself in experiencing." [49] All that the mind has is " the quality of consciousness which it enjoys in the contemplation of objects." [50] The object is thus entirely extramental and is not possessed by the mind even in knowledge. The categorical features of the object are also real and part of the object. They excite certain neural processes that the mind enjoys as experience.

Hegel's " absolute idealism " had succeeded in holding object and subject together in a compresence of knowledge. But Alexander's strict empiricist realism offers no sense of the unifying wholeness in knowing, in which subject and object are brought together in an embracing relationship that involves both. Thus, when mind emerges, it is thought of atomistically, whereas consciousness does in a real sense give a new wholeness to the world in the act of knowing. It is difficult to understand how a yet further emergent quality, " deity," emerging out of the lower increasing lack of comprehensiveness, should yet be all-embracing and represent the whole which is God. Alexander's thesis is inhibited in its development by his epistemology.

From the point of view of Christian philosophizing, Alexander's epistemology fails at just this point of involvement between knower and known. If Biblical realism be any guide, empiricist realism and complete separation of subject and object are impossible. Still more, however, do issues arise in the view of God. If God as actual is the universe in process to deity, we have no real God in the Christian sense, no over-againstness of God and man, and no true appreciation of human freedom and man's sense of estrangement. Alexander is almost compelled to declare that " we have to recognize that, not in deity, but in God, unvalues also are contained; not merely badness and ugliness and error, but in the end all impermanent forms of finite existence." [51] If God is the universe, that is to be expected.

Furthermore, if God is the whole, man's freedom must actually be a reflection of his being determined. The parable of the stone in flight [52] is reflected in a passage where Alexander states that

freedom is nothing but the form which causal action assumes when both cause and effect are enjoyed; so that freedom is determination as enjoyed, or in enjoyment, and human freedom is a case of something universal which is found wherever the distinction of enjoyment and contemplation, in the widest sense of these terms, is found. [53]

The absence of any thought of true transcendence — Alexander tries to speak of God's transcendence in terms of the future emergence of the quality of deity — together with the immanentist identification of the world process with God makes it impossible to have a Christian understanding of sin and evil and any other than a deterministic view of man. Beginning with a naturalistic empiricism, Alexander, like Lloyd Morgan, can only finish in a naturalistic pantheism. This is implicit in his starting point. It is significant that he himself confesses to having little experience of the religious sentiment.

Creative Evolution and the Life-Force — Intuition Displaces Intellect

The French philosopher Bergson seeks also to make evolution his key analogy and begins like Morgan and Alexander with a naturalistic base. But he differs in two ways. Morgan began with matter, regarded life and mind as emergent within it, and then postulated the directive presence of immanent mind throughout the process; Alexander began with speculative neutral Space-Time, regarded matter, life, and mind as all emergent qualities, and then postulated the immanent nisus to deity throughout the process; Bergson began with life, regarded matter as derivative from it, and then postulated an immanent life-force or *élan vital* throughout the process. In the first place, Bergson offers an " emergent vitalism " in contrast to Morgan's " emergent materialism " and Alexander's " emergent neutralism." In the second place, Morgan and Alexander were both basically empirical realists, whereas Bergson emphasized intuition, downgraded the intellect, and yet produced a philosophy with an idealistic flavor.

For Bergson, the basic fact of experience is change. Reality, therefore, is to be understood on the model of process and change, and the model is basically evolutionary. As for Greeks like Heraclitus, so for Bergson, becoming is the essential mark of ultimate reality, not being. Unlike the Greeks, however, he does not think of becoming as cyclic. It is a directed process of development in which time is meaningful and fundamental. He takes time seriously. Hence, he accepts the evolutionary viewpoint, and regards reality as a process in which an all-embracing life-force is creatively active.

Here we come to the first element in his position. For him, life is central as the key to reality. The process carries all the marks of life. The process is such that each stage of development embodies all that has gone before and yet modifies it so as to manifest new characteristics through it. There is, indeed, a creative advance in the process in which freedom is central and from which determinism in the sense of mechanistic causation is absent.

The latter position is possible, for Bergson, because of his emphasis on life as the prime reality. He regards matter, as we shall see shortly, as frozen life. Because it is derivative in this way, a secondary deposit of the living process, matter, and the mechanistic causation associated with it exercise no determinative role in evolutionary development. The key to the process is an immanent life-force, an *élan vital* that is completely free and creative. Reality is movement, becoming; reality is pulsating, dynamic, creative life. In its creative advance, life is unpredictable, always on the frontier of time and surging forward to the new. As Errol Harris puts it: " Exact prediction of living activity is impossible. We cannot calculate mathematically what it will be because until it has happened we do not possess all terms of the necessary equation." [54]

It is at this point that we must note the close identification of life with time. At the level of creative advance, time and change are synonymous. Time as science conceptualizes it is a spatial abstraction, a perfectly uniform *chronos,* spatially measured and possessing the character of reversibility. But time as it is concretely experienced is irreversible and unidirectional, possessing the quality of duration and cumulative in its effect. It is identified with change, and is time that is lived, that is experienced from within. It " is not a mere succession of moments qualitatively alike and related only externally to one another, but the mutual interpenetration of inward or psychic factors such as to constitute a real advance." [55] What we apprehend in the consciousness is time as duration, not as discrete points or instants. We are aware of a continuous, indivisible becoming. It is in this sense that time must be understood — as synonymous with change and as an expression of life itself. Time as duration is the actual process.

The second element in Bergson's position must now be noted. It is the intuition which grasps life and the durational nature of time. Bergson connects intuition with instinct, and finds the distinctive feature of instinct to be sympathy. He tells us that " instinct is sympathy," [56] and that, as such, it " is molded on the very form of life." [57] At the animal level, two divergent modes of knowledge are manifest — instinct and intelligence. Instinct involves both " the faculty of using an organized natural instrument " and " innate knowledge . . . of this instrument and the object to which it is applied." [58] Intelligence is essentially the capacity " to see the way out of a difficulty in any circumstances whatever "; it concentrates " on the relations between a given situation and the means of utilizing it." [59] Bergson, therefore, sees in intellect an innate tendency to establish relations which is grounded in a natural knowledge of certain very general relations. He suggests that intelligence basically has *formal* knowledge, whereas instinct has *material* knowledge.[60] Instinct, because it is sympathy, penetrates into the heart of life, participates in it. Intelligence examines and organizes life from without.

In evolutionary change, instinct was overshadowed by intelligence in the development of the vertebrates, because intelligence has shown itself to be a more flexible instrument. Yet "*there are things intelligence alone is able to seek, but which, by itself, it will never find. These things instinct alone could find; but it will never seek them.*" [61] At the level of self-consciousness, of man, instinct constitutes a vague nebulosity around the luminous nucleus of intelligence, yet it may be enlarged and purified into intuition. Bergson tells us that " if this sympathy (in instinct) could extend its object and also reflect upon itself, it would give us the key to vital operations." He then defines intuition as "instinct that has become disinterested, self-conscious, capable of reflecting upon its object and enlarging it indefinitely." [62] Such intuition is able sympathetically to participate in living things, expanding our consciousness and enabling us to understand from within life's domain with its endless creative movement.[63] In this way we are made aware of life as a continuous, creative surge of becoming and able to grasp it in its durational aspect.

In contrast to intuition, intelligence or intellect cuts up the living continuous process into manageable chunks of matter and organizes them into a relational structure. Intuition makes us aware of the living present as duration. Intellect freezes the present movement into a dead past and analyzes it. Indeed, it has been shaped in the process of evolutionary development for a very practical purpose, namely to help in the activity of consciousness. As life creatively advances, it stores up a deposit of habit, and thus it creates a contrary movement that must be controlled and made subservient to the evolutionary movement. Intellect has been shaped for this purpose. It carves up the world into frozen chunks, into matter. It is able to do so because it is concerned, not with the creative present, but with the immediate past, with that which has already been shaped and molded by the advance of life. Intellect steps into the advancing flow of life and consciousness, which alone is reality, and assists that flow by controlling the inertia of habit. It cannot actually arrest the flow, for time and life go on. But it does cut up the past.

In so doing, it transforms creative freedom into a realm of dead matter governed by mechanical laws and subject to mechanistic necessity. Actually such mechanistic determinism is only the result of dealing with the past. The creative center is the living present, in which life is freely advancing, and the past is the outcome of it, its deposit. Bergson can say that "*the mechanism of our ordinary knowledge is of a cinematographical kind.*" [64] The intellect, and modern science in particular, creates a rapid series of static pictures, all after the events, and relates them causatively in a structure of spatialized time. Intuition grasps the whole in its creative movement in the duration of the living present. The intellect, for the purpose of control, creates the illusion of a material order that is subject to efficient causation and in which succession in spatialized time accounts for a situation mechanically. The physical order is thus a distorted appearance, and reality is the continuous creative advance of life and consciousness. This would point to idealism and phenomenalism, and is the opposite to the realism of Morgan and Alexander.

Bergson evidently believes that the organism advances against an opposing reality which its intellect helps it to control. He is thus facing a difficulty. The life-force is immaterial and furthermore it is immanent in every organism which individually is an expression of it. Is the life-force struggling against itself? What is it that the intellect deals with, forming the illusion of a material order? Bergson's answer is to define matter as the result of the detension or relaxation of the life-force, in which the life-force casts off or sloughs off spent elements. These, like the drops of water falling back from the spent energy of a fountain, accumulate as they are left behind by the creative advance of life and form a dam to such advance. It is to control this dam and make it subservient to its movement that the life-force has created the intellect. Thus matter is not just illusion, but may be identified as earlier with the inertia of habit which the *élan vital* casts behind it as it advances.

This whole scheme raises its difficulties. If the life-force pursues its creative advance against opposition, the understanding of such resistance is made exceedingly difficult if the opposition is provided by the life-force itself. Why does it find it necessary to do this? Why does it have to put on a material appearance in its spent form? The whole system raises more questions at this point than it can adequately answer. Actually by objectively defining the material as spent life-force, Bergson has no reason to deny its physical reality and thus to treat the understanding of the intellect as illusory. The pure understanding deals with reality but with reality that has " already become," that has spent itself and become fixed. What living energy is in the present may, therefore, be far more than science can discover.

The whole difficulty of Bergson's system, as that of the systems of Morgan and Alexander, lies in the emphasis on immanentism and the rejection of transcendence. For Bergson, God is the immanent life-force. As such, he is creative freedom. Indeed, all action and creativity are manifestations of the *élan vital*, so that even man's freedom is actually an aspect of the creative activity of the life-force.

Morality and religion alike may manifest the characteristics associated with intuition and intellect.[65] Both these human activities may be open and closed. In closed morality and religion, men are captive to a social mechanism that is determined by habit and custom, a static structure of ethical legalism, dead gods, and institutional religion, which dams up creative activity. In open morality and religion, men advance by creative behavior and serve the ends of the immanent life-force. They give themselves up to the *élan vital*, which carries them forward and breaks through the conservative structures which would inhibit their creativity. In such open religion men intuitively unite themselves with the life-force and the fount of love which is God. Man's end is thus mystical union with God, the *élan vital*.

Yet there are insights of significance. We have already indicated the significance of intuitive insight in philosophical thought. We can be grateful for Bergson's emphasis on this, and yet we would be opposed to his unnecessary dichotomy between intuition and intellect. Reason is a necessary complement to intuitive apprehension. The two belong together.

Bergson's emphasis on creativity and rejection of mechanistic determinism open up an understanding of human freedom that is absent from the other philosophical systems examined in this chapter. It can be said that, despite the tendency to idealistic phenomenalism and his immanentism, Bergson has indicated how evolutionary categories may be used in a religious sense.

One other difficulty, however, in all the views discussed in this chapter, is their preoccupation with nature and their almost complete ignoring of that human history with which Christian thought is primarily concerned. Here Hegel's emphasis on process meets issues which these thinkers do not face.

IV

An Organismic Universe and God
the Fellow Traveler

WITH ALFRED NORTH WHITEHEAD the kind of philosophy that we
have been considering reaches its most attractive non-Christian
form. Whitehead, himself a mathematician and scientist of repute,
early showed marked native ability as logician and philosopher.
His influence in Britain still rests mainly on his contributions to
symbolic logic in association with Bertrand Russell. In this way
he contributed to the movement which issued in logical positivism
and, in so doing, paradoxically undermined any influence his
metaphysics might have exercised on British thought. Apart from
the outstanding study of the Incarnation which L. S. Thornton [1]
based upon the Whiteheadian philosophy and the interpretative
work of Dorothy Emmet,[2] Whitehead has been strangely ne-
glected in the British scene. One British Christian thinker and
philosopher, William Temple,[3] does show some of Whitehead's
influence. The fact that the major contributions of Whitehead
to metaphysical thought were made in America would partly account for this British neglect. It is certainly true that his influence

in the United States has been much more significant and especially so in circles of Christian thinking. Prior to the consideration of Whitehead, we shall look at one thinker who presented some of the ideas developed in depth in Whitehead's thought.

The Organismic Model

In the 1920's, one other thinker, besides those studied in the preceding chapter, Jan Smuts,[4] made some contribution to evolutionary thought. Not himself a professional philosopher, he did direct attention upon the holistic aspect of the evolutionary process. For him the model of the universe was an organismic one. Over against the preoccupation of biological science with the analytic approach, which reduced the study of life oftentimes to biophysics and biochemistry, he set the synthetic approach. He stressed the characteristic organization and wholeness of the biological organism and saw in this a model for the understanding of reality. He sees reality as being organized in ever new and more complex patterns of relationship, each such pattern constituting a whole. He tells us that

both matter and life consist, in the atom and in the cell, of unit structures whose ordered grouping produces the natural wholes which we call bodies or organisms. This character or feature of "wholeness" . . . has a far more general application and points to something fundamental in the universe, fundamental in the sense that it is practically universal, that it is a real operative factor, and that its shaping influence is felt ever more deeply and widely with the advance of Evolution.[5]

He uses the word "Holism" to describe this inner operative factor and sees evolution as an advance in the creation of wholes in the universe. The universe is one of whole-making. He sees the process moving from mere physical mixtures; through chemical compounds, which are more synthetic; living organisms, which manifest centralization of control and regulation of all the parts; minds where this central control attains consciousness; to personality, " the highest, most evolved whole among the structures of the universe." [6]

In developing his holistic system, Smuts makes use of the concept of " field." He sees a mutual interpenetration of the objects in the universe in a complex of relationships. No object may be thought of as a discrete and detached unit. It exists in an environment constituted by its relation to other objects, and each object is actually a " field " that interacts with and influences its neighbors. Smuts finds this " field " at the level of a physical body, where, of course, the concept is used in the case of gravitational, magnetic, and electrical interactions between physical objects. He would apply it, however, universally to all wholes at all levels.

Furthermore, he would give the concept a historical connotation. An organism can be understood only by reference to its past and future as well as its present. Smuts points out that

an organism much more than the physical body is an historic event, a focus of happening, a gateway through which the infinite stream of change flows ceaselessly. The sensible organism is only a point, a sort of transit station which stands for an infinite past of development, for the history and experience of untold millions of ancestors, and in a vague indefinite way for the future which will include an indefinite number of descendants. The past, the present, the future all meet in that little structural centre, that little wayside station on the infinite trail of life.[7]

As the wholes increase in complexity and move upward in development, Smuts sees each of them carrying a field of influence that reaches beyond its physical boundary. This field decreases in intensity of structure or force and shades off into indefiniteness, both spatially in the present and temporally into the past and the future. Here he seems to echo something of Bergson's understanding of duration. In some sense the holistic organism " contains its past and much of its future in its present." [8]

We are presented with a picture of the universe as a vast field of interacting organisms, at various levels of development or organization. Each organism is the center of a " field " of influence, manifested in the structure of relationships into which it enters with other organisms. Furthermore, such a field has temporal as well as spatial dimensions. The whole holistic process is dominated by a holistic factor, a drive to the production of higher wholes, culminating in human personality. This world is a universe of whole-making and must be conceived in " dynamic, evolutionary creative " terms.[9]

Smuts does not deny the presence of mechanical causality. Rather, he agrees that mechanistic causation does apply at the purely physical level. But he argues that once the holistic factor comes into play and wholes appear, such mechanistic systems are included within such wholes and are subservient to them. As the evolutionary process advances, mechanism recedes and holism advances, although there is a degree of mechanism everywhere. Indeed, he says that " mechanism is an earlier, cruder form of Holism; the more Holism there is in structure, the less there is of the mechanistic character, until finally in Mind and Personality the mechanistic concept ceases to be of any practical use." [10] Smuts argues that there is no need to introduce some vitalistic entelechy as a *deus ex machina* to account for life and mind. Rather, the lower stages marked by physicochemical structures are cruder manifestations of that inner holistic activity which is manifested in a deeper way at the levels of life and personality. The latter do not involve any interference with the lower structures of matter, but rather manifest higher structures. The latter are continuous with the lower, but they also show a new creative development to more direction and control.

The creative process of Holism consists in the intensification of structures, in small elements of newness appearing in existing structures until the basis is thereby laid for a new departure in structure; but still on the basis of the pre-existing structures, and so to say in line with the pre-existing structures.[11]

We are left with the vision of a creative process in which a holistic factor is ever creating new and higher wholes up to the level of personality. This is where Smuts leaves it. He offers us an immanentism without deity. His is a kind of emergent materialism with a humanistic flavor. Perhaps we might term it a naturalistic humanism. It is significant that he does not mention God or deity. Yet the system does not explain itself. It is purely descriptive and affords a remarkable tour de force. It leaves unanswered the question Why?, which man must inevitably ask. What is it all for? It is true that Smuts was optimistic in his humanism, but he seems to take little real account of the evil factors in the universe. He contributed a foreword to Breuil's *Beyond the Bounds of History,* in which he confessed that, when he looked at history, he was pessimistic about man. But he could also write that man's prehistory encouraged him to be optimistic and to have faith in man's future.[12]

Yet Smuts's emphasis on wholes as more than the mere summation of their parts, his conviction that organism offers a key model for understanding the universe, his concern with the whole movement of the universe as a creative holistic process should not be dismissed. He offers insights that other and more profound thinkers also employ. His concept of " field " and of the structure of interrelationship and interaction, without which no object in the universe can be explained, and his rejection of regarding such objects as discrete and isolated find sympathetic resonance in the thought of A. N. Whitehead, to which we must now direct our attention.

Whitehead on the Limitations of Science

As a scientist, Whitehead is a realist, but he is also very much more a rationalist than Samuel Alexander, to whose philosophy his own shows some degree of similarity. His empiricism is much more critical than that of either Morgan or Alexander. Although he might be said to begin from a naturalistic base, he is much more concerned with the nature of the scientific method and critical of its epistemology.

Whitehead held that science is a method of abstraction and that it cannot offer a full picture of reality. It abstracts certain aspects

of reality and ignores others. The roots of current " scientific materialism " or " scientism " lie in a preoccupation with discrete
chunks of matter related externally to one another in space and
spatialized time and interacting at the level of mechanistic causation. Whitehead declares that this point of view " presupposes
the ultimate fact of an irreducible brute matter, or material,
spread throughout space in a flux of configurations." [13] He argues
that this way of regarding the world is an abstraction, and that
our dilemmas have arisen because we have mistaken our abstractions for concrete realities. Whitehead is fundamentally rationalistic, at this point, in the great philosophical tradition that
stems from Plato and Aristotle. He points out that these thinkers
believed that nature is permeated by rational and teleological
order. They were far removed from the scientific division of nature into lumps of matter, separated spatiotemporally and related
externally by mechanistic causation. He terms this point of view
the " Fallacy of Misplaced Concreteness," and he defines the fallacy as regarding as real something which has been abstracted
from reality for the special purposes of thought. The influence of
Bergson would seem to be evident here.

Whitehead is influenced in his criticism by his basic presupposition that the universe must be understood by a model that is organismic. Here we have a strong resemblance to the point of view
adopted by Smuts, except that the universe is itself regarded as
an organism and not just a realm of whole-making. Whitehead
points out that if we separate a thing from its environment and
then describe it so separated, we are not describing it at all. Because we do this in science, there arises the concept of " simple
location." This sets a thing at a particular place at a particular
time. This spatial and temporal location implies that we may so
locate a particular configuration of matter that to understand it
we need not refer to other regions of space and time.[14] Moreover,
the state of the world at one time can be temporally isolated from
that at another. In consequence, Hume's [15] damaging criticism
of causation cannot be met by science. It makes " nonsense of the
scientist's scheme " and science lapses into positivism. Its task is

to describe and to draw up a system of external relations. If these relations hold, a certain state of affairs arises. Hume's criticism can be met only by introducing a tie between a cause and an effect. This is possible only when " simple location " is rejected. We must surrender the scientific view of reality as consisting of discrete configurations of matter spatially and temporally isolated. Whitehead describes this severance of cause from effect as " bifurcation."

This fallacy of simple location applies to more areas than the purely physical. The bifurcation of mind from matter, which can still be traced in the thought of Alexander, has introduced one of the most unfortunate dualisms into science. Since the time of Descartes, science has found itself left with two substances — mind and matter. These substances bear unreconcilable differentiating characteristics. Mind is characterized by thinking and is not extended in space. Matter is extended in space but is without the characteristic of consciousness. The two are separated by an apparently irreconcilable gulf, yet they incomprehensibly affect one another. Their causative interaction is as inconceivable as the causation between two spatially separated physical configurations.

Again, there is the bifurcation of substance from qualities. The scientist abstracts from nature all secondary qualities associated with color, sound, smell, etc. Descartes and his successors set the pattern for a picture of nature that is fundamentally one of extended matter in motion. Science leaves the commonsense picture of substance as the stuff which provides the foundation for all qualities and which, as Berkeley pointed out, cannot incidentally be observed or discovered. It leaves us with a world of electrical charges from which color, smell, and sound have been eliminated. To quote Whitehead:

The bodies are perceived as with qualities which in reality do not belong to them, qualities which in fact are purely the offspring of the mind. Thus nature gets credit which should in truth be reserved for ourselves: the rose for its scent: the nightingale for his song: and the sun for his radiance. The poets are entirely mistaken. They should address their lyrics to themselves, and should turn them into odes of self-congratulation on the excellency of the human mind. Nature is a dull affair, soundless, scentless, colourless; merely the hurrying of material, endlessly, meaninglessly.[16]

Modern science has, by its very method, majored on mechanism and tended to materialism, with the result that it has created real problems for itself while trying to solve others. It has confused abstractions with reality. This is Whitehead's contention. His criticism is still cogent, although we might express it differently. We would prefer to say that science works by models chosen from certain areas of experience and applied to other areas. Thus the mechanistic interpretation of reality is a model or analogue. The error in "materialism" and "naturalism" is to take the models literally and identify them with reality, rather than recognizing their analogical nature and heuristic purpose.[17]

Whitehead extends his criticism to evolution when this process is understood materialistically. He argues that "a thoroughgoing evolutionary philosophy is inconsistent with materialism."[18] If matter is the primal stuff, all we have is lumps of matter in motion related externally in space and time. But then evolution would have to be explained solely as due to changes in such external relations. The whole movement would be change without purpose and progress. Now evolutionary theory points to a movement toward increasing complexity in the structure of organisms. To explain this, Whitehead contends, we need "a conception of organism as fundamental for nature."[19] Mechanistic materialism does not provide a satisfying model. Evolution "also requires an underlying activity — a substantial activity — expressing itself in individual embodiments, and evolving in the achievements of organism."[20]

Whitehead agrees that the operation of natural selection upon random mutations could be used to support the materialistic interpretation. But he also points to the presence of cooperativeness in the evolutionary process and to the way in which such cooperation is geared to creativeness in communities of organisms.

Thus although there is, on the one side, a given environment to which organisms have to adapt themselves or perish, there is, on the other side, a degree of plasticity in the environment itself. What an individual organism cannot do on its own, a cooperating community of organisms can achieve in creating their own environment. "With such cooperation and in proportion to the effort put forward, the environment has a plasticity which alters the whole ethical aspect of evolution." [21] We can see signs " of struggle and of friendly help." [22]

The Organismic Model in Whitehead's Thought

We might describe the conventional pattern of the universe as nature extended in a spatiotemporal continuum and consisting of individual units of matter or bodies, mutually exclusive, into some of which there have inserted themselves life and mind. The presence of the latter means that it behaves in a way that laws of physics do not predict. It introduces into the universe an element of contingency which we call free will and which seems to challenge the orderliness of nature. We have already seen in the various theories of emergent and creative evolution an attempt to combat this mechanistic determinism and find some place for freedom and creativity. Bergson more than Morgan and Alexander succeeds at this point. The latter thinkers are too much influenced by Spinoza to offer a real understanding of personal freedom and avoid some form of determinism.

Whitehead contends that the naturalistic and mechanistic view of the universe is totally false. In its place he would substitute the picture of a process that is basically organic in structure. An organism is characterized by internal relations. In it all the parts are influenced by the plan of the whole. They behave differently in the whole from what they would in isolation. Whitehead makes organism his basic model for understanding reality. The universe is an organism embracing lesser groupings which are also organismic, the whole being characterized by internal relations. Thereby, he rejects the doctrine of simple location and avoids the fallacy of misplaced concreteness. The universe is a patterned process in which there is an intimate relation between all the parts, and in which, indeed, all the parts pervade one another. Becoming is a process of organismic development. He is more thoroughgoing than Smuts, as we shall see. Furthermore, what Smuts describes as a " field," Whitehead describes in a different way, yet both thinkers emphasize the intimate interpenetration and influence of the entities in the universe and their place within developing wholes.

In order to describe the process which is reality, Whitehead coins a rather elaborate vocabulary. The individual parts of the process are not individual in the same sense as a scientific object, for they are subtly bound up with one another in the whole. Whitehead defines them as " actual entities." He also calls these ultimate facts of nature " events," thereby indicating the presence of the temporal dimension and showing, like Alexander, the influence of the new relativistic physics. Actually " event " is a term that can cover more than " actual entities." The latter are the fundamental units and constitute " atomic events." The word " event," however, can also describe a large-scale grouping of such " actual entities."

When he comes to consider the interrelationships of his " actual entities," Whitehead returns to his concept of organism. Every " actual entity " is an organism. A grouping of actual entities, intimately bound together and influencing one another, is defined as a " nexus." It can also be described as an organism, since " there is a process of constitutive relationship between the members." [23] As an organism, an " actual entity " is regarded by Whitehead as a center or occasion of experience, and hence it can also be called an " actual occasion." It is a unity of experience. As such, it is pictured as possessing a bipolar structure. It has a physical pole and a mental pole. It is thus envisaged organismically as having both physical and mental activities. Here we find shades of Leibnitz' monadology.

At this point, we must consider the theory of " prehensions." The actual entities are described as prehending one another. This "prehension" would appear to be a rudimentary feeling. The whole universe is a process of feeling in which all the actual entities are mutually sensitive. Thus a prehension is a process of unifying. Whitehead tells us that prehension signifies

the essential unity of an event, namely the event as one entity, and not as a mere assemblage of parts or of ingredients. It is necessary to understand that space-time is nothing else than a system of pulling together of assemblages into unities.[24]

The universe is interdependent and interconnected. Its unity is constituted by each actual entity taking note of or perceiving the others. At the lowest level, we have rudimentary feeling. The prehensions in the universe attain their higher level in the consciousness that characterizes the human mind. Thus prehension pervades all things and is of the same order as cognitive perception.

In this way, Whitehead refuses to bifurcate matter and mind at any point in his picture of the cosmos. Everywhere, as in Leibnitz' monadology, we are asked to envisage the presence of mind, usually unconscious and rudimentary, and yet characterized by the mode of experience which we call feeling. Every event or actual entity has a feeling for the presence of everything else. "Actual entities" can be described also as prehensive occasions, "that is to say, events or concrete facts of becoming, which arise out of their interrelations with other events throughout nature."[25] The feelings for the past, the future, and the contemporary, which characterize human experience, are to be postulated as the models for all events and actual entities. Whitehead writes:

An event has contemporaries. This means that an event mirrors within itself the modes of its contemporaries as a display of immediate achievement. An event has a past. This means that an event mirrors within itself the modes of its predecessors, as memories which are fused into its own content. An event has a future. This means that an event mirrors within itself such aspects as the future throws back on to the present, or, in other words, as the present has determined concerning the future. Thus an event has anticipation.[26]

We have an active taking into relation of one actual entity by another, one organism by another. Some aspect or part of other actual entities is grasped or appropriated by each actual entity in the formation of its own nature.

It is in this matter of the formation of the nature of an " actual entity" or "actual occasion" that Whitehead's thought needs to be carefully analyzed. Especially significant is what he has to say about the "complete contemporary freedom" of actual entities. Whitehead seems contradictory at this point. As we have just seen he implies that actual entities prehend one another contemporaneously, and he openly claims that all actual entities do prehend each other. Yet, on the other hand, he evidently holds that actual entities can only prehend past actual entities, for he maintains that in its movement to "satisfaction,"[27] an actual occasion is completely free of contemporary occasions.

We can understand Whitehead's thought here when we remember that he bases his understanding of time on the theory of relativity, and not on classical Newtonian physics. He suggests that there is a "given" world which provides the data for the prehension of any actual entity. For this to happen, the characters of other actual entities have to be objectified. Here four things need to be remembered.

The first is that the actual entity is, as an actual occasion, but a fleeting center of experience. Each such actual occasion has its moment of "subjective immediacy"[28] when the data provided by its prehended "given" world are integrated into the new "concrescence" which constitutes this new actual occasion. The phase when such concrescence is fully attained is termed the "satisfaction" of the actual occasion. Once this integral satisfaction is attained, the actual occasion "perishes" and becomes an object to be prehended by subsequent actual occasions.

This brings us to the second significant idea. Until this objectification occurs and the actual occasion "perishes," it is completely free and self-determinate, employing the data provided by its prehensions for its own process of concrescence. The prehended data consists of the objectification of other actual occasions and the " subjective aim," which we must consider shortly. Since such objectification is possible only when the actual occasion providing it has attained integral satisfaction and perished, we are thinking of actual occasions which are past in time relation to the actual occasion now being realized.

The third significant point is Whitehead's use of relativity theory, which has altered completely the Newtonian understanding of contemporaneity. All time is relative to the experiencing subject. Hence Whitehead can define contemporaneity in a new way. He tells us that " actual entities are called ' contemporary ' when neither belongs to the ' given ' actual world defined by the other." [29] Thereby, he excludes prehension of contemporary occasions in the classical sense. Actual entities can only be prehended by other actual entities when they have become past in relation to the latter.

In the fourth place, the process of " perishing " and objectification does not mean that a past actual entity ceases to be. Whitehead tells us that " the various particular occasions of the past are in existence and severally functioning as objects for prehension in the present." [30] Thereby they attain objective immortality and become stubborn facts for future actual occasions to prehend. Every actual occasion enjoys " the past as alive in itself." [31]

The picture we have is of every actual entity synthesizing the past data or objects into which preceding actual occasions have been transformed. One special case needs to be noted. Whitehead rejects the idea of an enduring substance. He speaks rather of a succession or nexus of actual occasions. An " enduring object " is therefore a society of actual occasions that are temporally related. Thus an enduring atomic particle is actually a temporal string or society of atomic occasions. Each actual occasion in such a society has its moment of immediacy when it achieves something akin to self-determination. This is its moment of concrescence, when, by means of its prehensions, it attains a unity of feeling. It then " perishes " and becomes an object to be prehended by its successors in the society. In this way a " thing " persists through time. Generally we may say that every actual occasion reflects the whole course of past events. " The occasion arises from relevant objects, and perishes into the status of an object for other occasions. But it enjoys its decisive moment of absolute self-attainment as an emotional unity." [32]

With regard to the future, Whitehead thinks of each actual occasion as including in its experience or self-enjoyment " an enjoyment of itself as alive in the future." [33] There is a real potentiality for elements in the future within the present actual occasion, and the latter attains objective immortality in subsequent actual occasions in which such elements are realized. The synthesizing of past objects and the potentiality for future actualizations center in the prehension of its own subjective aim by each actual occasion. To this concept of subjective aim we shall turn our attention in the next section.

Every larger object in the world is a grouping of such atomic actual occasions in spatial relationship. We have an organic view in which the universe as a whole is an organism, itself an assembly of lesser organisms, all characterized like the whole by internal relations. Biology can be described as the study of the larger organisms, and physics as the study of the smaller. We are thus presented with a form of panpsychism.

The Universe as Process

The universe as an organic whole is not static but dynamic. It is a process of becoming in which actual entities are continually arising as new creatures and also passing away. Yet even when they pass away, they attain a degree of objective reality or immortality. For they pass into the continuing constitution of the whole and are retained as prehensions in the actual entities that succeed them. As T. M. Forsyth puts it:

At the same time every individual thing or creature, in perishing or ceasing to be as such, endures as a possible component in the constitution of any other such entity — a potential factor in *its* life or experience. [34]

Has this process any direction? It is here that Whitehead makes use of his category of " eternal objects." These have " potentiality for ' ingression ' into the becoming of actual entities." [35] Indeed, Whitehead can describe an eternal object as " pure potential." By " ingression," he means " the particular mode in which the potentiality of an eternal object is realized in a particular actual entity, contributing to the definiteness of that actual entity." [36] Divorced from the process, the flux of events, the becoming of actual entities, the eternal objects constitute an abstract world. They become real only as they become ingredient in the process itself and by their presence determine the nature of actual entities. In itself, an event is spatiotemporal. It gains all its other characteristics by the ingression of these eternal objects. Hence the latter constitute the differentiating characteristics between the actual entities. We may regard the eternal objects as forming an ideal realm of possibilities by which the actual process of reality is determined.

There is here something akin to Plato's realm of eternal ideas, except that Whitehead transfers reality from the realm of being to the realm of becoming. The world of eternal objects is the world of thought, containing all the possibilities which may be actualized in reality. Such actualization is possible because each actual entity receives a " subjective aim " by the ingression into it of eternal objects. It is this subjective aim which determines the nature of the prehensions that constitute the experience of an actual entity. The latter derives its character from its subjective aim rather than from its prehensions. These prehensions are subject to the inner drive or *telos* which directs the entity, and this drive has its mainspring or source in the subjective aim. Indeed, the experiences that prehensions make possible are integrated in the light of this subjective aim or ideal in which the actual entity is seeking creative satisfaction. The guidance of the subjective aim interrelates the various prehensions that help to make the actual entity. Or, in another way of saying it, the subjective aim integrates the feelings into a concresence of feeling and makes the entity an " actual occasion." Thus the subjective aim gives to an actual entity its identity. It makes it what it is. In the old classical language, it is its essence, but essence conceived in dynamic rather than static terms. The identity of a primal thing is creatively conditioned as the prehensions are directed by and unified around the subjective aim. T. M. Forsyth has expressed this well. He likens the issue to that of efficient and final causation.

Each actuality is bipolar. On the one hand, it is conditioned by its relation to other entities constituting and defining the actual world of its attainment, and their action upon it has the character of efficient causation. But, on the other hand, it reaches out towards fuller attainment, or to the realization of further value, and the value or end sought for operates in its activity in a way that is distinctively teleological.[37]

This viewpoint bears strong resemblances to Leibnitz' doctrine of a " pre-established harmony." There is an immanent *telos* or aim in every entity that determines its constitution and unifies its prehensions. We have just indicated that the actual entity can be regarded as a concrescence of feeling due to the integrating function of the subjective aim. This term " concrescence " is used by Whitehead to indicate an integrated event, and the subjective aim can therefore be described as a " principle of concretion."

Creativity and God

How do the actual entities derive their subjective aims? It is here that Whitehead directs our attention to the ultimate nature of the process. For him, ultimate reality, the ground of the real process of becoming, is " creativity." It is " creativity " that gives to the actual world its character of temporal passage to novelty. Creativity is, indeed, the formative ground of the world process. It is manifested in each concrescent creature, so that each actual entity is self-creative. It is the basic neutral stuff out of which all things emerge, closely akin to Alexander's Space-Time.[38] Inherent in it we may think of the possibilities or potentialities of existence, the eternal objects. There would seem to be Aristotelian influence here, for it is closely akin to the Greek philosopher's doctrine of form and to his peculiar definition of " act."

The real issue is how a particular pattern of development is assumed out of the variety of potentialities. How are the subjective aims of the individual actual entities determined? It is here that Whitehead introduces his concept of God. We are told that the selection of eternal objects for ingression into the process as subjective aims is the activity of God. God is the Principle of Concretion in Creativity, limiting the multiplicity of possible worlds to the one which is actualized in the process of becoming. He can be described as a uniquely different actual entity. As such he has two poles, a mental and a physical. These are described respectively as his primordial nature and his consequent nature.

In his primordial nature, God envisages or prehends conceptually all the eternal objects. The eternal objects subsist in God. In his primordial nature, God can be described as the first emergent of Creativity. Whitehead can write: "The primordial nature of God is the acquirement by creativity of a primordial character." [39] Thus God "does not create eternal objects; for his nature requires them in the same degree that they require Him." [40] They are potentialities in his primordial nature. What God does is creatively to arrange these eternal objects into the patterns of relationship and then to make these patterns available to the actual entities. As so arranged, the eternal objects enter into the experience of the world, not in disorder, but in relation and order. Indeed, Whitehead contends that the general character of the universe demands that there be such an entity as God. He must be both to organize the eternal objects and to make their patterned order available to the actual entities as the latter emerge out of the flux of creativity.

Yet Whitehead is careful to emphasize that God is *not Creator.* He does not create the actual entities any more than he creates the eternal objects. The actual entities are self-creating. Creativity comes to a focus in them. God does not force them to come into existence. He becomes related to them only as each one prehends conceptually an eternal object that he envisages. In this way he gives to them their subjectiveness. He makes available to them the eternal objects as he has ordered and envisaged them. So the free movement of creativity is kept open, and yet order and pattern are maintained. In this sense, God can be described as the Principle of Concretion. He is also " the ultimate irrationality." He must be accepted as the Principle of Concretion, and yet no reasons can be given for his mode of envisaging the eternal objects. There is no reason why the limitation of possibilities that God introduces into the flux of creativity by his patterning of the eternal objects should be as it is.

In his consequent nature, God realizes " the actual world in the unity of his nature and through the transformation of his wisdom." [41] In every actual entity, the mental pole makes possible the conceptual prehension of the eternal object which is to be its subjective aim. On the other hand, the physical pole provides the physical prehensions by which the actual entity is related to other entities and by which it is conditioned by them in its own development and self-realization. In the same way, God has both a mental and a physical pole. In God's primordial nature, his mental pole is central. He envisages the differentiated and patterned unity of the eternal objects and makes them available to all other actual entities. As such entities arise out of creativity and grasp their particular subjective aims by their mental poles, they become related to God by his physical pole. His mental pole envisages their subjective aims and his physical pole experiences their actuality. He physically prehends them. Thereby he finds his ideal pattern actualized in his experience. It is this which constitutes his consequent nature.

The becoming of the world is thus, at the same time, the becoming of God. With the physical experience that derives from the temporal world, God's consequent nature begins. He shares its actuality with every novelty which emerges out of creativity and chooses its subjective aim from the pattern that he has envisaged. The world creates itself. Yet it finds the vision or *telos* for such self-creation in the all-inclusive primordial valuation of the eternal objects by God. As it does so, God himself moves to full self-realization in his consequent nature.

There is something strongly akin to Hegelianism in this structure. The primordial nature of God might be likened to the Absolute Spirit in its mode of abstract Being ontologically prior to its dialectical movement into becoming, which, as it is wrought out, leads to the self-determination and self-realization of the Absolute. The abstract element is very evident when Whitehead declares of God in his primordial nature: " His unity of conceptual operations is a free creative act, untrammelled by reference to any particular course of things. It is deflected neither by love, nor by hatred, for what in fact comes to pass." [42] Indeed, we must ascribe to God, at this stage, " neither fulness of feeling nor consciousness." [43] To quote George Thomas:

God in His primordial nature is infinite, eternal, and unchanging. But He is " deficient " in that His feelings are purely conceptual, so that He is lacking in fulness of actuality and in consciousness. Therefore He requires other actual entities for His completion or fulfilment.[44]

This echoes Whitehead's own statement that, in his primordial nature and thus on his conceptual side, God is

free, complete, primordial, eternal, actually deficient and unconscious. The other side originates with physical experience derived from the temporal world, and then acquires integration with the primordial side. It is determined, incomplete, consequent, everlasting, fully actual, and conscious.[45]

This is not Hegel's monism, but it certainly has the flavor of Hegel's Spirit in its isolation and loneliness as abstract Being, moving through its dialectic to self-determination.

Whitehead tells us that God in his primordial nature is " the lure for feeling, the eternal urge of desire." [46] He can argue that God " adds Himself to the actual ground from which every creative act takes its rise," so that the power by which he " sustains the world is the power of himself as the ideal." [47] He confronts what is actual in the world with what is possible for it, and thus solves all indeterminations.[48] Thereby he moves to his consequent nature. We can understand, in the light of this, the suggestions that " the world lives by its incarnation of God in itself," [49] and that " the actual world is the outcome of the aesthetic order, and the aesthetic order is derived from the immanence of God." [50]

At first sight, Whitehead might seem to be advocating divine transcendence, and statements at the end of *Process and Reality* might appear to indicate this. He tells us: " It is as true to say that God transcends the World, as that the World transcends God." [51] Actually what we have is a veiled pantheism of the Spinozoistic variety. Undoubtedly, Whitehead has endeavored to reinterpret Platonism in a form consonant with the findings of modern science, especially biology. But the dualistic theism soon merges into pantheism. This is clear when Whitehead writes that " God and the World are the contrasted opposites in terms of which Creativity achieves its supreme task of transforming disjoined multiplicity, with its diversities in opposition, into concrescent unity, with its diversities in contrast." [52] This offers a vision of an all-embracing Creativity which finds expressions in parallel dynamic modes of God and the World, rather like a dynamic version of Spinoza's Substance. William Temple points out that " there is a force beyond God, called 'creativity,' and God in His primordial nature, is the first form of this." [53]

We do not have here the self-sufficient transcendent deity of Christian theism. We have an evolving deity dependent for consciousness upon the process of nature and history. He gives to the process its subjective aims, and he is for it " the great companion — the fellow sufferer who understands." [54] Indeed, the world creates God as much as God creates the world. God and the world are mutually necessary. He provides the rational ground for the world through his envisagement of the eternal objects, and thus supplies the process with an aesthetic order. But, on the other hand, the World makes possible the consequent nature of God, makes it possible for the deity to become conscious. God is not the first cause of the world, the creative and efficient ground of all actuality. He is dependent on the world for his own completion. " A process must be inherent in God's nature, whereby his infinity is acquiring realization." [55]

Even Whitehead has to confess that the meaning of God can be sought only in the world process and that such a mode of thought can lead only to an immanent deity. He writes:

Any proof which commences with the consideration of the character of the actual world cannot rise above the actuality of this world. It can only discover all the factors disclosed in the world as experienced. In other words, it may discover an immanent God, but not a God wholly transcendent.[56]

From the point of view of a final metaphysic, Whitehead's method cannot go so far as immanence in this sense. For the immanent deity is regarded then as the final ground of being. But Whitehead's deity is tied up with the process, so that the latter is as much necessary to give meaning to the deity as the deity is to give meaning to it. We cannot move beyond this duality. As William Temple puts it: " Professor Whitehead leaves us with a totality of God + World, wherein each explains the other but the totality itself is unexplained." [57]

Furthermore, on the basis of his own approach, Whitehead has no real justification for his conception of the primordial nature of God or even the postulation of God at all. Whitehead seems to believe that the general character of the world requires such an actual entity. Let us consider God's primordial nature. It is regarded as " the complete conceptual realization of possibilities relevant for any process of becoming whatsoever," a complete envisagement of the eternal objects. Now Whitehead has no transcendent realm of eternal objects which is the true reality, as had Plato. He adopts an empiricist approach and can give no reality to pure abstractions. His eternal objects are therefore the possibilities of actuality as envisaged and valued by God. God is the source of aesthetic order in the universe. But on the empiricist approach is Whitehead justified in declaring that the primordial nature that so selects the world's order is perfect and complete? There are many who would, on the basis of an empirical approach, doubt the necessity or even the probability of such a deduction from the facts of experience. They would not accept Whitehead's optimism.

Really this is the old teleological argument lifting its head. Its attractiveness does not make it convincing except to a prior commitment of faith. As a realist, can Whitehead really claim that the world as a process manifests increasingly a perfect aesthetic order? It is true, as he points out, that evolution manifests an "upward trend" and that life moves on to greater control over its environment at the physical level.[58] Whitehead sees the increasing modification of the environment as reaching its climax in man. There is a threefold urge — to live, to live well, to live better, and in man the function of reason is to make this possible.[59] Thereby the decay of one order is converted into the birth of its successor,[60] and ideal ends move man in a contrary direction to the aspect of physical decay.[61] But may not the whole be a *Götterdämmerung?* Indeed the struggle between goodness and sheer power by no means convinces one to view the process optimistically. At the empirical level, dysteleological aspects lift their head. Yet Whitehead infers an optimistic view and declares the completion of God's consequent nature because of the completeness of his primordial nature. William Temple's criticism is still apt. He points out that, for Whitehead, God's primordial nature is complete in any relevant sense only because "it is, by definition, the ground of all actual events." He continues:

But to infer from this the kind of completion posited is to assume the Leibnitzian theory of "the best of all possible worlds" which has previously been described as "an audacious fudge" (*Process and Reality,* p. 64). If on the other hand we are to estimate the character of the primordial nature of God from that of the events which it has occasioned, we have inadequate ground for concluding that, as He objectifies the world in Himself, "God is the poet of the world, with tender patience leading it by his vision of truth, beauty and goodness" (*Process and Reality,* p. 490).[62]

Perhaps Whitehead does show us his way out in his study of religion. For here he seems to point beyond God as a metaphysical necessity for his system to an intuitive awareness of God. Especially he thinks of God as the conserver of values. He tells us that "the fact of the religious vision, and its history of persistent expansion, is our one ground for optimism. Apart from it, human life is a flash of occasional enjoyments lighting up a mass of pain and misery, a bagatelle of transient experience." [63] He carefully denies that there is an intuition of a personal deity in religious experience. He holds that such personal nature is inferred,[64] but that there is "an apprehension of character permanently inherent in the nature of things." [65] Elsewhere, he tells us that

religion is the vision of something which stands beyond, behind, and within, the passing flux of immediate things; something which is real, and yet waiting to be realized; something which is a remote possibility, and yet the greatest of present facts; something which gives meaning to all that passes, and yet eludes apprehension; something whose possession is the final good, and yet is beyond all reach; something which is the ultimate ideal, and the hopeless quest.[66]

His rationalism is thus wedded to a warm emotional response to the apprehension of God. The vision of God lies in the background of his thought and comes out in the rich poetic forms that appear in his writings. Our values are worth pursuing and life is worthwhile, even though at the empirical level everything is perpetually perishing and life and its values are transient. This is because all are gathered up into God's experience and become a part of his consequent nature. Not only is God necessary metaphysically if our values are to be saved from loss, but "the vision of God . . . guarantees the worthwhileness of present life whatever may be its temporal outcome." [67] John B. Cobb holds that "in his own understanding, Whitehead's confidence was grounded in his vision of God." [68]

In this area Whitehead approaches to a personal understanding of God. Yet here difficulty arises. Tied as he is to his basic organismic model and to his understanding of enduring objects as societies of successive "actual occasions," Whitehead cannot really account for God's continuing identity. If God is an "actual entity," then it is difficult to account for him, on the one hand, as a succession of "actual occasions" and, on the other, as continually presenting all "other actual occasions" with their subjective aims, being himself enriched thereby, and moving himself to his full self-enrichment in his consequent nature. The very basis of Whitehead's philosophy with its idea of the rising of actual occasions to concrescence of feeling and their subsequent perishing introduces an inconsistency into the idea of God. How can God feel before he attains to his concrescence of feeling in his consequent nature? Yet if the model of an actual entity be applied to God, this must hold of God as of all actual entities.

The Strength and Weakness of Whitehead's Philosophical Theology

This philosophy has proved attractive to many Christian thinkers and has been especially used by the "process theology." We must examine in detail later some of the emphases therein employed, but we should here mention these and also note one major weakness, apart from those already noted in Whitehead's understanding of God.

This major weakness lies in Whitehead's basic analogy. In choosing "organism" for this, he has made it difficult to have any real understanding of human and divine personal being. Yet the Christian disclosure gives insight into God as personal and points to personal being as the key for understanding the total process. Whitehead is tied by his emphasis on the atomistic actual entities which are constituent of the configurations of larger events. This atomistic aspect has a temporal dimension. The actual entities are transient "occasions." Hence there arises the issue of identity, especially at the personal level.

Where he does deal with this issue, Whitehead speaks of a human "soul," yet even the soul is conceived as a society. Actually the soul is a part of nature like all other enduring objects, and like them, it is a series of occasions. As we have seen earlier, by "enduring object" Whitehead means a society in which the members are serially related, a nexus "which forms a single line of inheritance of its defining characteristic." [69] The higher animals also have souls, and what characterizes the soul is that it is the centralized control in an animal or human organism. Wherever the soul occurs it is a society of occasions characterized by consciousness, which is "a subjective form arising in the higher phases of concrescence." [70] As such it consists of a series of dominant occasions around which are organized the actual occasions that constitute the body and the brain. Particularly in the case of man, the presence of the soul makes possible a person as an enduring object. The actual occasions that thus serially constitute the soul involve a synthesis of the occasions in their past.[71] Thereby personal identity is possible.

The human personal being is marked for Whitehead by the use of language, the response of religion, and the aspect of moral behavior. Yet he finds it difficult to account for the continuing identity of a person. That is not surprising in the light of his atomistic and social view of the soul. He himself confesses this. He writes:

Any philosophy must provide some doctrine of personal identity. In some sense there is a unity in the life of each man, from birth to death. The two modern philosophers who most consistently reject the notion of a self-identical Soul-Substance are Hume and William James. But the problem remains for them, as it does for the philosophy of organism, to provide an adequate account of this undoubted personal unity, maintaining itself amidst the welter of circumstance.[72]

Attempts, such as those of John B. Cobb, to interpret Whitehead at this point do not resolve his dilemma. He is a victim of the key analogy which he has chosen.[73] All that Whitehead can say is that "we — as enduring objects with personal order — objectify the occasions of our own past with *peculiar* completeness in our immediate present." [74]

It is thus understandable that Whitehead does not really ascribe personal being to God. Also, his difficulty about theistic transcendence arises in part because of his organismic analogy. Personal self-transcendence points the way here where organismic wholeness does not. In consequence, Whitehead never escapes his naturalistic presupposition and even his God cannot escape from the process and transcend it.

Yet, allowing for the difficulties involved in Whitehead's understanding of the dual nature of God, he does offer some valuable
insights which correct the dominant Christian view of deity since
the medieval period. Whitehead's deity is much nearer the Biblical disclosure in his involvement with the world process. The
real significance of the Christian understanding of Creation and
Incarnation points to such involvement and the Cross points to
some degree of divine passibility. If we are to begin from the
divine disclosure and not from abstract Greek ideas, we shall
find that Whitehead has something to say to us at this point. His
understanding of God's relation to the world as one of persuasion
and not power says much to those who seek to express God's
essential being as love. His emphasis on process in God at least
reminds us that the God of the Bible is a living God and not the
static perfection of Greek thought. We may quote G. F. Thomas'
comment:

The problem of the relation between permanence and change, actuality and potentiality in God's nature has yet to be worked out in
a satisfactory way. But it may be predicted that the Theism of the
future will not abandon the Greek and medieval emphasis upon the
eternity, immutability, and perfection of the transcendent God, but
will seek a way to reinterpret them and synthesize them with the in-
sistence of Whitehead . . . upon His intimate relation to the world
and its profound effect upon Him.[75]

Part Two: *PROCESS IN CHRISTIAN PHILOSOPHIZING*

V

From Immanence to Transcendence

THE THOUGHT of Whitehead had the virtue, among others, of turning attention from the category of evolution to the more general category of process. In the past decades Christian thought has been in process of emancipating itself from the static categories current in its classical period. It has sought to replace them by dynamic categories more in keeping with the Biblical emphasis on history and the disclosure of God as the living God. Here it has been helped by the new historical perspective on nature made possible by the biological evidence for evolution and by our increasing scientific knowledge of cosmogony and the whole cosmic process. In addition, the new concern with the significance of history itself and with the nature of historical knowing has drawn fresh attention to the Incarnation, to the meaning of historical revelation, and to the place of history in the divine purpose. Finally, the success of science and technology has made it quite evident that we must have an empirical starting point if we would communicate reasonably with the contemporary mind.

All these factors are evident in the Christian thinker whom we shall now consider. William Temple,[1] Oxford don, headmaster of a British public school, Bishop of Manchester, Archbishop of York, Archbishop of Canterbury, social reformer, and world church leader, attempted to speak to the situation that we have just described. He does not show the influence of the linguistic philosophies of the last three decades, but his approach has many valuable insights which such philosophies in no way invalidate. Temple was himself greatly influenced by realists such as Lloyd Morgan and Samuel Alexander as well as by the creative evolutionist Bergson. He also came greatly under the impact of the thought of Whitehead. We shall find most of our material in Temple's Gifford Lectures — *Nature, Man and God.*

Dialectical Realism and the Structure of Reality

Temple begins as a realist on a naturalistic basis. That is to say, he accepts the data offered by modern science. Yet other ideas are ingredient in his thought. As a student and young don at Oxford University he was influenced by the Hegelianism of Edward Caird and Bernard Bosanquet. The Hegelian dialectic left its mark upon his logical procedure, as we shall see. The empiricist and realistic approaches of Lloyd Morgan and Samuel Alexander appealed to him because of his concern to speak to modern man. Modern science and the evidence for evolution demanded that he accept an empiricist approach to nature. Yet his empiricism was far more broadly based than sense perception alone could make possible. For him, empiricism embraced every aspect of experience — aesthetic, moral, and religious. He saw man as a person living in many dimensions of human experience and not just as a product of biological evolution, a higher mammal who was able to think.

To this empiricism he added the rationalism that he had imbibed from his Hegelian mentors. He believed that reality had a rational structure which the human mind was able to comprehend. He believed there was a kinship between the mind and the objects presented to it in its world.[2] He tells us that "the mind which knows is in a perfectly real sense equal to what it knows, and in another real sense transcends it, unless what it knows is another mind which also knows."[3] So the mind finds itself "at home in the world." Further, it is a unity, forming a rationally coherent whole. For mind is the principle of unity in the whole world process. "Mind is the principle of unity in Reality, or at least the fullest expression of that principle known to us."[4]

Finally, Temple faced the fact that Marxism had captured the imagination of many intellectuals and was a potent political force in our world. Its denial of the finality of moral and religious values, its reduction of man to the level of an economic animal, challenged him. So he termed his approach "dialectical realism" in opposition to "dialectical materialism." This description of his approach emphasized both the rational and the empiricist streams in his thinking.

When we seek to assess the absolute presuppositions of his thought, it is fairly clear that he believed the universe was a rationally structured whole. Also, he accepted at the empirical level what science offered but he believed other areas of experience pointed to a deeper understanding of the world than naturalism could give. Again, he believed personal being in its multi-dimensionality to be the key to the whole process. As we shall see, he sought to show that the whole evolutionary process led up to it.

Yet this basic totality of commitment had a Christian root. His is a Christian philosophy. What he chose as significant is made so by his Christian insights. In a letter that was discovered in Temple's own copy of the Gifford Lectures, *Nature, Man and God*, Emil Brunner points out that although Temple claims to be shaping a natural theology which is free of any Christian bias, actually the Christian faith regulates the movement of his thought and determines the conclusions to which his logical argument leads. It has been pointed out that Temple "was a man of profound Christian faith, and what he actually has done is to arrange the facts so that they give support to his faith."[5] But then it is highly doubtful, as we have seen, whether a committed man can do otherwise. Since Temple's time the understanding of the personal nature of all knowledge has made many aware that the idea of a rigorous and utterly unbiased reason is an illusion. Temple's philosophy was Christian in intention!

The term " dialectical realism," which Temple used to describe his philosophy, needs to be understood. In " dialectical material-ism " the dialectic is a process in matter itself and not funda-mentally in thought. At the historical level, as we have seen, it is an expression of economic forces. At the level of nature, it is re-lated to the movement of organization in matter itself. Temple, however, although a realist, is also a rationalist. His dialectic is fundamentally a description of his own logical procedure. It is re-lated to his thought processes by which he interprets his empirical data. Yet since reality is itself a rational whole, in a real sense his rational dialectic reflects reality. Hence, there is a Hegelian flavor in Temple's thought, and he never escapes the idealism that influenced his formative years.

By dialectic, Temple understands a logical method akin to that of Hegel. He dismisses the traditional logic because it was con-cerned primarily with universals, with general principles. Its grounding in mathematics makes this inevitable. But this means that it is unable to deal with the particular and least of all with the singular. Because of this, it is no fit instrument for the under-standing of history or of the personal, for the personal is dis-tinctively characterized by individual freedom. Such logic is valid in certain areas, but it is not universally applicable. Natural the-ology of the old type confined itself to this formal logic and, in so doing, has now put itself " out of business." The historical habit of mind has become a part of the modern thought world, and to this the old logic does not apply. " This mathematical ideal of knowledge," Temple writes, " has often been valued for those qualities which constitute its fatal defects: these are its indiffer-ence to time and its precision." [6] It looked for the unchanging and elaborated a realm of changeless universals, which it regarded as true Being, as reality.

This realm of reality is changeless, not only in the sense in which the Law of Nature is an unchanging principle governing a process of change, but in the sense of having no reference to change or process at all.[7]

But such unchanging universals do not exist. Rather, modern man is concerned with evolving existents, with evolutionary species. Evolution has destroyed the idea of an unchanging universal which deductive inference can securely choose as its starting point. It got rid of the fixity of species and replaced this doctrine by the development of species in a temporal series of existent entities. Thereby the unchanging universal or generic concept can no longer be basic. Historical development takes its place. We cannot divide sense experience from thought forms and regard the latter as alone truly real. Traditional logic offers us certainty on the basis of logical necessity, but it leaves us with forms that have little or no existential relevance. Existence is historical, not static.

What, then, of inductive logic? This argues from the many particulars but leaves us with, at the best, probability. As Temple points out: " The difficulty about Deduction is that we have no certain right to our starting point. The difficulty about Induction is that we have no certain right to any conclusion." [8] He reminds us that the only way to prove any such conclusion is to make a list of all possible conclusions and eliminate them one by one. But, at the practical level, this is an impossible procedure because of the difficulty of precise definition when we deal with existent things.

Hence Temple contends that the true approach is a blend of induction and deduction. He speaks of his methodology as dialectic and circular and makes much of the idea of the " concrete universal." The latter is a whole covering a developing group of facts. It is a system to which a succession of events contribute. Temple cites Michael Foster's attack upon " the determining activity of the generic concept," " the activity of the universal in determining its own specific determinations." [9] In this way we move by an "ontological argument from the organized complexity of a system to the necessity of its real existence." [10] This is the approach of traditional deductive logic.

But Foster also attacks the inductive idea, employed in the physical sciences, "that physical causation is the only active determinant." He contends that we must put in the place of the determining activity of the generic concept, "the development of the species through actual generations. The race which develops is the concrete universal which needs no ontological argument to add concreteness to it." [11] The idea of development of a concept introduces particularity into universality. It breaks down any radical dichotomy between sense experience and thought. The universal concept like race pervades the individual members in the historical development. But each member has characteristics not determined by it. The "race" *in toto* is a "historical individual" in which sense and thought come together. It is a concrete universal.

Temple sees living, logical thought moving in a circle. Thought starts with a group of particulars, experienced data, that point to some model or theory by which they may be better comprehended. When this model is applied to experienced data, it will have to be modified, and so the process continues until a system emerges, a concrete universal, a whole in which all the empirical material is embraced and made comprehensible. "Living thought is circular; it moves round and round a system of facts, improving its understanding of the system and its constituent parts at every stage." [12] A better understanding of the whole, the concrete universal is in step with a better apprehension of its particular differences. The facts of experience are brought into closer cooperation as the concrete universal is comprehended more fully. Temple cites, as concrete universals, occurrences like the Renaissance and the Reformation. [13] This circular way of thinking manifests the interaction of inductive and deductive thinking.

We note the Hegelian flavor in this method. Temple is a rationalist and an empiricist. He wants to give reason and the universal in some form a prime place. The method he outlines is much like the way modern science works. The parallel is even more evident when Temple finds a place for the aesthetic element. The presence of imagination and a creative appraisal of harmony and aesthetic order is evident in many of the intuitive hunches by which scientists have moved forward in nature.[14] Kant suggests, in his *Critique of Judgment,* that we are immediately apprehending the universal through the particular in the experience of beauty. This is echoed in Temple's statement that "art is, in structure, logic *in excelsis.*"[15] He points out that "intellect as a rule is content with a skeleton and persists in pushing enquiry further, while imagination clothes the skeleton with flesh and then contemplates its finished work until satiety overtakes it."[16] Artistic creations have a universal significance, and yet no one can dispute their particularity. It is not sufficient for a myth or drama to deal with a mere type. It illuminates because it particularizes the universal. Temple seems to be suggesting that myth and symbol take us to deeper layers of reality than abstract thought on its own. Imagination and the aesthetic aspect of experience clothe a concept in adequate imagery and draw out its meaning. This, as we have suggested earlier,[17] is what Plato did in his myths.

So Temple develops his dialectical movement in which imaginative thinking is an ingredient but of which the structure is still the Hegelian thesis-antithesis-synthesis. It is a circular movement in which the argument turns full circle to a synthesis that embraces all the facts in a deeper and more integrated way than the original thesis. He calls it realism because he is prepared to start with matter and see mind as emerging from matter. But his is no materialistic dialectic. In Marxism, mind and thought are responses to matter and are determined by it. Temple will not make mind so secondary and dependent. It is the aspect of the process that comes to dominate the material aspect and, because of its capacity for free ideas, to shape the material world.

Hence, he formulates his structure of reality much like the emergent evolutionists and yet with a difference. He sees a succession of levels in which each level draws up the constituents of the lower levels into a higher synthesis. Thus we have a movement from matter to life or sentience. As self-determination makes its appearance, so does individuality. We move through various stages of self-motion in which response to the environment begins to manifest more mental characteristics. From feeling we move to learning. At last fully self-conscious mind or personal spirit appears. The full potentialities of each lower level appear only as it is gathered up into a higher. Life discloses the possibilities in matter, and the potentiality of life only becomes evident when it is indwelt by mind. All that mind is capable of becomes manifest only as it becomes subservient to and is permeated by self-consciousness or spirit. The movement is a temporal movement, a movement increasingly away from the generic concept to individuality. Historical thought, and not static universals, holds the key to understanding. Selfhood is increasingly individual, and it is only by " concrete universals " that meaning can be expressed.

We must now examine, in detail, how, granted his presuppositions, Temple deals with this structure.

The Emergence of Mind and the Movement to Immanent Spirit

In the first stage of his thought, Temple adopts a realist approach to the natural order. He dismisses any idealistic contention that the objective world is the product of the knowing mind. He points to the healthy objectivism of the medieval mind. At their height, the medieval thinkers were realists. They believed that in their conceptual experience there was a direct grasping of the essential meanings of the objective world. Temple believes that it is necessary for us to return to this in a more comprehensive way. Here we see his dialectic and circular form of argument at work.

He sees that there had to be a revolt against the medieval establishment. Man had to throw off the shackles of medieval authoritarianism. Now the Cartesian approach in philosophy was one aspect of this revolt of the individual against authority. Manifested in the work of Luther and characterizing the Renaissance and the Reformation alike, this revolt is also seen in the Cartesian entanglement with the knowing self. Ever since Descartes, philosophy has been bound up with a fatal self-centeredness, a continuing appeal to consciousness. Its emphasis has fallen on " I think," severing man's thinking from the object that is thought. Descartes's *cogito ergo sum* marks the commencement of what Temple calls the " Cartesian *faux pas*." This artificial abstraction of the consciousness from the knowing relationship of subject and object has been labeled a dichotomy by Whitehead, as we have seen. It led to an isolation of man from the universe and his imprisonment within his own mental faculties. Here we see the principle of thesis and antithesis at work. The medieval thesis was destroyed at every level, including philosophy, by the individualistic antithesis.

The concentration upon the knowing mind and the rejection of a healthy objectivism has led to skepticism, and its logical outcome is solipsism. One result has been that mind has been taken out of the material order and a materialistic science has resulted. The reaction of philosophy to this materialistic emphasis was to assert, in an idealistic form, the supremacy of the spiritual. On the one hand, we find the scientist declaring, on the basis of his evidence, that the mind with which the philosopher was so preoccupied was a late arrival on the earthly scene. On the other hand, the idealistic philosopher was declaring that, despite its late arrival, it was the thinker's mind that made the world. As Temple puts it:

It is this assumption of the priority of intellection that gives such plausibility as it possesses to the notion that we begin with our mind and its ideas and then from these advance to the knowledge of external world by inference. Hence comes the whole farrago of Subjective Idealism, Pre-established Harmony, Psycho-physical Parallelism, and other outrages upon common sense.[18]

But this idealistic point of view and its preoccupation with human consciousness cannot be maintained in the face of an honest reading of the facts of science. The world, as we apprehend it, antedates our apprehension. It existed historically before anyone apprehended it. It is the testimony of our experience that "apprehension takes place within the world, not the world within apprehension." [19]

Once we recognize the late arrival of mind, Temple suggests that two alternatives are open to us. *Either* we may take the materialist approach and argue that our apprehension of the world is to be explained in terms of the interaction of the primary particles into which matter may be analyzed. He labels this a *reductio ad absurdum. Or* we may regard those very interactions at the atomic and subatomic levels as embryonic apprehensions. This is the approach of Whitehead. Temple suggests that, so long as we remain in the immanentist position and provided we intend to emphasize the continuity of the process, this approach is to be preferred. Believing in continuity and refusing the materialistic synthesis, Whitehead must find mind all the way through, in however rudimentary a form. Here we see the impact of Whitehead's thought on Temple. The latter moves from this approach in the movement of his dialectic, but does begin with it.

Temple's argument moves in this way full circle and takes up a synthesis at a higher level than the thesis. Let us now note how this circular comprehension of the facts proceeds. Consciousness appears in connection with organic life. It is upon this basis that our apprehension of the world must be understood. Experience may begin even at the inorganic level. Whitehead is certainly right in holding "that consciousness presupposes experience and not experience consciousness." [20] Vegetable life shows some degree of response to environment. We assume here that, in the absence of self-movement, there is no sensation, but we cannot prove that feeling is absent. Generally, we assume that self-motion and consciousness are concomitant, so that the self-motion of the organism is directed by consciousness. As the organism increases in complexity, we attribute to it more and more of the feelings and sensations which accompany similar reactions on our part. We only begin to have clear evidence of this where the physiological reaction is accompanied by a capacity to learn by experience. Self-motion would seem to indicate a clearer differentiation between the organism and its environment and thus to encourage the development of rudimentary consciousness. Thereby we would attribute consciousness to the animal but hardly to the plant.

Self-consciousness arises at what Bergson describes as the movement from instinct to intelligence. Temple [21] agrees that self-consciousness most likely arises under the conditions in which an organism moves from adjusting itself to its environment to adjusting its environment to itself. Self-consciousness is likely to be stimulated by the organism's necessity to adjust the environment to its needs. Temple is, however, very careful to add that this "can no more actually give birth to self-consciousness than self-motion can give birth to consciousness." [22]

Even in self-consciousness the arrival of cognition is quite late. The earliest form of self-consciousness is bound up with the feeling. It is emotion, sympathy or antipathy. We do not infer the existence of other selves by observing the motions of their bodies. Beginning with the intimate relationship of child and mother, we move to an awareness of others as we become aware of ourselves. We differentiate the elements from a primary unity of experience, a single apprehension. Cognition and thought are grounded in this continuing process of adjustment between organism and environment and are a continuation of it. Temple's realism finds expression here when he asserts:

The organism, now more mental than physical, is scientific, artistic, moral, and religious because in the mutual reaction between it and its environment it finds the environment to be possessed of the characters to which these activities are the appropriate response. [23]

Temple now bids us note that the mind, which is thus able to conduct this progressive apprehension of the process, itself emerges in the midst of that process.

That there should "emerge" in the cosmic process a capacity to apprehend, even in a measure to comprehend, that process is the most remarkable characteristic of the process itself. [24]

The mind will not allow itself to be dismissed as a mere episode in the process. Mind and consciousness are not homeless waifs in a material universe. Temple notes that the descriptive verb " emerge " denotes, at this point, an agnosticism with regard to the reason for the novelty. Yet it also indicates " a strong preference for continuity as against catastrophic irruptions of novelty " [25] and that Mind has a kinship with nature.

What then of the purely material? Man has not been successful in explaining mind in terms of the nonmental factors that preceded in the process. But mind does offer such a self-explanatory principle of explanation. It is, therefore, reasonable to give such a hypothesis the chance to justify itself. Nor must we cavil at its late arrival.

There is no insuperable difficulty in the view that the history of the universe is rational, though the ground of its rationality is only fully disclosed in its entire course, and though the element within it which supplies the unifying influence only appears late in that course.[26]

We might agree that an accidental collocation of whirling material particles, passing through endless permutations, might produce the universe as we know it. But when mind becomes a part of nature, that kind of explanation is not enough. Nature then has to be grounded in mind. We have to confess that " *the more completely we include Mind within Nature, the more inexplicable must Nature become except by reference to Mind.*" [27] We note that " mind " is here what Temple has described as a " concrete universal," a concept describing a historical succession in which all the members manifest the characteristics to differing degrees. We derive it as a description of a system of historical experience.

At this point Temple's argument has moved full circle and we come to his first dialectical transition. We have to move from naturalistic realism to an immanental form of theism. Mind pervades the process and is its basic reality, its ground. We have to do with immanent mind as a cosmic reality.

From Immanence to Transcendence

Temple now turns to an examination of mind and the values that mind finds in the process. The circular movement of his dialectic begins again. Mind, as we know it in general experience, is concerned with values as well as facts. It pursues truth, appreciates and creates beauty, obeys the claims of goodness. It reveres these values absolutely and for their own sake. They reside in the interplay of Mind and the environment supplied for it by the process.

In truth, the mind recognizes itself in its object. It finds that reality vindicates its own proper activity. The mind which emerges from the process finds the whole process to be informed by mind. " The little mind of man increasingly perceives that it is tracing out the workings of mind mightier than itself." [28] In beauty, the mind finds in the object what is akin to itself. " It finds itself in its other." [29]

As, in this pursuit of truth and vision of beauty, the mind of man apprehends Mind in the process, so it becomes increasingly aware of the transcendence and otherness of that Mind. In his scientific investigation of nature, man bows before the mystery and yet the order of the universe.

Nothing merely strange or alien can seem so incomparably transcendent as that Mind in the likeness of which our own minds are fashioned and yet before which they can only confess their impotence.[30]

As with truth, so it is with beauty. At its highest, beauty holds the artist in a way akin to the Beatific Vision.

When we combine with such reflections as these the consideration that mind historically appears as the flowering into consciousness of the organism's relation to its environment, there seems no valid reason for doubting the ultimate deliverances alike of the scientific and of the artistic consciousness. This testimony is an unambiguous affirmation of transcendent Mind apprehended by reason of its immanence in Nature, physical and spiritual.[31]

In this last quotation, Temple presupposes his next dialectical transition. But his thought has not yet turned full circle. He has to deal with the value of Goodness. He regards this as the supreme and inclusive value. Values of the order of Truth and Beauty consist of the discovery by the mind of itself in the object. But values can be present in absolute form only when the object is itself mind and not just the expression of mind. Hence, value becomes absolute in personal relationship, and this happens at the level of Goodness. From this fact the experience of uncompromising obligation takes its rise.

Temple admits the varying understanding of what constitutes duty. But he holds that it is always obligatory to perform that duty. There is no clear criterion as to what a man's duty may be, but there is still the absolute obligation to will the right so far as it can be ascertained. It is sufficient to remember that this obligation and the content of our duty are present in the complex of social relationships. As the multiplicity of persons lay their claims on us, we realize that the adjustments to others which constitute goodness require sympathy. What is required of us above all else is love. We ought to behave as persons in a society of persons, and thus we ought to love our neighbor as ourself. But here we realize our impotence.

Only by love can we fulfil the law, and love is not at our command. But if the ground of all the universe and of our own being is Personal Love, to which we owe our origin and our maintenance in being, then it may be that as we penetrate to that which is ever more than ourselves and yet is also the very life of our life, we may find the ability which we now lack.[32]

At this point Temple argues that a God who is merely immanent in the process leaves that process unexplained. We have indicated earlier his criticism of Whitehead in this connection. He contends that if God and the World are mutually necessary, the whole of God and the World remains unexplained. We cannot see why it is what it is. If we think in terms of personality rather than organism, we may find a more adequate category of explanation, the more so because we can then move from immanence to transcendence.

The hidden presupposition of Temple's thought then becomes evident. His argument has a rationalistic and idealistic bent to this point. The model would appear to be mind and reason. But with the concern with the value of goodness, with moral values and their accompanying sense of obligation, he has to move from an idealistic emphasis on rational mind to a concern with person as his model for understanding the universe. This would seem to be a movement in the basic position from which he starts. Quite clearly, from now on, he is more concerned with personal being in the totality of its dimensions than just the rational aspect. "Mind" becomes "personal being."

Personality is always transcendent in relation to process, for in self-determination we have also self-transcendence. "Personality always transcends its own self-expression." [33] Personality always acts within and yet stands apart from the process. Hence Temple contends that the only adequate explanation of the world process must be sought in a personal Will which, though immanent in it, yet transcends it. God is not outside the Process and acting on it from without, for he is its informing principle and life. Yet as personality transcends its self-expression, so God as personal transcends the process which he informs and guides.

The more we study the activity of God immanent, the more we become aware of God transcendent. The Truth that strikes awe in the scientist is awful because it is His thought; the Beauty that holds spellbound the artist is potent because it is His glory; the Goodness that pilots us to the assured apprehension of Reality can do this because it is His character; and the freedom whereby man is lifted above all other nature, even to the possibility of defying it, is fellowship with Him. Heaven and earth are full of His glory; but He is more and other than all that is in earth and heaven. [34]

So we are brought to the second dialectical transition in Temple's thought. We move from a God immanent to a God transcendent. Temple is careful, at this point, to avoid pantheism. Because God is Personal, he must express himself, but his self-expression is not himself. He indwells the world which is the medium of his personal action. We must assume, moreover, that his immanence means that he is unchangeably constant and that his transcendence implies that he "possesses a reserve of resource whereby He can from time to time modify the constant course sustained by His immanent action." [35]

Temple rejects the dichotomy between the normal and the miraculous. If the World Process is the medium of God's personal action, it is the expression of his purpose. Constancy of such purpose does not show itself in invariable constancy of personal action. Rather, it is manifested in such a perpetual self-adaptation to changing circumstances that the unchanging purpose may be fulfilled within the changing complexions of that process which is the medium of its expression. No scientific law, Temple contends, is ultimate. "It is a general statement of that course of conduct in Nature which is sustained by the purposive action of God so long and so far as it will serve His purpose." [36] He adds:

Our contention is that an element in every actual cause and indeed the determinant element, is the active purpose of God fulfilling itself with the perfect constancy which calls for an infinite graduation of adjustments in the process. Where any adjustment is so considerable as to attract notice it is called a miracle; but it is not a specimen of a special class, it is an illustration of the general character of the World-Process. [37]

Hence, Temple can hold that the so-called indeterminacy at the basis of matter, postulated by the quantum theory, is, in the last resort, not indeterminacy. All rests back upon that ultimate determinant which is the will of God.

There is an indication here of Temple's idealistic background. May it not be that the contingency and randomness about which science is increasingly speaking are aspects of the unfinished nature of the universe? It may be that God has created such an aspect of his world that within it man's personal freedom may operate creatively. If so, such a divine acceptance of self-limitation may mean that God himself voluntarily accepts the way of the servant and waits patiently on human cooperation for the fulfillment of his purpose. We miss this emphasis in Temple, probably because there is still a hidden strain of absolute idealism in his thought.

Temple would, however, have us take divine personality seriously. He contends that when we do, we shall know that the World Process is guided by an immanent principle which is also personal purposive Mind. In fulfillment of his inflexible purpose, that personal Mind guides the movement of the cosmic aggregates and the subatomic entities so that, for the main part, their behavior is constant and regular. But he can also vary that behavior when it serves the requirements of his purpose. "The cause of their constancy is itself the cause of their variation when it serves that one purpose best." [38] God is active in the World and its process is his activity. (Again we raise our question!) But God has created the world and, as Creator, he is transcendent to it.

From General Revelation to Special Revelation

In the next stage of his dialectical movement, Temple considers the divine activity in the world. We have already indicated his attempt to relate constancy of purpose to variation of activity if God be transcendent personal being who is also immanent in the world. The assertion of adaptability and variability does not introduce the ideas of chaos or caprice if we relate such an assertion to the immanent activity of personal deity. So Temple declares that " it is the Transcendent who is immanent and it is the Immanent who transcends." [39]

At this stage of his thought, Temple discloses increasingly the Christian insights that have shaped his presuppositions. It becomes evident that his is no natural theology in the old sense of that term, but Christian philosophizing. This is very evident in the discussion of revelation to which Temple now turns his attention. It is true that he talks about General Revelation, yet the Christian overtones are very present. There is a universal revelation of God that is manifested in all his activity, and special revelations must not be completely differentiated from this. All occurrences are to some degree revelation. For the very possibility of revelation at all is just this personal quality of the Supreme Reality. If a personal God is the ground of all existence, there can be nothing which is not revelation.[40] If the Supreme Reality "is not personal, there can be no special revelation, but only uniform procedure." [41]

In the ensuing discussion, it becomes very evident that Temple is taking the Biblical revelation as norm. He argues, in a way that has now become familiar, that revelation is not propositional, divinely dictated, and handed to man as infallible. It is "the co-incidence of event and appreciation," [42] the intercourse of mind and event. Temple regards the uniform world process as in some measure a revelation of God for minds capable of apprehending it. But he sees it as "less fully revelatory than specially adapted activities for the meeting of such contingencies as give sufficient ground for such activities." [43] Thus he argues for the possibility of special revelations against the background of general revelation. He adds:

There is obviously neither need nor possibility to draw any dividing line between the revelation which is continuously given in the whole course of the world process as men's minds are enlightened to appreciate this, and the revelation which is given in special and signal occasions.[44]

At all levels, however, we have the same principle — "the inter-action of the world-process and the minds, both being alike guided by God." [45]

Thus, though the primary medium for God's self-disclosure is the world process itself, within that process events arise which become particular media of revelation. Some of these may be miraculous, but not necessarily so. Whether miraculous or within the uniform activities of the process they all alike manifest God's immanence; all alike are revelatory as minds are alerted to grasp their significance. God may use any normal natural event or his-torical event in the world process as a special revelation, as, for example, the events that accompanied the exodus or the retreat of Sennacherib. He may equally use unusual and abnormal events.

In whichever form he acts, it is consistent with his personal nature and guidance of the process.

The argument comes full circle to the next transition as Temple moves from revelation to grace. The presence of evil in the world process becomes the occasion for this transition. Temple's thought now moves to a consideration of why evil should arise in a world that is grounded in the Divine Purpose. Once more the Christian intention and insights become very apparent. Indeed, although Temple claims to be dealing only with general revelation, much of what he writes is more Christian theology than Christian philosophy.

He begins with the biological level, pointing out that man, like the animals, is self-centered. But man also has the capacity for self-assertion because he is self-conscious. Man builds his values around himself, erecting them in an egoistical scale of which he is the center of criterion. It is on the basis of these values that he acts in opposition to the absolute values of truth and goodness. His own imagination serves to stimulate his desire. Furthermore, his solidarity with his fellows means that his actions and choices influence them.

We are, in part, reciprocally determining beings. We make each other what we are. Therefore the existence of one self-centered soul would spread an evil infection through all who come within its range of influence.[46]

So human society discloses itself, in one aspect, as a network of competing selfishness, tainting the personalities that are born into it.

Temple denies that such sin was necessary to the divine purpose. Yet he holds that God so made the world that "the dawn of moral self-consciousness was likely to be more of a 'fall' than an ascent."[47] In this sense, sin must be held to come within the divine purpose, even though things could have happened otherwise. Biological self-centeredness and the finitude of knowledge weight the scales of human decision. What God "faced was a probability so great as to be distinguishable only in thought from certainty."[48]

God could not, therefore, make a world with no provision to deal with sin. Temple finds a general grace operative in which the Divine Goodness seeks to lift man out of this self-centeredness. He holds that, in all religious experience, there is evidence of grace at work, seeking to uproot man from himself as center, and to draw him to find his center in God, "the Spirit of the Whole." The latter phrase is, at least, an indication that Temple has not really escaped from the Hegelian net. This becomes more evident as he moves to the end of his argument.

In general grace, God operates through the absolute values, seeking to break through man's tainted nature. With Truth and Beauty the call deals only with certain functions of man's life. In goodness the call is to a complete desertion of self-centeredness. Yet man's positive response to these values and the call that comes through them brings but a partial escape. Self remains the center. If God comes in the circle of the self, he is at the periphery. Hence, God must act in complete self-giving and self-sacrifice in order that he may win our freely offered love and make possible a complete break from self-centeredness. Such salvation must be all of God. All man can contribute is the sin from which he needs to be redeemed. It is true that man's will must cooperate. Yet even that cooperation springs from a purpose divinely implanted. Christian theology has now really taken over as Temple wrestles with the issue of election.

We are in this way brought to the final dialectical transition — that to special revelation and special grace. These fall outside the philosophical preparation and so Temple leaves us with a finger that points to the Incarnation.

Process and God

Before he arrives at his final transition, Temple, following his circular method, surveys the destiny of historical man and the significance of the natural order as these have been developed in his philosophical approach. Here his Hegelian indebtedness becomes very evident.

First of all, let us look at the picture of history. Temple holds, as all Christians should hold, that history has meaning for God. He rejects any Platonic idea of history as " the moving image of eternity." As he sees it, history is vitally united to God's eternal being. To say that history makes no difference to God is to reduce the ethical struggle to insignificance. The higher any religion is in the scale of spiritual, ethical, and intellectual values, the more it is concerned with the historical. Supremely is this true of Christianity. Sin is a temporal phenomenon. But the Christian faith affirms that it is so significant in God's eternal life that he is prepared to involve himself sacrificially in history in order to deal with it.[49] The moral experience of man in general points also in this direction. " For men, at least, it is true that fellowship with the eternal is most fully achieved by a certain mode of successive behavior in relation to the temporal." [50]

In considering the relation of history to the life of God, we cannot, however, regard the eternal entirely as the aggregate of historical events. We must not identify being with becoming. To say this is to involve eternity in the uncertainty that always attends history and becoming. Such a view does give history, as the scene of man's moral striving, supreme significance. " Its course positively constructs the content of that eternal experience, which is history as an integrated whole." [51] Yet it also implies that the content of God's eternal experience is dependent upon our moral action. Temple points out that if we avoid this by allowing divine intervention to a degree sufficient for the fulfillment of the divine purpose, then human freedom and responsibility become essentially fictitious. History is simply a projection of the divine nature.

We must, in some way, find a middle path between the two views so far attacked. History must make a difference to God, but the interrelationship of God and history must have its prime emphasis on the divine activity. The Eternal must always be the ground of the temporal and historical. Temple is careful to define eternity as " an experience that should include in a single apprehension the whole course of time, even though that course be endless in both directions." [52] Thus he eliminates the second view, for " the Eternal is not successive." [53] It is " a unitary synthetic apprehension of the whole process of Time and all that happens in it." [54] Eternity is transcendent and yet history is of ultimate importance to it. Temple declares that " *the eternal is the ground of the historical, and not* vice versa; *but the relation is necessary, not contingent — essential not incidental.*" [55] It is not a case of the Eternal being the substance and the historical merely the shadow. This eliminates the first view. Rather, the historical is evidence of the Eternal " as a necessary self-expression of a Being Whose essential activity is at once self-communication and self-discovery in that to which He communicates Himself." [56] Again, we are told that " the Eternal is self-expressed in History; but this act of self-expression is not epi-phenomenal to the Eternal — a mere by-product of its own unmoved perfection. The Eternal fulfills itself in its historical self-expression, so that if this were abolished it would in its own nature be other than it is." [57]

It is difficult to miss in such statements the shades of the Hegelian absolute and of idealistic monism. We have, however, to be fair to Temple at this point. He does endeavor to preserve the divine transcendence. Furthermore, he is careful to affirm the divine act of creation as a divine volitional act and no process of inevitable emanation from the divine being. God and the World are not " correlates, each depending upon the other for existence in some way." Rather " the world exists because God chose to call it into being and chooses to sustain it in being." God, again, is under no external compulsion to create and sustain the world. He chooses to do so freely " because it seems good to Him so to do." [58] That God should create cannot be " a mere accident of His being; it proves Him to be of such a nature as to create." [59] It is in the light of such statements that we must judge Temple's approach to the meaning of history.

Again, Temple does not assert that history changes God's essential nature or that God becomes self-conscious in the process or that through history he attains a " consequent nature " as personal spirit. There are no traces of the points of view already critically assessed in Whitehead and Alexander as well as in Hegel. Rather, Temple tells us that " history does not make a difference to God in the sense of making Him different at one time from what He was at another." [60] Indeed, in the light of his definition of eternity, it is difficult to see how he could envisage God otherwise. History cannot make a difference to God in the sense of God growing or changing his essential being, since eternity is not successive. " But in another sense History makes a great difference to the Eternal; for if there were no History, or if History were other than in fact it is, the Eternal would not be what the Eternal is." [61] Thus history matters to God because it is vitally united to his eternal essence. God being what God is in his innermost nature as love, he must express himself in creation and in history. If history ceased to be, then that would imply a difference in what he is, " as author, over-ruler, and fulfiller of History." [62]

The richness of God's own Being embraces the values that are manifested in history. The heroisms and aspirations, beauty and love that are manifested in the life of historical man must have value to God. Otherwise God would be inferior to the very process that he has created.[63] Temple holds that, on the basis of his analysis of value, the meaning of history lies " in the development of an ever wider fellowship of ever richer personalities. The goal of History, in short, is the Commonwealth of Value." [64] This commonwealth embodies individuality and fellowship, either of which cannot be manifested in richness without the other. " There can be no richness of individuality for men or for nations without fellowship, and there can be no fellowship apart from individuality nor depth of fellowship apart from rich variety of individuality." [65]

Indeed, it is in history that the divine purpose is being fulfilled. What God wills in his transcendence, he actualizes through his immanence in history. " History is the manifestation and working out of the eternal purpose." [66] We might say that history enriches God's life by the actualization of his loving purpose in a community of love. This community of love or Kingdom of God is what Temple terms " Commonwealth of Value." Historical process supplies an opportunity of actualization to the self-giving and the reality of victorious sacrifice, which religion apprehends as the heart of God's fullness of being. God's purpose will be accomplished when the world has been so transformed that finite spirits are united in " a fellowship which reproduces in the creature the love which is the essential being of the Creator." [67] " The spiritual richness of His [God's] eternal being is in some measure constituted by the moral achievements of His temporal creatures." [68] The Biblical testimony to God's involvement in history would seem to imply this. Actually its insights dominate Temple's viewpoint, and the Christian intention of his philosophizing becomes evident.

In this actualization of the divine purpose, Temple again avoids any monism that ignores individual freedom. If God's purpose is concerned with individuality and fellowship, place must be made for freedom and contingency. Now since God is the Eternal, in this eternal and transcendent dimension he sees history as a completed whole. Since " all that happens utterly depends on Him, He knows it all with utter certainty." [69] Yet finite personal beings are so created in resemblance to him that God must control them only in accord with the law of their being. But this means through their unforced affection and will as they respond to their apparent good. Therefore God " does not know *beforehand* exactly how they will respond to the various modes of His manifestation of Himself to them." [70] In the dimension of his immanent activity in history God does not know the precise mode of the future even though the fulfillment of his purpose be secure.

We are left with the paradox of God knowing all with utter certainty in an eternal dimension and knowing only with the succession of time in an immanent dimension. " To Him [God] the contingent is still contingent, as not being compelled by its own past; yet the whole is necessary, and therefore also all its parts; and the whole is the expression of His will. So He knows the contingent as contingent and yet knows it with certainty." [71] God both knows absolutely and knows in the dimension of temporal experience. This is a paradoxical situation which Temple makes no attempt to resolve. One must confess that it will remain so long as we endeavor to speculate on the meaning of time to eternity and so long as we affirm divine transcendence as well as immanence.

Some misunderstanding of Temple's thought would seem to be met in his discussion of the sacramental universe. He is clearly no idealist in his view of matter. Indeed, he attacks idealism and affirms that among the primary actualities of experience — matter, life, mind, spirit — " there may be degrees of reality if by that is meant that they represent, or express, the ultimate principle of Reality with varying degrees of completeness. But all truly exist." [72] The material order possesses reality. Where materialism fails is in rejecting the supremacy of Spirit. The material universe is not the enemy of the spiritual any more than it is not its product. It is created for and is capable of becoming the instrument of spirit and serving its ends. It becomes sacramental of spirit. " Matter exists in full reality, but at a secondary level. It is created by spirit — the Divine Spirit — to be the vehicle of spirit and the sphere of spirit's self-realization in and through the activity of controlling it." [73] Finite spirits, because they arise within organisms which are also material, express their spirituality not by ignoring matter but by controlling it. Spirit is real to the degree that it effectively controls the lower levels of being. What is natural to the animal is depravity for man when not brought under control by him as spirit.

In the light of this understanding of material nature and history, Temple can see the whole universe as sacramental. The processes of nature and history are expressions of, point to, and participate in the glory of God. Matter and spirit are united for Temple in the sacramental idea. By this he means that spirit, as the highest principle of unity, takes matter up into itself and uses it as a medium of its self-expression. At the human level, as we move beyond science, we see art using the material order in this way. " The conferring of spiritual quality upon inorganic matter, of which the bare possibility is sometimes denied, is one of the commonest experiences of life; the phrase is almost a definition of Art." [74]

At the divine level, God conveys, not just his meaning to the mind, but himself to the believer, through the sacramental process of the universe. Because he is Creator and Sustainer, omnipotent throughout his world, all aspects of nature and history are accessible to him. Temple sees no reason, therefore, to doubt the validity of the claim in sacramental worship that certain physical elements can be media of divine grace. Rather than being nonexistent or unreal, matter can subserve the ends of spirit. Sacrament is the spiritual utilization of the material whereby a spiritual end is attained.

God is continually doing this in the world process. The Divine Glory fills heaven and earth. And this Divine Glory is in one aspect the triumphant self-sacrifice of love. If heaven and earth did not contain this glory, God could not be what he is. He is what he is because he has creatures to redeem. His eternal redemptive love does not simply express itself in history without being affected. But, equally, what he does in history does not make him redeemer. Eternity and history interact here like spirit and matter. " Even to the eternal life of God His created universe is sacramental of Himself." [75] We can, in this sense, understand the statement: " His creation is sacramental of Himself to His creatures; but in effectively fulfilling that function it becomes sacramental to Him of Himself — the means whereby He is eternally that which eternally He is." [76] He is his eternal Self most of all as he creates a world and wins it back into union with himself. This is much more Christian than Hegelian!

The real difficulty in so much that we have discussed is that it is not what Temple initially intended it to be — natural theology. It is Christian philosophy. It is lit continually by Christian insights, especially as the argument develops toward its climax. Temple keeps deriving inspiration from the Incarnation and its attendant events, and openly refers to these to illustrate what he believes to be present in all religion. His emphasis on the personal is tacitly directed by his Christian convictions. Thus his argument increasingly shows itself not to be demonstrative, but analogical. It is an attempt to show how insights of the Christian revelation make a Christian philosophy possible and illuminate all experience. Brunner comments that Temple " seems to be striving towards a kind of synthesis of Christian faith with reason." [77] He adds:

So, for instance, your conception of religion is determined *a priori* by Christian faith, and is deduced from it; the same applies to your concepts of sin, love, personality, etc. This means, however, that in these passages your natural theology is natural only in appearance, whilst it is in truth Christian.[78]

The Christian faith, Brunner points out, determines the course of Temple's thought, despite every effort to conform to a natural theology. It culminates in the Incarnation because tacitly it begins there. Owen Thomas comments: " The lectures constitute a picture of what the world looks like when seen through the eyes of Christian faith. They are based ultimately on the suppressed premise of the truth of the Christian revelation." [79]

It would seem that criticisms of overmuch Hegelian influence are unfair to Temple. He has sought to evade any form of idealism while retaining the truth in its emphasis. He has taken from Hegel what is consonant with Christian insight into the divine involvement with the world through Creation and Incarnation. He rightly sees that the process of nature and history in some way enriches God's life without changing or creating his essential and eternal being. If, at times, he falls into language that is susceptible to an Absolute Idealist interpretation, other statements would challenge such interpretation. Undoubtedly his approach is partly passé. He ignores the existential aspect of man's being, but he does stress man's religious and moral dimensions. He is also very aware of man's historical consciousness and its supreme importance in human existence. He has nothing to say about the linguistic problem that now besets us, and he is far too rationalistic at points where today we would not speak with such confidence. Yet his work still stands the test of time. After thirty years he still has much to say to our day, not least about the significance of the world process for God. Be it noted, too, that he is not overobsessed by the evolutionary category. He is too aware of history and human freedom to make it universal. Rather, like Whitehead, he would make it one aspect of the wider category of " process."

VI

Beyond the Biosphere
and Toward the Omega Point

SINCE TEILHARD's death in 1955, this Jesuit paleontologist and
Christian thinker has exercised an increasing influence on many
minds. His books, suppressed by papal authority in his lifetime,
have become best sellers. In some ways, what he says has been
said also by many of the thinkers whom we have so far studied.
William Temple, in many respects, deals with issues that Teilhard leaves on one side, and actually speaks as much to our time
as the Jesuit thinker. The difference is that Teilhard was a trained
scientist and a recognized authority in his own chosen field. Hence
what he says as a Christian reaches contemporary man, obsessed
by science, a little more readily than the utterances of men less
well informed at the scientific level.

It needs to be added, however, that there are aspects of Teilhard's thought which suggest new lines of approach to the evolutionary view of nature and to the structure and movement of
the process of human history. He is, however, concerned more
with the evolutionary category than with the more general model

of process. In consequence he is overoptimistic where the movement of the cosmic process is concerned. As with Temple, his
system of thought leads up to and embraces the Incarnation. As
with Temple, his Christian intention underlies his whole development of the scientific evidence. Teilhard can no more be " objective " than his British contemporary. Unlike Temple, he offers a
very inadequate treatment of the mystery of evil and thus is less
concerned with the divine involvement in the process at the level
of redemptive suffering. His Catholic background further holds
him back from those insights into the significance of the process
for and the involvement in the process of the deity. This, too,
despite the suspicion held by many Catholics about his orthodoxy.

The Phenomenology of the Evolutionary Development

Teilhard, like the other thinkers we have discussed, assumes
that evolution is a scientifically established fact. This does not
mean that we have by any means solved the problem of how it
has occurred at the biological level. Darwinism and Neo-Dar-
winism offer us models that are only partially successful, and
yet so far, despite their deficiencies, they seem to be the most
acceptable and are established as the scientific orthodoxy. Teilhard was a paleontologist rather than a biologist. In consequence
he assumes these models adopted by contemporary biology, but
fundamentally he is concerned with the general array of phenomena which in themselves give considerable evidence of a
developmental process. It is significant that he argues more as a
paleontologist than a biologist and makes less use of biological,
evolutionary concepts like mutation, natural selection, survival
value, *et al.* Like other paleontologists, he also advocates orthogenesis, a viewpoint frowned upon by orthodox biologists. Also,
he would switch from a Darwinian to a Lamarckian model when
he comes to man. He writes: " Even if the Lamarckian view of
the heritability of acquired characteristics is biological *vieux jeu*,
and decisively refuted, when we reach the human level and have

to reckon with history, culture, etc., 'transmission' becomes 'tradition.'" [1]

Teilhard accepts evolution as an established fact and applies the category to the totality of the process, that is to say, from cosmogenesis through biogenesis to anthropogenesis. For him, it is an all-embracing model. He would agree that the "how" of the process in its various phases is by no means settled, but he would affirm that evolutionary development is now established. He can write concerning the biological phase of evolution:

Even if all the specific content of the Darwinian or Lamarckian explanation of life were to be demolished . . . , the fundamental fact of evolution would remain imprinted as deeply as ever on the whole experience of life. It no longer seems possible to defend our vision of the living universe, so far as its phenomena are concerned, without assuming the existence of a perceptible biological development. This is the factual and very firm position that the defenders of evolution must never abandon; they must never let themselves be deflected into secondary discussions of the scientific "hows" and the metaphysical "whys." [2]

With regard to the total process of the universe, he says:

From the smallest detail to the highest concentrations, *our living universe* (like our material universe) *has a structure* and this structure can only be due to a phenomenon of growth.This is the great proof of transformism and the measure of what that theory has definitely acquired. [3]

The difficulty about Teilhard's approach, from the scientific point of view, lies in the fact that what he offers is not just a phenomenal description derived from the purely scientific investigation. He is continually venturing beyond the scientific into the hyperscientific. He describes his method as phenomenological, but he does not mean by such a description what is meant by Husserl and his school. [4] What he seeks to do is to embrace thought as well as the natural sciences in his approach. In phenomena he would include man as a thinking being. He wants to employ the word "physics" in the Greek sense of "a systematic comprehension of all nature," and then it must have a place for thought. Thus he is really seeking for an approach that brings together the materialistic and idealistic interpretations of the universe. His problem is really that of Temple. Neither of these interpretations describes the true state of affairs, for each in its own way denies the intimate relationship between man as a thinking being and the actual material universe. Those qualities of man which we label "spiritual" also belong to any general construction of the world. He writes:

We have knowledge of man on the fringe of the universe, but still no science of the universe including man as such. Present day physics . . . as yet makes no place for thought; which means it is still constructed wholly apart from the most remarkable of all phenomena provided by nature for our observation.[5]

Teilhard, then, would see the whole evolutionary process from the human perspective. He tells us that a true scientific approach must embrace scientific phenomena as a whole. Any scientific phenomenon must be looked at in both its spatial and temporal contexts. The scientist ought to be concerned with its entire life history within the process of the universe. Most of all must this apply to the phenomenon of man, for man is the key to the whole evolutionary process. It is man who is doing the observing and yet man has also emerged in the process. How like William Temple! The observer is also at the center of the process that he is seeking to understand. "Man, the centre of perspective, is at the same time the *centre of construction* of the universe."[6] Hence we must see the story of man as "a single and continuing trajectory."

In viewing the universe from his human perspective the scientific thinker must develop a sense of spatial immensity, of temporal depth with its historical consciousness, of proportion between the infinitesimal and the immense, of novelty pointing to the absolute stages of growth and perfection without denying the physical continuity of the universe, of irresistible developments in the extremely slow movement of the cosmic process, and

---

of organic structural unity under the temporal successions and
spatial aggregations. Thereby Teilhard wishes "to develop a
homogeneous and *coherent* perspective of our general extended
experience of man. A *whole* which unfolds."[7] The scientist must
see the past, not from itself, but from the perspective of the ad-
vanced level that evolution has now attained. He must see it from
the point of view of man — "the momentary summit of an anthropogenesis which is itself the crown of a cosmogenesis."[8] Hence
he can declare that "the true physics is that which will, one day,
achieve the inclusion of man in his wholeness in a coherent picture of the world."

Because of this emphasis on man as a thinking being, Teilhard
also moves beyond the accepted scientific approach in his emphasis on the "within" of things. He moves beyond the exterior to
the interior aspect of the elements of the universe, contending
that account must be taken of a mental as well as a material aspect. This would clash with the strict scientific viewpoint which
would hold that a rigid scientific empiricism should deal only
with the observable. Teilhard, however, insists that matter at all
levels, inanimate as well as animate, has an inner side — it possesses a psychic as well as a physical aspect. By this description
"psychic" he does not mean "thought" but "consciousness." He
is thus quite near Whitehead. He himself writes: "The term
'consciousness' is taken in its widest sense to indicate every kind
of psychicism, from the most rudimentary forms of interior perception imaginable to the human phenomenon of reflective
thought."[9] In some sense we have a dynamic form of Aristote-
lianism here. Whitehead's criticism of the bifurcation between
mind and matter is met in the same way as Whitehead himself
meets it. What we call matter has also a psychic aspect or dimension.

All this means that Teilhard has a metaphysical bias at the
very commencement of his investigation. We would not quarrel
with this. Rather we expect it. Yet it is well that the movement
of his logic should be clear. Ostensibly he is speaking as a scientist, but his interpretation moves beyond the scientific. The natu-

ralistic thinker will object, but then he, too, has his metaphysical bias. Teilhard has opted in favor of man and in favor of mind. Furthermore, he has chosen evolution as his all-embracing model for the process of the universe. In this category he sees our understanding of the universe taking on a new dimension. He regards it so supported by the evidence that no phenomenon may be understood without or conceived of as falling outside its framework. Hence he can write: " Evolution has long since ceased to be a hypothesis and become a *general epistemological condition* (one more *dimension*), which must thenceforth be satisfied by *every* hypothesis." [10] He acknowledges that his description has an " aura of subjective interpretation." [11] " I do not," he writes, " pretend to describe them as they really were, but rather as we must picture them to ourselves so that the world may be true for us at this moment." [12]

What we are offered is not mere science. As with Whitehead and Alexander, the emphasis on mind or thought or the psychic aspect leads Teilhard to an ontological presupposition. He begins with the primacy of mind or the psychic in the stuff of the universe. Teilhard calls his general scientific explanation of the cosmos from this point of view " hyperphysics." He argues that it is not to be confused with metaphysics. It is questionable whether he can make such a distinction.

The methodology and its accompanying presupposition, as so far discussed, are at least weighted in favor of humanism. Yet there is a deeper faith hypothesis tacit in the approach. Teilhard would indeed draw humanism and Christianity together, for he sees inverse and complementary movements at work in the contemporary situation. He believes that the modern mind finds humanism lacking in Christianity which has appeared detached and otherworldly. He can write, however, that " in order to match the new curve of Time, Christianity is led to discover the values of this world *below the level of God,* while Humanism finds room for a God above the level of this world." [13] Teilhard's thought is Christian in intention, and this he is prepared in part to acknowledge. Thus he is quick to affirm that evolution imposes no metaphysics but it does imply one. This implication he is anxious to draw out, and he believes it to be Christian. He calls us to notice

that the systems of thought which suit it best are, perhaps, precisely those which thought themselves the most threatened. Christianity, for example, is essentially founded on the double belief that man is an object specially pursued by the divine power throughout creation, and that Christ is the end supernaturally but physically marked out as the consummation of humanity.

He asks:

Could one ask for an empirical view of things in closer accord with these statements of unity (by evolutionary science) than this, in which we discover living beings not artificially juxtaposed with the dubious aim of utility or ornament, but bound together by virtue of physical conditions in the reality of a conjoint effort towards greater being? [14]

From Cosmogenesis to Anthropogenesis

We must now examine Teilhard's understanding of the evolutionary process to the level of anthropogenesis. He begins with the origination of the cosmos, acknowledging that science cannot probe into the act of divine creation itself, but that it is able to describe the primitive state of the universe. We are not concerned here with his description of the development of the cosmos from the initial dispersion of energy in the formation of the chemical elements and the more complex molecules, the dispersal of the galaxies with their myriads of stars, the origination of the planets, and the story of our own earth. What concerns us is the way in which he seeks to build the findings of the various sciences — astronomy, geology, physics, chemistry, paleontology, biology — into one connected whole along a temporal development. It is at this point that he moves into what he calls " hyperscience " and his speculation is evident.

He seeks for dynamic principles within the scientific phenomena that he is describing. The most significant of these he terms the " law of complexification " — the movement toward increasing complexity of structure accompanied by greater internal unity and concentration. He is speaking here of the evidence for an increasingly centered complexity — what Smuts sought to express when postulating his holistic principle. The process of the universe shows developing unities, internally unified wholes, which at the same time manifest increasing complexity. Teilhard sees this movement beginning with the atoms, as the subatomic particles move into the complex patterns which constitute these unities, and moving upward to the molecules with increasing complexity until organic wholes emerge. Thus we have a developing process in which new entities appear that are both more complex and more unified.

The primitive stuff of the universe is energy. At the physical level this may take the forms of matter or of radiation. Moreover, physically it is characterized by a capacity for action. Material particles are "transient reservoirs of concentrated power. Though never found in a state of purity, but always more or less corpuscular (even in light) energy nowadays represents for science the most primitive form of universal stuff." [15]

Teilhard agrees that at the physical level science has observed two principles in operation with regard to this primordial stuff — the principle of the conservation of energy and the principle of increasing entropy. According to the first, the amount of energy in the universe remains constant. Thus the energy required for the ascending complexity is fixed. We have a closed quantum of energy, not an open one. In the mechanical functions of the universe "nothing progresses except by exchange of that which was given in the beginning." [16] But this exchange of energy involved in the synthesis and breakdown of structures always involves a dissolution of energy; that is to say, the energy available for the building-up process is decreasing. This is the consequence of the second principle, commonly known as the Second Law of Thermodynamics. Entropy is the measure of the loss of available energy. Energy is continually being irrevocably entropized, dissipated in the form of heat. The total energy of the universe is running down to a final state of lifeless equilibrium. "The more the energy-quantum of the world comes into play, the more it is consumed." [17]

Thus the ascent of the world to life and mind, with their increasing complexity of structure and unification into wholes, has a twofold aspect. On the one hand, it is possible because at the physical level there is a reservoir of available energy for such an advance. On the other hand, the availability of that reservoir of energy is steadily decreasing. What is capable of action in the reservoir is being used up. Physical science, therefore, holds up the pessimistic view of the universe, like a rocket, rising to the height of thought and self-consciousness and then falling back spent because the available fuel has been used up. Life at all its levels is living on negative entropy and one day, in final dissolution, the universe will lapse into a fatal equilibrium, in which the complex wholes that bear life and mind will have ceased to be. Teilhard points out that the picture of the world thus presented depicts consciousness as "an eddy rising on the bosom of a descending current." [18] No final value can be placed, on this basis, on the new entities that appear in the ascending complexity.

Yet Teilhard believes that the emergence of consciousness and of thinking man holds the key to the whole process. He can do so because of the other interpretative approach to the scientific data. He holds that the pessimism of the physical scientist arises because he has concerned himself with only one dimension of energy, the physical dimension. There is a "within" of things as well as a "without." Science has concentrated on the latter and almost, if not completely, ignored the former. The tendency has been to regard "consciousness" as an isolated phenomenon, because it is only fully manifested in man.[19] Science has never troubled to look at the world other than from the "without," but there is another kind of energy which begins to manifest its presence at the biological level and becomes fully evident at the human level. This is psychic energy. This inner aspect, which we know deep within ourselves, points to an interior aspect of the whole universe. "Since the stuff of the universe has an inner aspect at one point of itself, there is necessarily *a double aspect*

to its structure, that is to say in every region of space and time —
in the same way for instance, as it is granular: *coextensive with
their Without, there is a Within to things."* [20] So Teilhard can
contend that a proper perspective of the world process requires
that we should see an interior preparation for life, a " pre-life,"
as far back as the eye can see. [21]

This stance leads Teilhard to the conclusion that energy is
really psychic [22] and that the physical is only one dimension of it.
He postulates two aspects of this energy — a physical or tangential component and a psychical or radial component. These two
components or dimensions of energy are complementary. [23] No
dichotomy is thereby involved, and man as the supreme manifestation of " consciousness," the " Within " of things, can then be
made a part of the universe that science describes. So long as
science concerns itself only with the " Without," it is not possible
to offer a coherent view of the cosmos that includes man.

The tangential component of energy is responsible for linking
elements together at the same level of complexity. It shapes the
outward form of the process, providing an externalized observable
connection between an individual and all others of the same
order and complexity. Its results are scientifically observable, for
they constitute the material complexity of organization at any
stage of the process. The radial component is responsible for the
movement to higher levels of organization and for producing
greater interiorization, more centered wholes. It draws the universe " towards ever greater complexity and centricity — in other
words forwards." [24] It constitutes the inner aspect of the process,
the spiritual aspect, and it is responsible for the increasing in-
wardness, for the greater centricity and unity that accompany
the increasing complexity of organization. Thus the radial component of energy is responsible for the movement to more " centered " molecules in the early stages of the earth's history, while
the tangential component is responsible for their proliferation. In
the same way, at the biological level, the tangential energy causes
cells and organisms to reproduce themselves at the same level of
organization. On the other hand, the radial energy leads them

on to higher levels of complexity and makes possible the great unity and organization that are manifested as consciousness develops toward self-conscious mind.

Teilhard agrees that this radial component of energy is opaque to science. The spiritual aspect of man is very evident. His moral nature and reflective capacities confront us. Yet "the nature of this inner power is so intangible that the whole description of the universe in mechanical terms has had no need to take account of it, but has been successfully completed in deliberate disregard of its reality." [25] The result has been an irresoluble dichotomy between mind and matter. It will be remembered that Whitehead has made the same point and sought to give every actual entity a mental as well as a physical pole, and that Alexander sought partially to avoid the dilemma by defining Time as functioning like the mental component in his primordial "Space-Time" stuff. Teilhard contends that science cannot ignore the issue, for it confidently believes it can discover a coherent unity in the phenomena of the cosmos, despite its sensibly observable multiplicity. Now such a coherent unity is impossible to attain if man in his spiritual aspect is not included. Thus Teilhard would hold that his position can be justified from the point of view of the scientific quest itself.

The law of complexification and interiorization which Teilhard sees throughout the process is thus given an ontological basis in energy itself. And it is the radial component of energy that is responsible for the advances which the law seeks to describe. He sees certain "critical points" at which the process passes through a profound transformation and a completely novel phenomenon appears. There always has to be a "first instance" of a novelty. The process is historical, and every new phenomenon has a historical birth. Teilhard writes:

In every domain, when anything exceeds a certain measurement, it suddenly changes its aspect, condition or nature. The curve doubles back, the surface contracts to a point, the solid disintegrates, the liquid boils, the germ cell divides, intuition suddenly bursts on the piled up facts. . . . Critical points have been reached, rungs on the ladder, involving a change of state — jumps of all sorts *in the course* of development.[26]

This has happened in the evolutionary process. He sees a process of involution, of coiling up. Along the axis of increasing complexity " the universe is, both on the whole and at each of its points, in a continual tension of doubling-back upon itself, and thus of interiorisation." [27] Teilhard likens it to a vortex, in which the center or core is a continually growing " consciousness," getting deeper as there is a higher degree of interior organization, that is to say, as the vortex has a greater tightness of coiling.

Teilhard sees such critical points as those at which life first appears and at which " hominization," the coming of man, occurs. Life he envisages as arising because a fairly thick layer of protein-type molecules was formed on the earth's surface in an area where temperature conditions and radiation possibilities were favorable. Within this " temperate zone of polymerization," the pre-life emerges from the torpor caused by its diffusion in space. A process of complexification takes place and tensions begin to arise until the whole arrives at a point of supersaturation and life bursts forth.[28] Thereby the earth is covered with a thin skin of life, which Teilhard describes as the " biosphere." The " Within " is in operation. The universe is folding " in upon itself until it is interiorized in a growing complexity." [29]

We are asked to see a multiplicity of forms " groping " toward greater complexity and higher interiorization. This groping or randomness is not, however, mere chance. It is directed chance. Nature is consciousness " pervading everything so as to try everything, and trying everything so as to find everything." [30] Teilhard sees this as the reason for nature's recourse to a profusion of forms and to expanding multitudes. All the random activity, of which " natural selection " makes so much, is somehow being shaped by an inner drive, an organizing principle. Individuals at a lower level are wrenched up into the constitution of a more complex whole. What at the lower level is itself a centered entity is built up by association in a chain of entities in a new complex whole with its own center. Thus there is in nature an indifference to all that does not lie ahead and is not a centered wholeness.[31] The individual at a lower level is merged in the collective of the higher level and stretched out into the future movement of the process. This organization principle, radial energy, is not alien to the laws holding at the physical level but works within them.

Once more Teilhard is under scientific criticism, for he identifies this inner movement to consciousness with orthogenesis, an inner adaptiveness that drives the organisms ever forward. It is significant, however, that Dobzhansky, an authoritative Neo-Darwinian, can say of Teilhard that he does not use the word "orthogenesis" in the technical biological sense but in a philosophical mystical sense. His final comment is of interest: " [Teilhard's] Mystical 'orthogenesis' need not be incompatible with modern biological theory." [32]

Teilhard evidently sees a freedom in the basic energy stuff, however rudimentary, which is consonant with its radial dimension. If consciousness is, as he contends, present in a diffused state at the level of the corpuscle even though it is imperceptible, then the " groping " is understandable and interpretative of the random aspect of the evolutionary process. But let us be clear that, at this point, Teilhard is no longer speaking as a scientist. Science can deal only with the " Without." Directly Teilhard moves to the " Within," he cannot claim to speak as a scientist and he does not. He has moved to metaphysics, and his fundamental presuppositions are becoming evident.

As life ascends in complexity, it increasingly folds back upon itself and interiorization develops. Many stems grope upward toward increasing centricity, but in one stem, that of the zoological group known as the vertebrates, we see the process of coiling up, interiorization, increasingly taking over. In the mammals and the primates, the complexification is increasingly associated with the brain and the centralized nervous system. The movement now takes the direction of increasing cerebralization and, with it, of developing consciousness. Indeed, the radial component of energy becomes more and more dominant. The proliferation at the base of the tree of life manifests the operation of the tangential component of energy, and divergence is the order of the day. But with increasing cerebralization, life is led up to a new critical point, the appearance of thought and reflection. Now the process is marked by convergence. The physical forms become less differentiated and consciousness becomes more evident.

Because the specific orthogenesis of the primates (urging them towards increasing cerebralisation) coincides with axial orthogenesis of organised matter (urging all living things towards a higher consciousness) man, appearing at the heart of the primates, flourishes on the leading shoot of zoological evolution.[33]

For Teilhard, the Ariadne's thread of evolution now becomes clearly mapped out. It follows a line of increasing complexity and also increasing interiorization. As it moves forward through the biosphere, the proliferation of types and the divergence from the unicellular base decreases. Concentration takes place around the vertebrate stem of the tree of life with more complex cerebralization and unification of a central nervous system. When the primates are reached, an evolutionary ferment occurs in the area from central Africa across to Indonesia where the physical conditions for a major change are possible. "*In this singular and privileged case* [the primates], *the particular orthogenesis of the phylum happened to coincide exactly with the principal orthogenesis of life itself.*"[34] Now the most powerful brains found in nature "become red hot. And right at the heart of that glow burns a point of incandescence."[35] Life began to transform itself in depth, as another point of supersaturation was reached. The appearance of man was, indeed, "an explosion of consciousness." "Once life, along this particular ray, reached a critical point of arrangement (or as we call it in this context, of convolution) it became hyper-centered upon itself, to the point of becoming capable of foresight and invention."[36] Consciousness was folded back upon itself to become self-consciousness. Hominization took place at this new critical point, reflective thought appeared, and a new layer, the "noosphere," was stretched around our planet.

From Man to the Omega Point

Once the noosphere is reached and hominization occurs, convergence takes over. Teilhard points out that, from the morphological point of view, there is little to distinguish primitive man from the higher primates. Man has a maximum of physico-chemical complexity, but his physiological structure is still mammalian. Yet, although the structural leap is so slight, the centralization in man separates him from his antecedents by a large gap. We have both continuity and discontinuity.[37] Man may be, from one point of view, the final link in a chain of animal forms. But the threshold of reflection is a major mutation, and Teilhard finds it hard to imagine any intermediary being at this psychic level.

Either this being has not yet reached, or it has already got beyond, this change of state. Look at it as we will, we cannot avoid the alternative — either thought is made unthinkable by a denial of its psychical transcendence over instinct, or we are forced to admit that it appears *between* two individuals.[38]

After the critical point of hominization, newly emergent man quickly spread around the planet. Mankind multiplied, divided into ethnic and cultural groups, began to exercise control over the planet and the biosphere. The divergent and diversifying function of the tangential component of energy was thereby manifested. But now divergence began to be replaced by convergence. With man the presence of the radial component of energy became more evident. The process of interiorization which had led through increasing cerebralization to man now continued its centralizing task. As mankind spread around the globe and became packed more tightly in certain confined areas, social pressures arose. Men began to exchange material goods and ideas. Spiritually and physically interrelationships arose and were built increasingly into a close-knit network of trade and communication, sharing of ideas and technological skills, cooperating in inventive genius and in the control of all lower life and natural forces. Thus the envelope of the noosphere, the envelope of reflective thought and self-consciousness, has also illustrated the law of complexification — interiorization. It has witnessed the spread of a skin of mankind all around the globe and also an increasing socialization and collectivization of individual humanity.

The noosphere is thus characterized by the personal and the social. By our own time the divergent lines of mankind's development around the globe are beginning to converge. The critical point of hominization produced the personal, and the personal has gone on developing until, in the last century, the value of the autonomous individual reached its highest point within the social group. The rights of man and the age of democracy emphasized the value of the individual citizen and supported the idea that "there now lies ahead of it [mankind] no biological necessity nor destiny other than to generate (and release in a state of isolation) particles that are increasingly more self-sufficient and self-centered." [39] But this tendency in the West of the noosphere to culminate in individuation, in separate persons, has been challenged in this century by "the massive and as yet undreamt of forces of totalization."

Teilhard sees certain forces within the noosphere moving toward the convergence of the human group into a new social interiorization.[40] Ethnic compression is increasingly present with the approach of our human population to saturation point. Economic-technical organization has sought to meet the challenge across the centuries of man's existence by continually finding "new ways of arranging its [mankind's] elements in the way that is most economical of energy and space." [41] Now Teilhard sees a rise in "psychic-temperature," for the increase in man's mental interiority and inventive power have brought about both an increase in the individual's range of influence and in his power to penetrate into relationships with other persons.

It takes the form of all-encompassing ascent of the masses; the constant tightening of economic bonds; the spread of financial and intellectual associations; the totalization of political regimes; the closer physical contact of individuals as well as nations; the increasing impossibility of being or acting or thinking *alone* — in short, the rise, in every form, of the *Other* around us. We are all constantly aware of these tentacles of a social condition that is rapidly evolving to the point of becoming monstrous.[42]

Teilhard goes on to ask whether this is just a natural catastrophe that we must seek to avoid if possible or just blindly accept, or whether it has deeper import in the light of his law of complexification — interiorization.

We are asked to see all this as a continuation of the movement of evolution. The process of human history must, like everything else, be understood on the basis of the evolutionary category. The Darwinian model gives place to a Lamarckian one at this level, for we have to do with thought, with the transmission of culture and tradition. What we are now seeing is a movement of " socialization " or " collective cerebralization." The radial component of energy is moving humanity toward a new critical point in which the human phylum is coiling itself up around the surface of the earth. *" The social phenomenon is the culmination and not the attenuation of the biological phenomenon."* [43] Evolution must continue onward in its interiorization, its coiling-up process, accompanying increasing complexity. The movement is ever toward greater consciousness, and this does not end with self-consciousness. It moves toward a yet further stage in which the social consciousness is involved.

Teilhard therefore endeavors to trace the trajectory forward and to extrapolate into the future. He sees ahead the " Omega " point upon which the whole process is now converging and in which the movement of interiorization and centricity will be complete. Yet he is quick to add that such a forward movement is not inevitable. In the past there have been developing stems in which, at a certain stage of complexity, the constituent elements have not come together in a centered unity and so have not moved forward to a new level. The process has manifested waste and sidetracking in the past. But now with man it has become self-conscious, and the situation becomes more critical. Man is free to cooperate with or to oppose the forces that operate upon him and that would move him forward. Men must face their responsibility toward " evolution " and confront the issue of their destiny. This is the " grand option " before them.[44] Yet, despite the pressures forcing them together, " thinking units do not seem capable of falling within their radius of internal attraction. . . . Deep down men exclude and repel one another with all their might." [45] At every level where interior centering does not occur, the aggregate falls apart. Mankind faces this danger. Men may fall back into determinism and materiality. Man may become depersonalized. We may become an anthill rather than a brother-hood.

At the moment we seem to have unleashed a monster that threatens to engulf us. The process has now become conscious of itself, and man knows that he has it in his power to determine his future. The fear of losing the little that has been gained so painfully across millions of years drives man to oppose the apparently blind whole. The reflective aspect of man experiences a radical anguish before the challenge of the collective.[46] Instead of adding his indispensable cooperation to the forward surge of the process, he lapses into outmoded individualism or national-ism, seeing in front of him the totalitarian whole as a monster that will entwine its tentacles around him. Yet this will be his doom unless he moves on to the true hyperpersonal that is grounded in love. " All that matters at this critical moment is that the massing together of individualities should not take the form of a func-tional and enforced mechanization of human energies (the to-talitarian principle), but of a ' conspiracy ' informed with love." [47]

As Teilhard sees it, the true extension of the noosphere cannot be the impersonal, but a hyperpersonal. Man's opposition to the whole or all that lies ahead of him would be dissipated if he rec-ognized that the whole is centered.

Because it contains and engenders consciousness, space-time is neces-sarily *of a convergent nature*. Accordingly its enormous layers, fol-

lowed in the right direction, must somewhere ahead become in-
voluted to a point which we might call *Omega*, which fuses and con-
sumes them integrally in itself.[48]

But such a movement means the "personalization" of the universe. Each of us transmits his inventions, education, etc., into
the mass of humanity, but these are only the shadows of our true
selves, our works. We are each an absolutely original center in
which the universe reflects itself in a unique way. We are selves,
persons. It is unthinkable that the interiorization of a conscious
universe could mean other than the reassembly of all consciousness: " each particular consciousness remaining conscious of itself
at the end of the operation, and even . . . each particular consciousness becoming still more itself and thus more clearly distinct from others the closer it gets to them in Omega." [49] Teilhard contends that this is supported by the fact that, at all lower
levels, union differentiates. " In every organized whole, the parts
perfect themselves and fulfil themselves." [50] Thus socialization
does not mean the end of the personal but the beginning. The individual only becomes truly personal as he universalizes himself.

Such a synthesis in a union that preserves the personal and
also perfects it is possible through the energy of love. This is the
highest form of what Teilhard calls the radial component of energy. By love, persons are joined together at the deepest level of
their being. This holds of the richest understanding of sexual
relationship, at the level of the family, of the mutual enrichment
of friendship, and even, to some degree, in patriotism. " In order
therefore for men to continue in freedom towards that unity in
the noosphere which is their destiny, their power of loving must
gradually develop until it is capable of embracing the whole of
mankind and the whole of the earth." [51] Love superpersonalizes
men. " True union, the union of heart and spirit, does not enslave,
nor does it neutralize the individuals which it brings together." [52]
What we have in love is not the pressure of external forces but
internal attraction. The coercion of the " Without " can lead to collective tyranny unless man responds to this internal attraction and
moves to " unanimity in a common spirit. . . . It is through sym-

pathy, and this alone, that the human elements in a personalized universe may hope to rise to the level of a higher synthesis." [53] Thus it is in love that there will issue a creative socialization of humanity.

This says much, according to Teilhard, about the point Omega. His Christian intention, which has colored his premises from the start, now becomes very evident. He believes that the whole process must be leading us on to a personal center as a *present reality.* He follows the Thomistic-Aristotelian tradition by postulating a *Prime Mover,* the point Omega.

If the Omega is to attract man's efforts, certain statements must be made concerning it. First of all, it must be not only personal, but loving and lovable. As Christopher Mooney puts it: " Unless the modern impetus towards union is leading us towards ' Someone,' it must certainly end up by plunging us back into matter." [54] Or to quote Piet Smulders: "The force of attraction centering mankind at last upon itself must be a person: a person to whom all men can direct their love and in whom they can love their fellows." [55] Love is devotion and the most emancipating devotion is that directed upon person. But a collectivity is essentially unlovable. The Omega point must be a " centre of centres," evoking love and directing it in the personal centers of the noosphere. Teilhard declares that:

there is but one possible way in which human elements, innumerably diverse by nature, can love one another: it is by knowing themselves all to be centred upon a single " super-centre " common to all, to which they can only attain, each at the extreme of himself, through their unity. [56]

Thereby universal love can become a reality.

Secondly, it must be a present actuality. It is not sufficient to postulate point Omega as something in the future, which emerges in the process. Omega must be an actual presence, a personal Being, " loving and lovable at this very moment," [57] not some vague future existence. As Teilhard puts it: " Neither an ideal centre, nor a potential centre could possibly suffice. A present and real noosphere goes with a real and present centre. To be supremely attractive, Omega must be supremely present." [58] If equilibrium is to be attained in the personal interactions of human beings, it is possible only if Omega acts " with equal force, that is to say with the same stuff of proximity." Teilhard holds that the very movement of evolution shows that Omega is already active in this way, radiating love energy and moving the whole toward union.

In the third place, Omega must transcend space and time. Teilhard sees the tangential component of energy as weighted by entropy. The universe is " running down " materially, and yet the radial component of energy is driving toward the hyperpersonal. Now the whole evolutionary ascent would be certainly doomed if this prospect of total dissolution is the sole prospect for the future of the universe. Yet man feels that the creative products of reflective thought and the whole spirit of humanity should escape from the destructive aspect of time and the universe. Consciousness and personal being should not crash back into the abyss of the material. There must be irreversibility, immortality, in the process. Teilhard argues that the great stability of the process does not lie in its material base but paradoxically in its spiritual apex. Something in the cosmos is increasingly escaping from entropy. Hence Omega must be beyond such dissolution as is suffered by the tangential envelope of the world. " To satisfy the ultimate requirements of our action, Omega must be independent of the collapse of the forces with which evolution is woven." [59] The universe is a conserver, not of mechanical energy, but of persons. It is being built in the inverse direction of matter which is moving to dissipation. This is possible because Omega transcends the whole process, drawing it to itself by the radiation of love energy. " While being the last term of its [evolution's] series, it is also *outside all series*. . . . If by its very nature it did not escape from the time and space which it gathers together, it would not be Omega." [60]

Thus it would appear that the universe is converging upon an Omega which is also a present actuality, providing the lure for the ascent of the universe and transcending its involvement in space and time. As the process draws nearer to point Omega, it increasingly moves to a socialization of the personal, until it coils back upon itself under the love energy released from Omega. Then, in an evolutionary ferment, the "hyperpersonal" emerges around point Omega which is truly a Personal Center of personal centers. It would seem that, at this point, Teilhard contemplates the transfiguring of the material universe and a movement into a totally spiritual and personal order.

Unless it is to be powerless to form the keystone of the noosphere, "Omega" can only be conceived as the *meeting-point* between a universe that has reached the limit of centration, and another, even deeper, centre — this being the self-subsistent centre and absolutely final principle of irreversibility and personalization: the one and only true Omega.[61]

It is at this point that the idea of God is interpolated by Teilhard into the evolutionary process. But tacitly such a premise had directed his whole inquiry.

Evolution and the Christ

That the Christ should be the summit of Teilhard's development is not surprising. We have continually pressed this point and would here gather our comments together. He himself admits that

scientific transformism, strictly speaking, proves nothing for or against God. It simply notes the fact of a chain of connection in reality. It presents us with an anatomy of life, certainly not a final reason for it. It affirms that "something organized itself, something grew." But it is incapable of discerning the ultimate conditions of that growth. To decide whether the movement of evolution is intelligible in itself, or if it requires a progressive and continuous creation implemented by a prime mover, this is a question that depends on metaphysics.[62]

The emphasis on the directiveness of the process, the supreme value placed on human self-consciousness and personal being, the postulation of a radial component of energy directed toward the development of the psychic aspect of reality — all point in a personalistic direction. Furthermore, it is evident that the hidden premise is not humanism, for a humanist might be far less optimistic, accept the final triumph of entropy, and still affirm human values. That Teilhard's intention is theistic becomes evident in his extrapolation to point Omega. That it is Christian becomes increasingly apparent as he develops his emphasis on love. That it is idealistic in intention, as well, might seem to be implied by his suggestion of the transfiguration of the material in the final critical movement to the hyperpersonal. We must examine the last point more closely in the following section. Here, let us note that Teilhard's whole argument is colored by Christian insights and is actually Christian philosophy. What could be said of William Temple can, with equal justice, be said of Teilhard. That his arguments appear to be reasonable is true only if we grant his premises. His faith directs his logic. For a humanist or a naturalist the latter would move otherwise.

It is evident that Teilhard's intention is so to build up his interpretation of the evolutionary process that it points to God. It is not a demonstration but an analogical picture based on the model of consciousness and colored continually by insights gained from the Christian doctrines of Creation and Incarnation. What he does is to show that the universe, as he sees it from such a standpoint, poses questions that cannot be answered from within it but that require the transcendent personal and actual "centre of centres" to make the process intelligible. Thus he has built up his interpretation to the point where what has been tacit may become manifest. Omega point is the Creator God, the *prime mover*. The advance to man, the advance of men to socialization only make sense for him if there be an all-embracing advance to God. In the privately printed "How I believe," Teilhard states his credo.

I believe that the Universe is an Evolution.
I believe that the Evolution goes toward Spirit.
I believe that the Spirit achieves itself in the Personal.
I believe that the Personal Supreme is the Universal Christ.[63]

This sums up the movement of his apologetic. He significantly points to what we have said when he confesses:

Doubtless I should never have ventured to envisage the latter [Omega point] or formulate the hypothesis rationally if, in my consciousness as a believer, I had not found not only its speculative model but also its living reality.[64]

It is in Christ, his Incarnation and Resurrection, that Teilhard finds the guarantee for his vision. Here is the assurance that the great stability of the pyramid of evolution rests in its spiritual apex and not in its material base. "Instead of the vague centre of convergence envisaged as the ultimate end of this process of evolution, the personal and defined reality of the Word Incarnate, in which everything acquires substance, appears and takes its place."[65] The Christian Phenomenon thus caps the phenomenological study of the process. Indeed, when Teilhard writes openly, and no longer covertly, as a believer, he sees the whole movement of the biosphere and of human history in the noosphere moving to the Incarnation.

The long ages which preceded the Nativity were not empty of Christ, but penetrated by his powerful influx. It is the shock of his conception which put the cosmic masses in motion and which directs the first currents of the biosphere. It is the preparation for his birth which accelerates the development of instinct and the flowering of thought on Earth.[66]

Always when Teilhard speaks of Christ, in however mystical and cosmic a sense, he has a fixed point of reference — the Incarnation, the phenomenon of the historical Jesus. He must match his phenomenology of evolution with a historical base. The activity of the Christ in the noosphere required at its inception an operation of a transcendent order, " grafting — in accordance with mysterious but physically regulated conditions — the Person of a Deity on to the Human Cosmos."[67] Yet, from the historical Jesus, Teilhard launches out into the Johannine and Pauline visions of the Eternal Word, who was always immanent in the creative

movement of the cosmos. The Christian sees the Creator and Redeemer penetrating all things so that "the world is full of God,"
but:

This aggrandisement is only valuable in his eyes so far as the light, in
which everything seems to him bathed, radiates from *an historical
centre* and is transmitted along *a traditional and solidly defined axis*.
The immense enchantment of the divine milieu owes all its value in the
long run to the human-divine contact which was revealed at the
Epiphany of Jesus.[68]

The divine omnipresence is a metaphysical dream without this
historical reality.

Teilhard sees Creation, Incarnation, and Redemption intimately interwoven. In the light of his vision of the universal
power of the Christ, Teilhard writes of "the world . . . as sus-
pended from the Omega focal point where Christ, by virtue of
His Incarnation, appears, invested precisely with the functions
of Omega." [69] He is indeed "the Head of Creation," giving consistency to the entire structure of matter and mind. The movement toward harmonization in the hyperpersonal has Christ as
its organic principle. Hence "the whole universe . . . finds itself
marked by His character, planned by His choice, and animated
by His form." [70] The Omega point by the revelation in the Person
of Jesus Christ shows itself to be personal, loving, and lovable.
God unifies the universe by becoming a part of it, a person among
persons. From this point of vantage, he is able to control and
guide the whole process.

Christ, principle of universal vitality because sprung up as man among
men, put himself in the position (maintained ever since) to subdue
under himself, to purify, to direct and superanimate the general ascent of consciousnesses into which he inserted himself.[71]

Elsewhere Teilhard declares:

By virtue of the characteristics which at first would seem to particu-
larize Him too much, *a historically Incarnated God*, on the contrary,
is the only one who can satisfy, not only the inflexible rules of a uni-

verse in which nothing is produced or appears save *by way of birth,* but also the irrepressible aspirations of our spirit.[72]

Christ accomplishes his purpose by incorporating humanity into his Mystical Body. The Cosmic Christ pervades the whole process from the focal point of his Incarnation and Resurrection. The power of the Incarnate Word penetrates all things, even matter itself. We are surrounded by a divine milieu, in which "we recognize an omnipresence which acts upon us by assimilating us in it, in the unity of the Body of Christ." [73] Indeed, the universe is in process of "Christification" or "Christogenesis."

Since the time when Jesus was born, when He finished growing and died and rose again, *everything has continued to move because Christ has not yet completed His own forming. . . . The mystical Christ has not yet attained His full growth.*[74]

Thus the natural process of evolution with its movement to the hyperpersonal becomes transformed by faith into the physical and literal incorporation of the cosmos into Christ. At the core of this incorporation are the faithful in Christ. Piet Smulders points out that the mystery of the movement to the hyperpersonal in point Omega, God, becomes deeper still and more ineffable "in the incarnation of the Son of God, which positions the union of all men to God in the union of the elect to the Mystical Body of the Incarnate Son, so that men approach the Father incorporated into the Son." [75] The Incarnation will be "complete only when the part of chosen substance contained in every object — spiritualized first of all in our souls and a second time with our souls in Jesus — has rejoined the final Centre of its completion." [76] In Christ everything is reunited and all things are consummated. This is possible because the Christ whose omnipresence pervades the cosmos is the Incarnate Christ, dead and risen.[77] The world is in process, and Christ is completing himself in it. The divine omnipresence becomes a "network of the organizing forces of the total Christ," and the presence of Christ is to be found silently growing in all things.[78] The kenosis of the Incarnation is extended throughout the universe and so there is a promise of ultimate transfiguration of the whole.

So, for Teilhard, the whole cosmos is moving to the completion of Christ, " Christification," in his Parousia. In his mystical vision he sees the full Christ at the Omega point, incorporating the cosmos as well as personal beings in the greater unity of himself. Men *must* die and rise on the pattern of his resurrection that they may be incorporated in his fullness. Even matter itself will be transfigured. In Christ's plenitude the hyperpersonal and a New Earth will come into being. He stands at the end, the ultimate pole of attraction, as he stands at the beginning and in the center. In the midst of history, we ourselves are being incorporated in this Christogenesis. The Parousia is the last " critical point," the catastrophic movement into the ultimate union with God.

In this section we have seen Teilhard move from Christian philosophy to Christian theology and increasingly to mystical vision. He has reinstated for many in our time the cosmic dimension of the Christian faith. His understanding of the Cosmic Christ or Eternal Word as the creative, revelatory, and redemptive principle in the universe is a salutary recovery of early Christian thought and, at the same time, one very relevant for the defense of Christian orthodoxy in a scientific environment. His connection of the Incarnation and the Church with the whole cosmic process and his suggestive understanding of the Incarnation itself as a dynamic movement through which the Christ is forming himself by the incorporation of the whole cosmic process are challenging, even if highly speculative. He resurrects for many a cosmic eschatology where so often eschatology has become bound up with personal immortality. Further, his realism and acceptance of this world is commendably Biblical. He does not consider the significance of the whole process in the divine life and the meaning of creation and redemption within the divine experience. Yet his suggestive idea of Christogenesis has real bearing on this.

Teilhard's emphasis on the movement of the process to self-consciousness in man is significant. He does see man as a cooperator with God and views the process as unfinished. His emphasis on " groping " at various levels of evolution is indicative of this. He finds such cooperation between man and God consummated in the Incarnation and in " Christogenesis." One could wish, however, that he had more to say about its implications in a growingly secular world. In his own way, he is echoing Bonhoeffer's declaration that " the world is coming of age." Yet his shallow view of evil makes him more optimistic than even Christian eschatology would permit him to be.

His weaknesses lie mainly in his tendency to immanentism and in his shallow treatment of the issue of evil. He has been accused of pantheism. This is certainly unfair, for he clearly does not suggest the absorption of the personal in the One, the Omega, nor the identification of the core of individual personal being with the divine. In his vision of the hyperpersonal, the person remains a center although now he is centered in the " Centre of centres." The emphasis on love is a solid effort to retain the value of the person while pointing to that greater whole in which the " socialization " is consummated. If men have to die and rise in Christ and thereby find true personhood and real freedom, this emphasis should not surprise us. If Teilhard is pantheist here, so is Christian orthodoxy! His mysticism is a mysticism of love and communion, not of absorption; of personal commitment but not absolute identification. It has, however, to be confessed that Teilhard does not say too much about transcendence. Because of his scientific bent, he is almost bound to emphasize the immanent. Yet in his envisagement of the Omega he points to a beyondness and transcendence. In addition, he speaks of the birth of Christ as a " critical point." The Omega comes by birth and assumes a human life, but there is the suggestion of transcendence even in Teilhard's description of this catastrophic and eschatological event.

Teilhard's treatment of evil is patchy. He treats sin too statistically and does not take the challenge seriously enough. The Incarnation, the Cross, and the Resurrection would have to be dealt with at a deeper level if the mystery of evil is to be treated adequately. Actually the surd nature of evil would raise very serious questions for the kind of system Teilhard offers with its tendencies to monism and immanentism. This is not, however, a theological investigation, and we shall leave the criticism at this point.

VII

Being and Becoming — A Dipolar Deity

THE IMPACT of Whitehead's thought on American theology has been felt in the development known as " process theology." Its advocates have been especially associated with the University of Chicago. They include a considerable diversity in approach and vary from Wieman's view of God as purely temporal [1] to the much more balanced views of Charles Hartshorne [2] and Daniel Day Williams,[3] who retain much of the traditional Christian emphasis on divine being but also postulate becoming as an aspect of the divine nature. In the last few years, significant contributions have also been made by John B. Cobb, Jr.,[4] Schubert Ogden,[5] and Richard H. Overman.[6] It is to this school of thought that we must now turn our attention. We shall take the approach of Hartshorne as basic and include the contributions of other thinkers within this framework.

We have already pointed to the difficulties involved in Whitehead's organismic model when this is applied to an understanding of personal being and personal identity. However, since

Whitehead's thought is employed by the thinkers under review, it is clear that it will need considerable transformation when used as a basis for specifically Christian philosophy. Cobb terms his own usage of Whitehead *A Christian Natural Theology,* and we have already pointed to the difficulties he faces on the issue of personal identity.

The problem of modifying a non-Christian philosophy is by no means new. It has been with Christian thought from the very early days. Origen, Augustine, and Aquinas all had to deal with it. If we are to speak to our day, we need to harness the contemporary structures of thought to our Christian understanding. Only so can the latter be made intelligible to our generation. That Whitehead's system has not been acceptable to " scientism " and that much current naturalistic linguistic analysis would reject all metaphysics should not deter Christian thinkers from employing some of Whitehead's insights. We have, however, pointed to certain implications of the Biblical disclosure that should be normative in our employment of secular thought and in its baptism into Christian usage. So long as the Christian intention of our philosophizing is maintained, we can be grateful for a system of thought that offers some basic contributions to Christian apol· ogetics.

The Social Nature of the Cosmic Process — A Panpsychic Universe

Like Teilhard and Whitehead, Hartshorne would see the universe, even at the physical level, as fundamentally psychic. Consciousness, in howsoever a rudimentary form, and its accompanying individuality exist even at the physical level. Because a mineral object is apparently inanimate, that does not mean that it is so. Everything, in other words, has an inner side or a mental pole (in Whitehead's terminology). In consequence, Hartshorne develops a panpsychism which takes as its model, after Whitehead, human experience at the mental level. He tells us that " experience " must not be confined to the human level, but must apply throughout the ordered structures of the universe. This does not mean, of course, that human experience in all its aspects is paralleled at all levels. Rather, the kinship between the human level and all subhuman ones must be expressed by understanding " experience " in terms of sentience or feeling. " The minimum of experience . . . is feeling." [7]

"Experience" has a social dimension — the cosmic process is social. Thus Hartshorne has as the adjunct model to " experience " that of " society." He is careful to point out that, in his understanding of society, human society is not the norm but one form among the diversity of forms which society assumes throughout the process.

By "social" is not meant "human," though, since human beings do form societies, there will, according to the theory, be an analogy between any reality whatever and a human being. . . . But the analogy need not . . . be close or specific; thus the social theory rests upon the utmost generalization of the resemblance between the various types of social beings, of which man is but one.[8]

Hence the " experience " that Hartshorne ascribes to every thing in the universe must be more specifically defined as " shared experience," " the echo of one experience in another." [9] It is on this social basis that Hartshorne defines minimal experience as feeling, since " creatures are social if they feel, and feel in relation to each others' feelings." [10] He is not satisfied, however, with limiting such feeling to the higher animals, where its presence is indubitable. He wants to carry his category of " experience " down to the lowest level of the inanimate. Thus he can hold that " the insentient, dead, and mechanical is secondary to, or even a mere appearance or special case of, the sentient, living, and social." [11] He agrees that the inner life of animals which do not possess a brain or a centralized nervous system will involve feelings of a different order from the human. But the difference of physiology does not imply the absence of the psychological aspect. It may be the absence of a centralized nervous structure betokens a more elementary level of feeling. Just as a creature without muscles may move, so one without nerves may feel and move in response to its feelings.[12] Even unicellular organisms may have a psychological nature.

Comparative psychology cannot perhaps derive much profit from considering the joys and sorrows of an amoeba. But this is hardly evidence that the amoeba neither suffers nor enjoys.[13]

Indeed, in defining the lowest limit of experience, Hartshorne writes: " Is it the lowest vertebrates, the amoeba, the virus ' cell,' radioactive molecule, or what? " [14] He continues:

All in some fashion respond to their environment, and the radioactive molecule even initiates activity without having to be stirred up by its environment. The whole gamut of levels from atoms to man is for science basically one system. From this it appears that the poet's notion of his kinship with all nature may in principle be correct.

Here Hartshorne follows Whitehead in developing an organismic model. He is also, as his many essays demonstrate, considerably influenced by the monadology of Leibnitz. He tells us that the problem of mind and matter is not that of two kinds of stuff but that of oneness and manyness at numerous levels.[15] Thus all natural wholes are organic, and an organism is defined as " a whole whose parts serve as ' organs ' or instruments to purposes or end-values inherent in the whole." [16] He denies that there are two types of wholes, organic and inorganic, but rather opts for an organic monism. He agrees that there is a limited dualism in the sense that some wholes, such as man, are organic and others, such as a mountain, are not, within his definition of organism. But all wholes do constitute parts of a larger organism. The mountain may be included in a cosmic organism, and it is itself built up of molecules which are themselves organisms. However, all wholes are not purposive or organic. " Any whole which has less unity than its more unified parts is not an organism in the pregnant sense here in question." [17] All such organic wholes are built together by feeling, for they are fundamentally psychic. The social dimension is central.

Hartshorne defines two types of society — the type in which *all* members are on the same level and the type in which one member is radically superior and dominates the assembly.[18] The inanimate world provides the best examples of the first type, as, for example, a pile of sand. Yet at the atomic and molecular levels we cannot so confidently affirm a lack of dynamic integrity or wholeness. Every individual thing above the electronic level has a social aspect. Some, at the inorganic level, do possess a supermember, and others do not. Because the members of such societies are at such a low level and have no organizing supermember, they appear to our limited knowledge as dead machines or inert masses. Yet no individual, even at such a level, is "totally without sensitivity or responsiveness to other individuals."[19] If we define life as "response to environment, adaptation, seeking and avoiding reactions," even molecules, atoms, and subatomic particles may have a fundamentary psychic life.[20]

The second type of society is very evident at the organic level. Certain multicellular creatures and the plants do not act as wholes and would fall more under the first category. Yet this would not mean a denial of a psychological aspect to the individual cells. "Each of the cells of a tree has more functional unity than the whole tree," declares Hartshorne, and then proceeds to quote Whitehead's dictum that "a tree is a democracy."[21] This description might also apply to a creature like the worm. But the second type takes over at the level of the vertebrates. Such animals are not democracies. The animal acts as a unified whole. A plant may bend to the light because its cells nearest the light respond to the stimulus. The bending results from a group reaction. But the higher creatures respond as feelingful wholes with some dominant master "mind." They possess a quality of integration absent from societies of a lower grade.

In this way, Hartshorne would attack what Whitehead termed "the fallacy of misplaced concreteness," and, in particular, the differentiation of matter from mind. "Experience" or "feeling" characterizes the whole universe; and the various grades of things all manifest such "experience" in a social structure.

The shape, size, and motion, which we associate with matter, are manifestations of psychic activity, even at the most rudimentary level. At the human level, Hartshorne would not ascribe space to body merely, for man is a psychic society in which his mind is the monarchical center. Since for science "a thing is where it immediately acts," he contends that mind has place. It does act immediately through various parts of the body and thus at definite locations. It is thus in many places at once. In consequence, its spatial pattern will be fixed by the pattern of the places where it acts at a specific time and its motion by the pattern of places where it acts at successive times. Hartshorne writes:

It can be inferred with some probability that the human mind, at any given moment, is not drastically different in size and shape from the pattern of activity of the nervous system with which at this moment it interacts, and as this activity moves about somewhat it follows that the mind literally moves in brain and nerves, though in ways unimaginably various and intricate.[22]

Extension is primarily given in enjoyed, suffered "matter," that is to say, in "matter" that is connected with mind. All matter is spatially located by its relation to my most intimate transactions which arise within and through *my* body. The locus of "matter" is meaningful only because of its interaction with minds. Spatial extension is initially observed not in dead matter but in living experience. Hence the extension and motion attributed to matter are explicable on the basis of psychic societies bound together in experience.

Hartshorne can contend that even electrons are social beings endowed with sentience. An electron as a point of energy is, "as it were, a disembodied spirit." Its "radius" marks off the space in which it is able to interact with other particles. All this is strangely reminiscent of Leibniz as well as reflecting strongly the influence of Whitehead.

Hartshorne follows Whitehead also in the denial of "substance" and the emphasis on the temporal aspect of things. There cannot be a "purely timeless or immutable existent." [23] When we postulate that reality is social, we have also to envisage a temporally as well as a spatially extended society. A social reality is a temporally extended succession of experiences. Thus individual things consist as much in changes as in enduring self-identity. Every such existent individual involves changes, even though Hartshorne would not deny the presence of " an unchanging factor." " A changing whole," he writes, " may have some unchanging factor, since the change of any factor suffices to change the whole. And a changing individual must have some unchanging factor, since the change of all factors and properties would abolish the individual." [24] Thus, at the human level, the self at this moment is a society of psychic entities that make up the body, presided over by a monarchical mind. But at the temporal level, it is a succession of such selves, each a center of experience. Thus the self both undergoes changes and at any moment is not totally identical with all its past selves, although its identity with its immediate past is very close. The connection with the past is so close, however, that personal identity is evident. This latter, Hartshorne seems to ground in memory, again reminiscent of Whitehead. He writes: " Memory is direct verification of the hypothesis of different individuals with more or less similar feelings." [25]

We are presented with a picture very similar to that of Whitehead. The cosmic process consists of social groupings at various levels, some democratic and some monarchical. The societies are characterized by a psychic nature. They are gatherings of centers of experience or feeling, the intensity and quality of the latter depending upon the level of existence of the individual entity concerned. All individual centers of feeling experience other contemporary centers of feeling and also, by something akin to memory, past centers of feeling, especially those which constitute their own past as individuals. Thus Hartshorne defines " relation " as " the ability of a thing to express in its own nature those other things which, among alternately possible or contingent things, happen to exist." [26] In the monarchical social groupings, of which man as mind and body is the supreme example, there is a center of experience, the mind, which gathers into its own experience all the experiences of the lower centers which are immediately gathered around it and which constitute its body. It also is related to past such societies which have previously constituted its selfhood. This is possible by memory. Furthermore, it interacts with the other societies at various levels by which it is surrounded and which come within its effective radius or "space" of interaction.

Hartshorne speaks of human enjoyment as social, since it is shared with "a multitude of individuals of a non-human kind." [27] He is here referring to the bodily cells which he envisages as feeling, in their own characteristic way, at least our physical pleasures. Our bodies are bound to our minds by "feeling of feeling." [28] Physical pleasures and pains are objectified and localized in our phenomenal or bodily space, and thus they have a certain detachment from the self. There is a certain "feeling of feeling" involved here, so that I can distinguish a pain in "my" finger as "there" whereas I, as spectator, am "here," "vaguely in the head and chest region" (as Hartshorne puts it).[29] Thus there is a kind of spatial contrast involved in it. Hartshorne acknowledges that "with certain of the less definitely physical, the more subjective joys and sorrows, this detachment is more difficult or partially impossible." [30] He is adopting Whitehead's organismic model and contending that it involves an immediate sympathy between the constituent elements. Man communicates with at least parts of his body "by a direct transaction which nothing further can explain, but which may well be the type of transaction which, adequately generalized, explains everything else." [31]

It is at this point that Hartshorne finds it possible to move to the higher satisfactions. The human mind is a "group mind" in the sense that although simple it yet embraces in its "feeling of feeling" a group of lesser psychic entities which constitute the human body. But we may not speak of a "group mind" at the level of human societies because of the lack of integration.[32] Higher satisfactions involve increased differentiation from that for which we have a "feeling of feeling." They arise when the word "social" is applicable in its narrower and more generally acceptable sense of mutually conscious and explicit communion. As Buber would put it, they are within the I-Thou relationship. "The higher feelings are participations wherein that in which we participate is adequately distinguished from the participation, and reciprocally distinguishes itself." [33] Thus the enjoyment of moral activity is never private but involves the enjoyment of the whole social community. At the highest level such enjoyment ought to arise out of love, and even the humbler values which man enjoys at the physical level are best interpreted as "love in an embryonic stage."

So far no mention has been made of God. Hartshorne's development of his panpsychism points, he believes, to the necessity of deity. Here he is once more like his mentor Whitehead. Yet let us note at once that the whole movement of his thought is directed to such a necessity because of its starting point, the assumption that the universe is basically psychic.

A Dipolar Deity

As Hartshorne sees it, a universe structured as a panpsychic process points to a deity in whom its organismic wholeness is completed. Hence, in one line of argument, he begins with his analysis of the process as social. He contends that it is "difficult if not impossible" to view this universe at the level of what he has defined as a democratic society. At the human level we have a "monarchical society," in which the human personality directs the lesser members of the psychosomatic whole. On this analogy, he thinks that even though there be many democratic societies, at different levels, in the universe, they are all merged within a monarchical whole. Without a guiding and controlling center, democratic groups at all levels tend to be noncooperative and diversive. "Nothing would guarantee the continuance of the society from moment to moment save the infinite good luck that they all happened to use their freedom in ways serviceable to the society." [34] Plato's insight that democracy is the next stage above anarchy has truth in it. There has, at least, to be an imposed structure of law and order. In the same way, unless, in the universe as a whole, there be some centralized guiding principle, which nullifies the chaotic state of affairs arising from individual choices and freedom, science could not claim that the cosmos is, as its name implies, an ordered whole. The whole would dissolve into a chaotic and warring jungle at all levels. Now, Hartshorne argues, that it is radically unverifiable that the universe is *not* a society. Such a supposition must be dismissed. Here we might raise a demurrer if we remember entropy and the Second Law of Thermodynamics. It is certainly true that his panpsychic bias presumes that the universe is social. If social, it must be monarchical. In this way it points to a God. If it becomes disordered, a disorderly society cannot restore itself, but a central controlling and guiding principle can constrain it in the right channels at every level of its constituent members.[35]

Another position also arises in the course of Hartshorne's thought. This turns upon his understanding of time as the creative dimension of the universe. He accepts Bergson's dictum that "time is creation or nothing." As we have noted above, every event is related to past events and includes them in its present experience. In Hartshorne's picture of the universe, such relationship is unidirectional. The present cannot envisage the future, for many possibilities are open, but it can and does include the past. The future has many potential directions, and the concrete actualization waits upon the creative movement of time. As Hartshorne puts it:

The chance-character or freshness of the particular can, in truth, be viewed from two perspectives: from that of the antecedent phase of process which involves various relatively well-defined alternatives for the next phase; and from that of the particular itself which is the actualization of one of these alternatives.[36]

A previous phase of a process is destined to be succeeded *somehow,* but there are certain limits of variation. Not all logical possibilities for the future are actual possibilities, because of the circumstantial situation, but there is openness. When, however, the future has become an actual present, it includes within itself, in a determinate way, the past out of which it has issued.

The antecedent possibility is as innocent of the precise quality as it is of the actuality of the event in question, and indeed the precise or particular quality *is* the actuality.[37]

Yet even so, at the human level, the past events included in experience are at most but a selection. Individuals of the past can be predicated in the present in experience. Shakespeare can be related to Shaw in a way that would not hold in the reverse order. The former could not predict the latter, but the latter can include the former in his present experience. The present constitutes a whole which includes the past but is not included in anything. When it itself is included, it will have become past, and the new whole will be the present. Now " our human consciousness has, of course, but a feeble direct awareness of the inclusion of the past in the present, via memory." [38] Hartshorne cannot, however, believe that past events which are not so remembered in present experience at all levels have ceased to have reality, become nonbeing. " If the past once for all ' has been what it has been,' then *something* does preserve, and as it were remember, all that happens." [39] Then new experiences, additional values, need not mean losing any of the old. This would point to a literal and all-embracing memory and thus to the need for God.

So Hartshorne brings us to his own understanding of deity. The indications in his development outlined above would be that such a God is involved in and includes the individual experiences of the cosmic societies at all levels. Hence he suggests a dipolar model for God. By this he means the inclusion of both being and becoming in the concept of deity. He argues that the classical statements of both theism and pantheism have emphasized being. Out of the polarities — the one and the many, the necessary and the contingent, being and becoming — they have chosen the first member in their understanding of God. Classical theism has allowed a place for the second member in its concept of an order " outside " God. Classical pantheism, as in the case of

Sankara, has denied any reality whatsoever to the second member; the many, the contingent, becoming, are human illusions. The one — theism — assumes the " all " to be God + what is " outside " God; the other — pantheism — rests with God and denies the inferior polarity. Hartshorne argues that this dilemma need never arise if we envisage deity as inclusive, the whole which is both being and becoming.

Accepting the " Law of Polarity " as regulative at the level of human experience and logic, Hartshorne regards the ultimate contraries as " correlatives, mutually interdependent, so that nothing real can be described by the wholly one-sided assertion of simplicity, being, actuality, and the like, each in a ' pure ' form, devoid and independent of complexity, becoming, potentiality, and related contraries." [40] He contends that classical theism and pantheism have ignored this law, which can be traced from Heraclitus to Hegel. They have postulated God as an absolute exception and developed a monopolar conception of deity. On the one hand, they have affirmed the insufficiency of human conceptions to define God. Yet, on the other hand, they have opted for one pole only of the contraries, seeing for it a transcendent analogue and regarding the other pole as theologically unacceptable. But there is a breach of logic here, Hartshorne contends, and adds that " classical theism is far from a consistent doctrine of modesty with respect to human conceptions. Certain categories are favored over their contraries." [41] If experience is to be the final arbiter for such a position, Hartshorne argues that this gives no justification for the evaluation " superior-inferior " in regard to the contraries. Such an evaluation holds within the poles themselves but not between them.

In consequence, he postulates what he styles panentheism. He conceives of deity as all-inclusive and thus as including in itself the contraries that characterize human experience. Both being and becoming must be ascribed to God, and the word " superior " must be applied to both aspects in relation to our human experience of the contraries. Both these categorical contraries admit a supreme case, a supercase, and therein they are descriptive of

God's own life. God will have an individual *essence* but will also have his *accidents*, to use the classical expressions, " so that what is ' in *him*' need not, for all that, be in *his essence*." [42] The use of the preposition " in " is a reminder that, for Hartshorne, deity is inclusive. God is not the world, for he is the Supreme Creative Reality, but he includes the world in himself and all things are constituent elements in his life. Thus he is in the world, and the world is in him. On this basis, Hartshorne can affirm that God is both being and becoming; he is dipolar.

God's essence is the unchanging aspect of his life. It constitutes his character and makes him what he really is. It is his, no matter what be the changing experiences of his life. He is always " himself," and thus there is an " absolute " in God, his inner unchanging character, his " individuality." As Hartshorne puts it: " God's ' essence ' is not accidental — that is indeed required by the premise, which implies that in any possible state of affairs God will be included, and this means that there will always be something by which he may be identified as God, and no other. This something is his essence." [43] He continues by noting that knowledge of God's " essence " by no means carries with it knowledge of the contingents or accidents or possibilities to which God's life is open. Such will be present in him according to circumstances. This arises because the whole world and its becoming are included in God. In the universe we can know the genus without knowing all the species and " certainly without knowing the individual natures which the genus makes possible." [44] So too with God! He does not know all the individual instances which may be included in the generic.

The accidents of God come under the genus of possible states of God, a genus inexhaustible through any series, even though infinite, of actual states, it being part of the meaning of possibility that it cannot be translated without remainder into actuality. [45]

God's essential aspect is his *that*, as he is in himself, " apart from having created just this world as it now exists." [46] It is his abstract aspect, " his purpose as laid down before all the worlds." [47]

The world process that God has actually created is, however, present in God, in Hartshorne's panentheistic model. It is this which provides for the aspect of becoming in God's life, his accidents. At the human level of personhood, the world as nature and history is experienced as becoming, and thereby the person himself grows through experience. We are persons in relationship who grow in and through the relationships. Hartshorne argues that, in an analogous way, the process must be meaningful to God. In God's relationship to the world, which is included within him, we cannot think of him as immutable. Creation, providence, incarnation — the classic affirmations of the Christian faith — point to the involvement of God with his world at all levels.

Hartshorne's Christology is certainly not Chalcedonian. Indeed, he admits that he has "no Christology to offer." But he adds:

beyond the simple suggestion that Jesus appears to be the supreme symbol furnished to us by history of the notion of a God genuinely and literally "sympathetic" (incomparably *more* literally than any man ever is), receiving into his own experience the sufferings as well as the joys of the world.[48]

God is a related being in this aspect, and he cannot be thought of as immutable and impassible. He must experience his world in its change and becoming, its evolution and process, for he is constantly in relation to it. Though he is absolute in his essence, his abstract being, he must be changing in his experience. "Even the mediocre forms of being will be contained in the supreme being by entering into his accidents."[49] Hartshorne argues that the traditional concept of God which treats him as immutable Divine Substance does not provide a basis for a personal understanding of deity. He writes:

A personal God is one who has social relations, really has them, and thus is constituted by relationships and hence is relative.[50]

He believes that the doctrine of the Trinity preserved the truth, though it furnished "a social relation between persons all of whom are perfect" and it did not explicitly define what is enjoyed in this relation.[51]

The difference between God and human persons lies, in part, in the superior quality of his unity. It is the difference "between a partial and a maximum realization of the principle. God identifies himself as the same in basic purposes through all the details of the past and all the general traits of the future." [52] On the other hand, man with his limited existence and partial memory cannot do this. Yet what guarantees God's individual personal being, identical through all changes, is the presence of his abstract and determinate aspect over against his concrete, indeterminate aspect — his essence as contrasted with his accidents.[53] As personal, however, he is supremely relative. Since the universe is in him and thus in his experience, he retains all past actualities in his perfect memory. They are concrete constituent elements of his experience. Here we link up with Hartshorne's postulation of God, discussed above. Furthermore, all future actualities will also be gathered up as concrete elements in his own life. Thus God is the Absolute only in the realm of abstraction. In the realm of concreteness and actuality he is the Supreme Relative.

This is not, however, pantheism. There is nothing outside deity, and, in this sense, he is the All. But God is not a cosmic aggregation. In his individual essence he is "utterly independent of this All, since any other possible all (and there are infinite possibilities of different totalities) would have been compatible with this essence." [54] The pantheists have no place for such transcendence. But for Hartshorne, both God and his creatures are free. The universe is open-ended toward the future, and God, in his inclusive actuality, is "as truly contingent and capable of additions as the least actuality it includes." [55] His essence is compatible with any *possible* universe, which is external to his essence although included in his life. The word "possible" does, however, refer to the nature of his essential purposes, with which alternative concrete experiences or states are compatible. Hartshorne's panentheism agrees with classical theism "on the important point that the divine individuality, that without which God would not be

God, must be logically independent, that is, must not involve any particular world." [56]

The use of the word "perfect" to describe God in such a philosophy has to be defined. How can God be perfect if he is becoming in his relatedness? If he includes in himself the concrete actualities of creatures who are imperfect, his perfection will be less than if all his included constituents were perfection. Hartshorne, however, defines "perfection," not as "that which in no respect could conceivably be greater," but "as that individual being . . . than which no *other individual* being could *conceivably* be greater, but which *itself*, in another 'state,' could become greater (perhaps by the creation within itself of new constituents)." [57] To define the perfect being as he who cannot improve or in any sense increase in value is to deny the happiness of the supreme individual who includes all in himself and rejoices in his creatures. [58] God in his relative aspect includes all the past of the world process in himself and thus is always surpassing himself. He surpasses all others, for he possesses the values of all concrete actualities from the time such values exist. Yet he also is continuously surpassing himself in his own relativity.

Thus, Hartshorne sees a third alternative to the two usually postulated. These two are either there is a Being absolutely perfect or unsurpassable in all respects or there is no Being in *any* respect absolutely perfect. He opts for the third alternative — a Being in some respects perfect and in others not so, yet perfect even then in the sense that such a Being can only be self-surpassable. [59] God is unchanging in his essence but constantly surpassing himself in his advancing experience. Hartshorne contends that this is much nearer to the Biblical view of God.

At this point, we need to emphasize Hartshorne's conviction that God in his essential being is love. He endeavors, above all else, to build a metaphysic which safeguards this revelatory insight of the Christian faith. He thinks of God as "a God of love and responsiveness and interaction with man." [60] He finds this in the person of Jesus. "To say that Jesus was God . . . ought to mean that God himself is one with us in our suffering, that divine love is not essentially benevolence — external well-wishing — but sympathy, taking into itself our every grief." [61] Hence Hartshorne reminds us that love involves sensitivity to and participation in the joys and sorrows of others, and he sees traditional Christian theism failing just at this point because "we cannot infect God with our sufferings (since he is the cause of everything and effect of nothing), and our joys can add nothing to the immutable perfection of God's happiness." [62]

Such theism, as Hartshorne sees it, makes God's love totally altruistic, but he finds it absolutely unacceptable that we can do nothing for God and that he will gain nothing from our actions.[63] Rather, he holds that egoism is perfectly consistent with altruism in God, as he envisages deity. " For whatever good God may do to any being anywhere he himself, through his omniscient sympathy, will inevitably enjoy." [64] Since the future welfare of all his creatures is involved, God takes upon himself their sufferings as well as their joys. God's love does not mean his unqualified happiness. God's love means that our interests are his and that our failure or tragedy is his also. If we say that God is love, then we mean that God desires the good of all his creatures and for God, in his all-inclusiveness, this is coincident with desiring his own good.

An Inclusive, Social God and His Relation to His Creatures

Hartshorne, on the basis of such an understanding of God, argues that religion is a fraud unless God is related to his creatures "by a sympathetic union surpassing any human sympathy." [65] He enters lovingly into his creation, becomes involved with it, and takes into his own life all the surges of feeling that move through the lives of his creatures. He is no "unmoved mover." Rather, he finds his own joy in the happiness and joys of his world. They are "in" him and he is "in" them to such a degree that he participates in their diverse states, their sufferings and defeats as well as their joys and triumphs. In this way God is himself enriched in and through the experience of his creatures, gathering up their lives into his own life. His perfection lies not only in the integrity of his own being as love but also in his capacity to enter into the fullest and deepest relationship with his world.

Yet in this relationship, God, who is immanent in all things, also maintains his ontological distance. He grants his creatures their freedom at all levels. His is a supreme relationship to others, as ours is not. His creatures live their own life "according to their own free decisions, not fully anticipated by any detailed plan of his own." [66] But in this relationship to his creatures, God also orders his world. He is no supreme autocrat. Rather, his is an "infinitely sensitive and tolerant relativity, by which all things are kept moving in orderly togetherness." [67]

Following Whitehead, Hartshorne describes this as "persuasion," by which he means that God incorporates his aims and ideals into his world through the experiences of him which the creatures enjoy. Here the emphasis on the panpsychic nature of the universe and on "feeling" becomes central. "God can rule the world and order it, setting optimal limits for our free action, by presenting himself as essential object, so characterized as to weight the possibilities of response in the desired respect." [68] God presents "at each moment a partly new ideal or order of preference which our unself-conscious awareness takes as object, and thus renders influential upon our entire activity." What happens at the human level is also true of the way God molds the entire process.

We are asked to envisage a cosmic process which God orders by his wisdom and persuades by his love. In this way the world is constrained and ordered to achieve the ends which lie in the divine will. Hartshorne suggests that God grants to his creatures a wide range of capacity and response. Since all beings, on his view, are greatly free and deeply sympathetic, conflict and disharmony will introduce an element of chance. But God sets an optimum of conditions for this freedom whereby a balance is maintained between overmuch risk and security which is too costly to freedom. "A too tame and harmless order and a too wild and dangerous, even though perhaps exciting disorder — these are the evils to be avoided in some golden mean." [69] The whole emphasis falls on God's love. His relativity to his creatures is a sympathy in which giving and receiving are both involved. As he does so, his world is constrained to fulfill his purpose for it, as his creatures enter into feelingful relationship one with the other. Each creature builds its own life out of strands which it receives from others. At the same time it gives its own life to be woven as a strand into the life of others. [70]

We may well ask at this point: What of the divine omnipotence and omniscience? Hartshorne is quite clear that God's omnipotence rests in the supremacy of his relativity and in his love. By his love, God, as the supreme power in the universe, influences the activity of all his creatures. But he does not coerce or determine them. Rather, he " persuades " them by his continuous and loving activity to go his way, while leaving them free. His influence is always present. It may be thwarted but it cannot be destroyed. It is continually swaying the feelings of the creatures at all levels toward the ends ordained in his loving purpose.

It is " irresistible " only in the sense that none can evade it. In this way, the reality of evil can be affirmed, for each being is granted its own power, and in such a social reality, disorder and mutual tension is bound to arise. Hartshorne comments: " A best possible power in God need not imply a best possible world; for any possible world is in part self-determined, a world of partly self-made and self-making constituents." [71]

Such a view has repercussions on the understanding of the divine omniscience. Traditionally this means an " all knowledge " that applies to future events in all their determinate detail, as well as to the present and the past. Hartshorne, with his dipolar view of God and his emphasis on divine relativity, holds that God's knowledge is relative to the feelings and actions of his creatures. It is not a changeless whole, but dependent upon the decisions and actions of the beings in his world, upon their free activity. Insofar as the actuality of the world is contingent, God's knowledge must be seen as growing with the cosmic process, new elements continually being added. Such knowledge must be understood as a perfect sensitivity to the creatures. God's dipolarity is evident in it. What is absolute, nonrelative, and unchanging is his cognitive adequacy. His knowledge is unchanging because it is always perfectly sensitive and adequate to its objects. It is infallible. But it is also relative to the concrete actuality of God's creatures. God knows all things with perfect adequacy, but he also knows them in their concreteness. Thus the future is not yet detailed and determinate, and God knows it as such. He knows the possible as possible. Only in this way can his knowledge be adequate to the future. He must know things as they truly are — the actual as actual, the possible as possible. He knows the future as indefinite and unsettled.

God's knowledge is, moreover, direct and immediate. He knows his creatures from within. In his perfect sensitivity, he knows the feelings and shares in the experiences of his world. This must hold if the world is within God. It does not, however, imply that God shares in the ignorance of creaturely beings. Because he sees the future as indeterminate, God can understand ignorance, for ignorance is "the absence of determinate awareness." But God is aware that the object is indeterminate, whereas the creature, because of his limitations, is only aware of a lack of determinate awareness.

God knows the positive aspects of ignorance and of sin, too, without being either ignorant or sinful. Ignorant and sin are, for Hartshorne, essentially negative. They are exclusions. Ignorance is a lack of that knowledge which is available to an all-inclusive deity. Sin is the lack of concern for another's interests and feelings. A whole, Hartshorne argues, includes all its parts, whereas the latter may exclude one another in sin and in ignorance. But the whole does not exclude any part that another part may have excluded. Thus God does not participate in the exclusions of his creatures, but he does know that such exclusions exist.[72] Furthermore, he shares in the positive aspects of such exclusions. Hence he suffers in the sufferings of his creatures.

We are left with a picture of God's relativity to the process much like that of Whitehead. God's dipolarity means that he is enriched by the experiences of his creatures and grows in his own experience. He finds joy in sharing their lives and is himself fulfilled as he feels their happiness. But he also suffers. His perfect and adequate relationship to his creatures means not only that he contains their sufferings in his inclusiveness but also that he suffers. Indeed, " it is in his character to suffer, in accordance with the suffering of the world." [73] Hartshorne finds here a metaphysical expression of " the Christian idea of a suffering deity — symbolized by the Cross, together with the doctrine of the Incarnation."

Process Philosophy and the Christian Faith

It is significant that others besides Hartshorne have been influenced by Whitehead and that the " process philosophy" is becoming a significant claimant as a possible metaphysic in which the Christian revelation can be expressed. John B. Cobb, Jr.,[74] in particular, has sought to find a Christian natural theology in this approach. Like Hartshorne, he leans heavily on Whitehead and does so more directly and explicitly. He significantly refers to Hartshorne at certain points where he feels the inadequacies of Whitehead's organismic model. He does, however, accept Whitehead's theory of actual entities and his theory of prehensions, so that his philosophy is couched much more in the categories of Whitehead than in those of Hartshorne. Indeed, the panpsychism of the latter seems to have been presupposed in Hartshorne's thought prior to the direct impact of Whitehead himself. Hartshorne was strongly influenced by both Royce and Hocking in his own thinking, and Hocking has written an appreciative introduction to *Reality as Social Process*.

Cobb believes that Whitehead's organismic philosophy can be modified sufficiently to provide Christian thought with a metaphysical base. He defines " theology" as a " coherent statement about matters of ultimate concern that recognizes that the perspective by which it is governed is received from a community of faith." [75] In this way he endeavors to remove any mention of God or the sacred. He does this because he wishes to make a place in his definition for the advocates of "religionless Christianity," who would place their emphasis on the this-worldly concern of the Christian faith and would liken it to this-worldly but atheistic movements such as communism. Whether Christianity can thus be divorced from mankind's religious experience and whether attempts to naturalize it and remove the idea of the supernatural are legitimate must be deferred to the discussion of the last chapter. Immediately, however, we must note that any philosophy grounded in Whitehead's philosophy will tend to have a naturalistic basis. This is very evident in the philosophical thought of both Cobb and Hartshorne.

As we have already seen, Cobb has difficulty in defining personal identity on the organic model, as did Whitehead himself. Hartshorne has the same difficulty. In both cases we have the personal defined in social terms as a succession of temporal occasions. Hartshorne has to fall back upon memory as the root of the identity of a personal self; so also does Cobb.[76] Curiously there is little, if any, mention of the experience of self-transcendence, and Cobb has to admit that, in his own view, the treatment of personal identity "is still not entirely satisfactory." [77] So long as models are adopted from a lower level than the personal, we may expect such unsatisfactoriness.

The same issue arises when we turn to the issue of immortality. Hartshorne quite emphatically rejects personal survival in any concrete sense. Rather, he postulates survival as an abiding and meaningful memory within the divine experience. He confines man's active personhood to this earth and contends that "God loves us in our present reality for the sake of that reality." [78] He rightly says that such reality cannot be destroyed. He then argues that we are themes in *the* divine theme, of which we are so many variations. God enjoys us in his inexhaustible selfhood, continually reforming his awareness of us forever.

We function as a theme for literally endless variations in the use God makes of us as objects of His awareness to be synthesized with ever additional objects. But these endless variations are *nothing we shall experience,* save in principle and in advance through our devoted imagination, our love of God.[79]

We do not have the divine privilege of living everlastingly, but we may earn everlasting places in the divine experience, by virtue of our earthly lives.

Cobb is more careful at this point and indicates passages in which Whitehead guardedly suggests the possibility of the immortality of the soul.[80] He shows that Whitehead's philosophy left open the possibility of personal survival of death, but that Whitehead held that " the philosophical *possibility* that this occurs is no evidence that it in fact occurs." [81] Cobb shows that " the usual philosophical and commonsense arguments for the impossibility of life after death are removed by his [Whitehead's] philosophy." [82]

Cobb does, however, look at the problem of where such existence beyond death may have a " place." Now that mind has become a part of the natural order, the spatiotemporal continuum, this raises difficulties. Cobb acknowledges that our own spatiotemporal structure is the form taken by the universal extensive continuum in our world. This continuum is necessary and universal for actual entities to exist in relation, since Whitehead views some kind of extensiveness as a function of such relatedness. But this extensive continuum may take another dimensional form appropriate to man's survival as soul. Here Cobb can claim no direct support from Whitehead, and he refuses himself to regard his own speculations as offering more than a possibility of survival. The nature of the soul as such does not imply continued existence. Cobb can write, however, " If man continues to exist beyond death, it can only be as a new gift of life, and whether such a gift is given is beyond the province of natural theology to inquire." [83] We would agree with this judgment which is much more in keeping with the central Christian disclosure in the Resurrection, upon which alone the Christian hope finally rests. Hartshorne's position is, at this point, a denial of the fundamental Christian insights.

Cobb finds difficulty with Whitehead's understanding of God. We have already indicated this difficulty.[84] He is not prepared to accept Whitehead's definition of God as an actual entity, but rather would regard God as supremely personal in the same way as Hartshorne.[85] God is not an "actual entity," as Whitehead postulates. Both Cobb and Hartshorne, however, can still think of God in social terms as a cumulative temporal succession of experiences. Presumably, as is not the case with finite individual persons, this is associated with the perfect adequacy of the divine memory. "God," Cobb tells us, "then, at any moment would be an actual entity, but viewed retrospectively and prospectively he would be an infinite succession of divine occasions of experience."[86] He adds, however, that such a succession has "special continuity," because of the unified nature of God's experience.[87] Cobb finds this unity both in God's perfect experience of the past of the world as well as of himself and in the idea that the passage of time does not entail loss in God's experience as it does in ours. Presumably Hartshorne would find here what he regards as God's essence in his dipolar view of God. Both thinkers suffer here, as at the level of finite personhood, from a deficient view of what it means to be a self-transcendent person.

One weakness of Hartshorne, as with the somewhat similar philosophical system of Hocking, lies in its evident rejection of the Christian emphasis on *creatio ex nihilo*. His panentheism seems to require this rejection. The inclusion of the world within God and the implications of Hartshorne's development of God's relativity and "accidents" point to the cosmos and its creatures as in some sense derived from God's own "stuff."

Cobb is much more in keeping with the Christian insight. He regards God as "the ground of our being, our purpose, and the order that sustains us."[88] In the light of his own interpretation of Whitehead's somewhat ambiguous term "creativity" Cobb can think of God "as the cause of the being as well as the form of actual occasions" and can suggest that Whitehead's thought was moving in this direction. On the other hand, Cobb does accept the idea of God as an all-inclusive whole. He thinks of God as

" absolutely present " and yet " as *numerically* other, and qualitatively, incomprehensibly other." He is careful to add that such otherness of God does not imply spatiotemporal distance. Rather, God extends himself so as to include " all the regions comprising the standpoints of other occasions." [89] God possesses omnispatiality. He possesses a standpoint, and " since that standpoint could not be such as to favor one part of the universe against others, it must be all-inclusive." [90] His region " includes all other contemporary regions." Such a view of transcendence and immanence would appear to be much more in keeping with the Biblical testimony.

Both Hartshorne and Cobb are helpful and provocative in the emphasis on God's enrichment in and through the creative process of nature and history. Here traditional Christian theism has been strangely deficient, and other Christian thinkers have, as we have seen, sought to modify it in this direction. The whole burden of the Christian disclosure points to divine involvement and relativity. Cobb wisely points out that " if we believe that God knows us in such a way that he knows our subjective aim and its relation to the ideal possibility with which he has confronted us, our own motivation gains in our own eyes an urgency otherwise lacking." [91] We must defer till the next chapter a more constructive discussion of what Hartshorne terms God's " dipolar nature " or in Whiteheadian language, God's movement from his primordial to his consequent nature.

VIII

Theistic Faith in a Secular Society

THE EMPHASES in the studies so far undertaken must now be considered in relation to Christian philosophizing as we define it in the first chapter. It is very evident to all serious Christian thinkers that any realistic presentation of the Christian standpoint must take note of the data provided by contemporary scientific investigations, including the facts which underlie the evolutionary viewpoint and the models by which scientists seek to understand such facts. Furthermore, the importance of history in the Christian faith needs to be matched by the deeper understanding of history which has emerged in the last century. Finally, the secular society, which in a very real sense is the result of the Christian emphasis on this world, has resulted in a radical challenge to traditional Christian theological conceptions, especially because of the value placed upon this world and its processes, both at the level of nature and at the level of human history. To speak to such a world intelligibly, theology must find a philosophical bridge, a natural theology or Christian philosophy which provides some point of contact with the preoccupations and attitudes of " secular man." All the philosophies so far studied and critically assessed have attempted to do this in their own characteristic ways.

We need to remember that the present stage of secularity is a result of the Christian disclosure and its claims. For one thing, the triumph of the Christian faith in the ancient and medieval world meant the expulsion of the nature deities and demonries from their habitat in man's world and set that world free from any claim to be itself divine. The Christian emphasis on creation and on God's otherness from his world meant the de-divinization of the world. It also meant that man was set free from bondage to the powers of this world and liberated to be responsible in controlling and directing it. He was set free, however, under God, in faith. As R. Gregor Smith reminds us:

He [man] is not taken out of the world, rather, he is now lord over the world, and responsible for it: he becomes fellow-heir with Christ, he is now son and heir. He is henceforth responsible for his own history. In faith, therefore, the world belongs to him.[1]

In the second place, Christianity helped to shape the method by which man's control of his world could be facilitated.[2] Greek rationalism had provided one strand, but it remained for Christianity to point the way to the experimental and empiricist strand. By de-divinizing the world and stressing the divine otherness, Christianity denied to man any participation in the divine reason. Man's creaturely rational powers could be exercised in understanding the plan of the Creator, not by looking within at his own rational structures, but rather by investigating the works of the Creator. Thereby man could seek, by his rational powers, to piece together a rational structure in his world. Hebrew-Christian realism emphasized the reality and significance of this world as God's creation and the setting for the Incarnation. It equally stressed God's otherness and mystery, and thereby pointed to empirical and experimental investigation.

In the third place, we need to remember that the Christian

faith is world-affirming. At its center there are the doctrines of Creation and Incarnation. When God created the world he declared it to be good and made it the scene for the actualization of his purpose of love. In the Incarnation, God took a human life up into his own and so identified himself personally with man's psychosomatic nature that his redemptive love is effective at all levels of our world. Paul sees the whole creation groaning and waiting for the final unveiling of God's purpose, and our Lord healed men's bodies concomitantly with forgiving them their sins. The Old Testament men manifest a healthy realism toward nature and history, finding in them the media of divine disclosure and the arena for the actualization of the divine purpose. The New Testament writers do not preach escape from this world but the living of eternal life in their own *Dasein*. The life of the Kingdom is already a present reality to be wrought into the texture of human history here and now. It is true that the eschatological note is never absent, but even that has cosmic dimensions. There is the vision of a new heaven and a new earth. Personal survival is rarely envisaged apart from such a setting, and the symbolic framework of the latter means that survival is pictured in terms of resurrection rather than immortality.

The word "secular" means "this age" or "world." In the medieval period it came to be set in contrast to the "sacred," concerned mainly with the other world, the spiritual order. This is false to the Biblical understanding which, in its disclosure, affirms this world and rejoices in it, even though it sees it marred by sin and evil and in need of redemption. The Church's attempt to preoccupy itself increasingly with heaven and the "spiritual" realm and to leave the "secular," the this-worldly, on one side has led to a perversion of secularity. In secularism, we have an attitude of mind that rejects the divine, concentrates on the things with which science and technology deal, and sees nothing impossible to the triumphant onward march of the scientific method. Often allied with naturalism, it also takes a humanistic form, secularizing Christian values which have been grounded in the divine disclosure and divorcing them from any belief in God.

In attacking such secularism, the Church needs to have a positive and redemptive attitude toward secularity. It is the virtue of the approaches that we have been considering that they challenge us to do this. Christian salvation is not from this world but in it. Evolution and process, natural development and historical movement, have meaning for us because they are also meaningful to and in God's own life. We must now seek to gather some insights from our study and seek to find pointers toward a Christian metaphysic.

The Basic Model for a Possible Christian Metaphysic

We have seen, at the present juncture, a renewed interest in Whitehead and a return to a panpsychic view of the universe. It appears evident that despite the triumphant assertions of empiricists and naturalists, idealism is by no means dead, although it will have to take a postcritical form, listening to what has been said, on the one hand, by the linguistic analysts, and on the other hand, by the existentialists. It is significant that, in the past decades, thinkers like H. H. Farmer[3] and Karl Heim,[4] who have endeavored to deal with the intricate issues posed by science for the Christian faith, have found themselves moving toward some form of panpsychism. We have noted that Temple never escapes an objective form of idealism, despite his initial realism. Furthermore, Teilhard has to postulate a dimension of energy, which might be termed its psychic component, and evidently sees consciousness, in however rudimentary a form, at least as potential in what appears to be brute matter. Finally, Whitehead and his Christian disciples see the whole world as a unity of "feeling" or "prehension," so that the most elementary entity in the universe has both a mental and a physical pole, through which it prehends other entities and also its own peculiar subjective aim.

The tendency of the last group to assume that the basic model is organic raises real difficulties for them in their discussion of personal identity, so much so that they break from Whitehead when they seek to define God. In making God enduringly personal, however, they still regard human persons as social chains of successive occasions of experience, bound together by memory. It would seem wise to break a little more loose from the White-headian structure, attractive though it be, and move from the organic model to a personal model as basic in the interpretation of the universe. It has seemed to the present writer that H. H. Farmer has made a valiant effort to do this in his book *The World and God*, a book that in many respects has not received the notice or exerted the influence that its thesis deserves.

What all these groups would seem to be agreed upon is that a basic dualism of matter and mind, of the Cartesian variety, must be rejected. Either a naturalistic/materialistic stance or an idealistic/psychic stance may be adopted. The position of Harts-horne and Whitehead might be described as "naturalistic theism," but its naturalism is quite a remove from that form of naturalism which regards mind as the description of how matter behaves at higher levels of organization. For them, the mental or psychic is central, and consciousness, at however rudimentary a level, must be ascribed to all "actual entities." Temple concluded that, be-cause the natural evolutionary process produces minds that can understand and control it, much is implied about the process itself. This is a reminder that there is in matter something mys-teriously akin to mind. His attack upon the Cartesian *faux pas* with its false dichotomy between subject and object is matched by the parallel attack of Whitehead with his rejection of the fallacy of simple location. Whatever matter may be, it has kin-ship with psychic reality and must not be treated as some alien stuff. H. W. Robinson comments: "'Matter' must be ultimately spiritual, however much lower its level of reality than 'Mind.'" [5]

We have seen how, each in his own way, both Temple and Teil-hard point to the emergence of self-conscious spirit, personal being, as a key to the understanding of the process of nature and history. In unanimity with this we have the verdict of Lloyd Morgan. Even a naturalistic thinker like Julian Huxley can re-mind us that "the primacy of human personality . . . is a *fact* of evolution. By whatever objective standards we choose to take, properly developed human personalities are the highest product of evolution." [6] W. H. Thorpe can declare that " with the coming of self-conscious life the evolutionary process can be said to have become conscious of itself," [7] a thought echoed by Teilhard. The present writer has argued elsewhere for the reality of self-conscious mind or spirit as the focal point of the natural and historical processes.[8] We cannot repeat the process of thought here, but rather note that it is supported by the arguments and positioning of many of the thinkers surveyed in this volume.

We need to differentiate the personal nature of man from the organic nature of other animate creatures. Man's psychosomatic nature and the connection of his physiological and psychological aspects with the lower animal order are increasingly evident.[9] Evolution has made us very aware of the continuity, but we need also to note the differentiating characteristics which emerge with man. Here man's self-consciousness with its accompanying self-transcendence must be stressed. Man has intense subjectivity, an " I-ness," which differentiates him in a new and characteristic way from his environment. He exists as a self and he knows that he exists as a self.

John Macmurray, in his Gifford Lectures which have not received the attention that they deserve,[10] has sought to analyze this self-awareness. He points out that man is primarily agent rather than subject and that the emphasis should fall upon the dynamic and active aspect of the personal rather than upon the reflective and objectivizing aspect. He holds, like Temple and Whitehead, that the objective attitude of so much philosophical thought has ignored man's involvement in the processes of nature and history and isolated the knowing mind from its object. This criticism is in line with that of the existentialists. Man should be characterized by the phrase " I do " primarily and not by the phrase " I think." Macmurray differentiates " knowledge " from " thought " in the sense of primary or immediate awareness. Such knowledge involves what this writer has termed the intuitive aspect of the consciousness.[11] Macmurray contends that this knowledge is bound up with action. In acting, I meet the Other, become aware of the Other as the support of and the resistance to my action. This is of the very structure of personal existence, and the awareness of my own existence and of that of the Other accompanies my activity as agent. " I am aware of the Other, and of myself as dependent upon and limited by the Other." [12]

Thus an immediate mark of the personal is this awareness of the self and of what is not-self, the Other. Consciousness at the personal level means that we know ourselves to stand in relation to what is not ourselves. As Macmurray points out, this " is the very essence of our experience as persons, and so is all-pervasive." [13] He describes it as a capacity for objectivity and regards it as a differentiating characteristic of the personal. Objectivity might suggest the reflective process of conceptualizing, but he is referring here to the immediate consciousness of over-againstness, from which the reflective process of objectivization or conceptualization is an abstraction. Self-consciousness is born of my nature as agent and arises as I encounter the Other; as I become differentiated from my subpersonal environmental process and become aware of personal " Thous " confronting me and making claims on me. This is in keeping with the way in which self-consciousness arises in the small and developing child, the Other taking the form of the immediate presence of the mother. This means that knowledge of existence as a self and of the existence of the Other is a given. Existence cannot be proved, and self-awareness is immediate and intuitive. " The ' I do ' *is* existence and includes, as its negative aspect, the knowledge of existence." [14]

In this dynamic situation I become aware of the Other as limiting my own selfhood and, at the personal level, as personal claim. Indeed it is our awareness of other persons which awakens our own self-consciousness to its full functioning. The subpersonal world evokes a response from me but does not draw out all the full capacities of personal being. It may, for instance, evoke a quest for truth and an appreciation of beauty. But I need to be related to that which is so akin to my own personal being that it evokes the rich capacities of personal consciousness. " It is only the personal aspect of the world that can do this, and, therefore, it is only the objectivity of our conscious relation to other persons which can express our rationality fully and so reveal its essential character." [15] I become conscious of myself as a person most of all when I become conscious of another person to whom I must relate myself. " The basic fact about human beings, in virtue of which they are human," comments John Macmurray, " is that they know one another and live in that knowledge." [16]

At this level we become most fully aware also of our freedom. Our action results from a capacity to choose and, at the level where the personal claim of the Other is experienced, we become most fully aware of the distinction between right and wrong action. Personal activity is always bound up with motive, and the motive is sharpened as we are met by moral claim. Our " I " becomes shaped as we make our decisions. The significance of the existentialist analysis lies most of all in its exposure of human freedom and of the centrality of that (existential) decision in which an I determines its essential being.

At this point, the process of reflective thinking arises. Macmurray contends that " I think " is both essential and subsequent to the I do/I know situation. Philosophy has tended, except in existentialism, to major upon objectivization and to emphasize the self as subject rather than agent. In consequence, the self ceases to be the true I and becomes isolated from the process in which the actual I is intimately involved. What has been styled the " balcony " approach leads to the impersonal attitude. The world including other persons, becomes " It," the area of conceptualization, the object of my thinking. Perhaps most of all this becomes evident in dealing with other persons, where their " Thou " becomes my " It." Generally we may say that we concentrate upon the actions and external manifestations, seek to generalize and universalize their appearance into manageable concepts, and thus attempt to control and manipulate them. This holds of the whole of process, history and nature alike, persons and the lower entities that constitute our environment.

The Other thereby is removed from our immediate awareness of limitation and resistance, challenge and claim. We seek to con-

trol it and turn it into an object to be manipulated in our reflective thought. Yet this impersonal attitude is only a necessary, yet
negative, aspect of the personal approach to our world. Objectivity in the full sense means our being related objectively in action as well as in reflection. It thus requires personal relationship.
We do not know the personal in this way, however much it may
help our comprehension of that of which we are immediately
aware. It is a mark of our secular and scientific society that it
tends to neglect the personal and to major in the impersonal attitude to our world and to other persons.

The personal is, however, most known in mutual relationship,
in which we recognize ourselves as responsible beings who are involved with the Other and subject to his claim upon us. It is at
this point that disclosure situations arise in which the Other discloses himself to us in words and gestures. The truth of the Other
lies in the dialogue and mutual commitment in which the revelation of the one person awakens a sympathetic and imaginative
response in the other person. In words and actions the active
agent evokes in the Other an active involvement. That reflective
thought, the impersonal attitude, follows this personal dialogue
is to be expected, but it is not completed until there is some return
to dialogue and the personal attitude. Dynamic interchange and
involvement are central here. We have to descend from the balcony, accept the finitude and limitation of our freedom by the
presence of the Other with his claim and challenge, and realize
that the Other is not there for our use and enjoyment but as person on equality with ourselves. Such a person has his rights, and
we may not adopt toward him the instrumental, impersonal attitude.

It is in this personal dimension of relationship that we truly
become aware of ourselves in our inner dimension of being. Just
as we do not really know the Thou by turning him into an object
of thought, so we do not know ourselves fully by introspective
processes. Our knowing "I" is always separated in such thinking
from the psychological and physiological processes which we are
contemplating.

The nature of this self-transcendence in which the " I " is iso-lated from the objective self becomes evident to us as we become aware of the absolute values in the active involvement with our world. It is in the light of these that the self-critical processes of reflective thought are undertaken. We pursue the Good, the Beau-tiful, and the True. In reflective thought and moral judgment we subject our own thinking and behavior to their claims. As Temple pointed out, man is characterized by his appraisal of experience in terms of the pursuit of truth, the claims of the good, and the feeling for the beautiful. Here is the sharp dividing line between man and the animal order, however much the roots of this " spir-itual " dimension of man's life may be found within the levels of the higher organisms.[17] Man's self-transcendence is bound up with his awareness of claim from beyond himself. If we define the Other as the total process in which he is involved, his deepest im-mediate experience of the Other is of the claims that it lays upon him at all levels and to which he must consciously subject his own thought and behavior.

Another aspect of this self-transcendence lies in the capacity of personal being to unify past with present and to be conscious of a self-identity which can be extended into the future. The hu-man self is able to unify its experience in time. At the ethical level such self-identity is the root of the sense of moral responsibility and of the experience of guilt. The power of an ideal is rooted likewise in man's self-transcendence with the capacity of the self to extend itself in the future. Already at this ethical level, the re-ligious level is very evident, especially in the dimension of guilt and decision. All this would suggest that there is a dynamic con-tinuant which persists through the flux of becoming constituted by human experience. There is a continual unifying of experience and enriching of self for which memory is not a sufficient explana-tion. There must be a persistent center of dynamic activity, a con-tinuing ego, which is continually shaped and enriched by experi-ence, retains that experience through memory, and extends itself into the future by decisions in keeping with its essential nature. The latter is directed by that existential choice in which the individual ego decides its destiny. It is significant that though Hartshorne, following Whitehead, might seem to deny this aspect of being in human personal being, he yet has to postulate it in his bipolar understanding of a personal deity.

We may define this highest manifestation of the world process as " spirit." " Spirit " is the personal, and the movement of the universe is directed toward the emergence of the personal, of " spirit." For Christian thinkers such a valuation of experience springs directly from the Incarnation. Philosophizing that is Christian in intention will tend to choose " spirit " or " person " as the basic model or analogue rather than organism and, in this sense, the process theology and philosophy need to be modified.

Let us now look at the process as a movement toward the emergence of Spirit. Teilhard's suggestion that energy has what we might call a psychical as well as a physical component, the suggestion of thinkers like William Temple and H. W. Robinson (quoted above) that energy is akin to mind or spirit, the panpsychic views of Whitehead and his disciples, all indicate a new approach to the problem of matter. Three options are before the serious thinker as he looks at the major levels of reality — matter, organism or life, and person or spirit. The materialist will emphasize matter as the fundamental principle and regard all else as derivative. The naturalist increasingly tends to emphasize the organic model as fundamental. He never escapes his naturalism even if he postulates God, for even his God is conceived on the organic model. We have seen the difficulties faced by thinkers like S. Alexander and A. N. Whitehead at this point. We have noted how Hartshorne has, as a Christian thinker, to adopt a personalist position in seeking to frame an intelligible picture of deity. Equally, he and other naturalistic theists have difficulty in picturing personal self-identity and finding a place for what we have analyzed as personal self-transcendence. Finally, they so major on this world order, with which the dominant scientific method is concerned, that they have real difficulty in any case with divine transcendence also. Yet many of the insights garnered in this point of view need to be utilized by Christian thought, and the Christian thinker can be grateful for it. The third option is to emphasize the personal as the fundamental principle, recognizing that finite personal being, as we know it, has always a psychosomatic form, is embodied spirit.

Instead of speculating specifically along a panpsychic line that follows Leibnitz' monadology, it would seem to be more cautious to suggest that matter or energy has within it potentiality for the ultimate emergence of spirit and to regard the organismic level with its increasing psychic aspect as the first manifest sign of the emergence of spirit. This would suggest the kinship between matter and spirit or mind, and remove the danger of an ultimate dualism, without removing the ultimate mystery of reality. Furthermore, matter must be considered in its more dynamic aspect as energy and the temporal dimension acknowledged, as relativistic science has required. Teilhard's position would, at this point, seem more viable, with its emphasis on increasing complexification concomitant with increasing interiorization and developing consciousness, however rudimentary and confined, at the lower levels, to feeling. Here there is considerable agreement with the emphases of Whitehead and the process thinkers on "prehension" and feeling.

Whitehead's emphasis on the necessity of an extensive continuum gives a basis for the physical aspect of energy. The increasing differentiation of selfhood and the ultimate emergence of personal being in its uniqueness and freedom would seem to require such a differentiating medium.[18] The characteristic element of objectivity or over-againstness in the human consciousness and the differentiation of personal beings, the I from the Thou, point in the same direction. The realism manifested in both the Biblical disclosure and the various thinkers studied would likewise support this position. We might even suggest that such a physical and extensive continuum is a safeguard against any possibility of pantheistic mergence, with its denial of the true nature of the personal. Furthermore, the temporal aspect of this continuum makes process and the fulfillment of purpose both possible and a reality. If evolution and history are to be directed and meaningful, as Christian insight demands, we might expect development and differentiation in the temporal aspect also.

As spirit emerges more and more within this physical flux, we see certain aspects of its activity. In the first place, the movement toward increasing complexity of the energy is accompanied by increasing unification. Hence we have the development of higher wholes which manifest a capacity for response, increasingly conscious and also increasingly marked by a capacity to learn. At the biological level, organisms evidence a pattern of increasing differentiation in the functions and nature of their parts, and yet also a developing centralization of the nervous system. As Teilhard points out, there is evident a movement of interiorization, of feeling or consciousness. At the human level, we have a personal whole, a somatic and psychic structure integrated around a self-conscious center. The complex nervous structure of man, centralized in the cerebral cortex, is directed by an inner side, personal spirit, that makes him a psychosomatic whole. The integrating nature of the human spirit is manifested in the temporal aspect, as we have indicated above, in the operation of memory and anticipation, in which the psychosomatic nature of man and especially the cerebral cortex plays its full part. Man's body is not merely a differentiating medium; it is an integral aspect of his personal being. Through the long process of evolution, energy has been increasingly unified and centralized in its patterns until fully self-conscious life can emerge within its developed wholeness. This inner side of man's own being, his self-transcendent, self-conscious I-ness, points to an inner side that is more and more evident throughout the process.

In the second place, as spirit emerges within the increasing complexity of energy, there is manifested a capacity to transform the lower levels of reality out of which the new quality has emerged. The biological shows a transformation of the physical, just as the personal means a transformation of the biological. We can see this at the human level in the way in which the neurological phenomena and their cerebral accompaniments are transformed by spirit into sensations. As H. W. Robinson suggests: " They have been baptized, so to speak, into the spirit of man, when they emerge in consciousness." [19] By a kind of alchemy, the physiological becomes a sensation, the sensation is transformed into a percept, and the perceptions are integrated into concepts. We may believe that this kind of alchemy occurs wherever consciousness is present at however rudimentary a level.

This aspect of spirit immediately brings its corollary. So in the third place, let us note that spirit always works through and with the lower levels of reality as its media. As Bergson emphasized, life is grasped intuitively, an immediate feelingful awareness. So it is also with personal being or spirit, not only in the dimension of relationship to others, but also in our own self-consciousness. Yet this intuitive awareness is mediated to us through the physical or somatic structures of organisms and personal beings. Furthermore, the awareness is enriched as sympathetically we enter into the inner side of the other through the disclosures to us. At the human level, words and acts alike create disclosure situations in which the physical media make mutual communication and imaginative and sympathetic understanding possible. The initial apprehension thereby moves to a growing comprehension, although the mystery and hiddenness of the Other always remain. Whitehead, as we have seen, has argued that our human conscious experience suggests a paradigm for all entities, and the process thinkers have made a like contention. Intuition, disclosure, sympathy, imagination — all make possible a penetration into the inner side of reality. But let us note that this is the result of involvement. It is the self as agent that primarily grasps the presence of spirit at the various emergent levels of its activity.

The Involvement of God — His Transcendence and Immanence

It is significant that, at the human level and thus in dealing with history, both Teilhard and Hartshorne see love as the motivating principle. Teilhard sees spirit as a unifying principle binding persons together in love around a personal point Omega, already actualized in the process in Jesus Christ. He suggests a hyperpersonal goal for the whole created order in which individual persons, far from losing their individuality, become more fully individual and personal as they realize their personality in the mutual relationships of love. Hartshorne and the process thinkers likewise emphasize the historical process as directed by the love of God for his creatures and their love for him. Yet the difficulty of their line of thought in dealing with personal identity and personal survival makes their solution questionable. If God be personal, as they contend, it is difficult to understand how the value of personal beings to him as objects of his love can be understood unless they survive death as more than a memory in his developing experience.

The real difficulty in this line of thought lies in its fundamental adoption of an organic rather than a personal model. In that case, as with Hegel too, individual persons are but parts in a whole which is God. They serve their purpose, play their part in the divine theme, and give place to others. It is hard to perceive how the theme of love can really be fitted into an organismic model. As with personal being, so with the relationship of love in its full dimensions, such a model breaks down. Teilhard's approach avoids this. For him, God is not an inclusive organismically conceived whole, but a personal being whose transcendence is as significant as his immanence. There is an over-againstness, as well as a creative and sustaining presence in this way of thinking, which safeguards personal values. Panentheism is replaced by true theism.

We need, at this point, to look at how a personal model for the universe differs from an organic. The organic model recognizes the essential differences between the parts but regards the parts as complementary to one another. Its concern is fundamentally aesthetic, and it is at this level of order that Whitehead takes his stance. Individuality in the full sense is not possible in such a model, for differentiation is functional and within a whole. Indeed, it is only the whole that has full individuality.[20] This holds of the process philosophy, where only God is really pictured as personal in the full sense of that word. But personal being and human freedom demand more than this type of limited individuality. Moreover, personal relationships require more than aesthetic order. They require a moral order in which personal differences are matched with individuality, responsibility, and freedom of response. We cannot speak of complementarity at the personal level, for, in the full sense of personality, such a term does not apply. Furthermore, we cannot speak of a group of mutually related persons as constituting a personal whole. Hartshorne recognizes this when he states that he does "not see much to be said . . . for any group mind above the human individual." He adds, of course, "And below the mind of the entire cosmos." [21] But he can only hold fast to his last statement because of his organic model. As Macmurray reminds us: "Groups of persons are not individuals." [22] In a personal universe we have to think of relationships that allow for independence and individuality and that require a moral order. This is another reason why to speak of love is not applicable to what is basically organismic.

One other very evident weakness of the organismic model is its failure to find a place for the Christian understanding of creation. Much as the many insights of process-thought help a developed understanding of the Christian disclosure, the weakness at this point must be counted a major defect. It is at the root of the weakened presentation of the Christian understanding of man and of personal identity. The world and men are all derivative from the divine being. It would seem, on the reading of Whitehead which we have here accepted, that this philosopher thought of creativity as ontologically prior to both God and the world. God is not thought of as creator but as the one who gives the world its aesthetic order. The actual entities themselves are creative. Any philosophy grounded in this viewpoint will tend to have a weakened understanding of creation. Like Hegelian Absolute Idealism, it will tend to regard the creatures as moments in the divine experience. The organismic model inevitably moves this way, however much it may speak of the freedom, creativity, and independence of the various components of the world structure. In the end, as with Hegel, the world becomes a process in which

God, like a master egoist, is enriching his own life. Even his love for the creaturely is, reflectively, a love for himself. Human beings can persist through death only as themes in the divine memory, which plays upon them in ever-new combinations.

Such a view of God's immanence in the created order robs the creatures of the deep awareness of God's over-againstness. None would quarrel with the picture of God's inclusiveness as the creative ground of the being of his world. The creatures who are sustained and directed by his immanent activity have been called into being by an act of God's will and have been given by him a mode of reality appropriate to his purpose. As his creatures, he is ever present to them, but they are not simply passing elements of his experience, least of all man himself.

This does not indicate a denial that the created order, through its creation and providential ordering, is drawn up into God's experience, enriches his life, and serves in the fulfillment of his purposes. At this point, Hartshorne's understanding of God as bipolar offers a valuable insight to Christian thought. That God may be both being and becoming, as Hartshorne has contended, resolves many problems that classical theology and philosophy never have resolved. If a personal model of God be accepted, instead of an organismic one, this in no way reduces the cogency of this insight. God who is love may yet be thought of as so involved with his created order that his own life is enriched thereby. The Biblical testimony to the divine disclosure in history, culminating in the Incarnation, points to this. The Christian emphasis on a divine purpose, fulfilled in and through the created order, would seem to imply it. The Greek emphasis on divine perfection and impassibility has created an impasse for Christian theologians in past centuries. It sets the Biblical witness at odds with metaphysical expression and has imported alien ideas into theological thought. We shall here accept Hartshorne's definition of perfection, accept the essential Biblical disclosure of God's personal being as love, and suggest that this love is enriched through the experiences in which God is involved with his creatures.

This point comes to a metaphysical focus in the issue of time and eternity.[23] Evidently eternity in the sense of timelessness, as for the Greeks, finds no place for historical time and meaning in the divine life. The modified idea of eternity as gathering all temporal existence into God's " eternal now " so that our past, present, and future are always present in God's consciousness raises very real issues. How can the future be present to him, if it is still future to us, without raising real difficulties about divine omniscience and human freedom? Further, if purpose is already present to God as fulfilled, we have difficulty in envisaging what the historical actualization can mean to God. Problems like this have been dealt with adequately in Hartshorne's discussion of divine omniscience, already considered above, and we shall not fall into a needless repetition of them. At this point we would concur. If, then, we define eternity as " God's time " and regard his personal being as involving a dimension of enriching experience, we may suggest that one aspect of his perfection lies in a truth that the " eternal now " image seeks to emphasize. God's " now " is a moving now. As the living God, he lives through his experiences in a succession over which he has perfect control. By this we mean that the past of himself and his creatures is always perfectly retained in his present. Furthermore, although the details of the future lie within the free future activity of his creatures, God's intention for the future is sure and the ultimate outcome is certain. It is part of the divine self-limitation in the creation of the world that God knows the future as indeterminate, and lives in his own experience through his relationship to the free decisions and contingencies present in his created order. God knows the actual as actual and, in the future, the possible as possible, so that his knowledge is adequate to the future as it is adequate to the present.

In speaking of God's involvement in this way, we have yet to seek to understand what we mean by transcendence and immanence. Here the issue has become acute. The two-tier universe was long since discredited, but dimensional analogies still remain and are liable to misunderstanding, while they do not speak to the modern mind. Once more, it is to personal analogies that we must turn at this point. Two models suggest themselves, neither adequate alone but together offering a possible way of thought. They are personal self-transcendence and intrapersonal relationship.

The first model suggests that God is related to his world on the analogy of the self-transcendence of personal being. In this, the ego is both immanent at every level of the psychosomatic whole and yet transcends it in critical reflective and moral judgment. This analogy raises difficulties if pressed to the point of the panentheistic position, where the world becomes analogous to God's body. Our emphasis on the nature of creation means that God's immanence in his world must not be pressed too far. This model does, however, provide some understanding of what we might call the personal depth of our universe, reminding us that God is both personally present at every level of his created order, and yet transcends it as its dynamic directing and creative center. Always the world must not in any way be identified with God.

The last statement is met by the second model of intrapersonal relationship. Here an I and a Thou are personally related and also mutually transcendent. There is an over-againstness in which mutual involvement obliterates neither " Thou." Rather, they become more personal through their very relationship. Furthermore, sympathy and imagination make possible some penetration of the one by the other, while love and the subtle thing which we call influence help us to understand how personal being can stretch beyond its somatic frontiers to envelop the other. Now when we are speaking of infinite personal being, not limited by somatic frontiers, we may begin to understand how the infinite is related to the finite at the personal level. There is a transcendence and yet an immanence of God in his creatures which complements the insights of the first model. Yet further, true finite personhood is attained only through positive relationship to the infinite love which is God. This does not mean the annihilation of such personhood but its fulfillment, and is portrayed for us, in the history of Christian thought and experience, in the mutual indwelling of Christ and the believer.

The mutual envelopment of personal being at the finite level and still more in the relation of the believing man to personal deity may help us also to understand the trinitarian structure of the Christian thought of God. Hartshorne, as we have seen, suggests that God is social. Not quite in his sense but in accord with the views of the Cappadocian Fathers, we may think of God as a mutual involvement of three personal centers of infinite being in which each perfectly envelops the others and manifests that perfection of love which Christian disclosure declares to be the essence of God.[24] The classical trinitarian formula of *Perichoresis* or coinherence [25] gathers new meaning with this intrapersonal model as but an imperfect analogue. Father, Son, and Holy Spirit abide fully and perfectly in one another and yet each has his own personal subsistence. In the divine disclosure, the differentiation of the divine persons is in part functional. We might picture the Father as the mysterious depth of the divine being as love, the Son or Word as the personal movement of the triune God in creation and redemption, and the Holy Spirit as the immanent personal presence of God within the created order, including finite personal beings. It is at this point that we must return to further consideration of the divine involvement.

A Suffering God and an Unfinished Universe

The suggestion that the divine control over the world is that of " persuasion " presupposes that the world has an organic structure down to the most infinitesimal atomic entity. Attractive as this panpsychic hypothesis is, it raises serious questions in the light of the fact that the physical and the psychical manifest a prima facie difference. We have taken the line that energy is akin to spirit and has the potentiality for being ordered and transformed by it into higher orders of reality. It would not, however, appear justifiable to make any more sweeping judgment. Rather, we may think of the Creator as endowing energy at the physical level with certain inborn habits or modes of activity, which it is the task of physical science to investigate. Leonard Hodgson suggests that the analogy at this level might even be that of the potter and clay.[26] This suggestion is, he agrees, too deistic, for we have to do at this point also with a divine immanence. At the physical level, the created order must be envisaged as open to the divine directing and sustaining activity, and we may see the latter in the habitual forms of behavior which have been given to it. It provides the raw material within which the Creator intends to accomplish his purpose. As the energy becomes patterned into greater complexities, the new phenomenon of life begins to appear. At first, this, too, is so little different from the lower material level that it appears to move with the ebb and flow of energy itself. Then there comes evidence of sensation, feeling, rudimentary consciousness, and so, ultimately, personal beings emerge.[27]

It is at the level of the organic and the personal that we may speak to the divine relation to the created order as increasingly one of persuasion, of the constraint of love. Always, however, we need to envisage the divine immanence. God is personally present within his created order. Hodgson cogently expresses it.

His control of the whole process is continuous and intimate, and every fresh development in the course of what we call evolution is due to His communicating from the richness of His own being some new capacity to the more highly organised matter.[28]

The Old Testament vision of the Creator Spirit brooding over the deep at the moment of creation may point to a personal presence, within the created order, of a God who is also transcendent to the universe and who creates from such transcendence.

But if the creative Spirit is so involved in direct sustaining and creative activity, we need to remember also the element of kenosis. Infinite " Spirit " must always limit itself when it indwells and acts within the created and finite. H. W. Robinson defines " kenosis " as " the self-emptying and humiliation of Spirit when it expresses itself, as it always must, in ' degrees of reality ' lower than itself." [29] Thus God, who is present in and through the process of the created order at every level, yet hides himself with it and is to be found in, with, and under the activities, the emergent qualities, the unconscious and conscious responses, the free decisions of his creatures. He accompanies and directs the movement of his order, and increasingly, as consciousness develops and sensitivity of response becomes evident, his way with his creatures takes the form of a " persuasion " suitable to their level of being. In such an accompanying and direction, God accommodates himself to his creatures, so that his presence is not evident to scientific analysis. The hiddenness of God in his creation at every level is a sign of the kenosis of the Creator Spirit as he acts in intimate relationship with his creation.

Nor may we think of the divine experience at this level as without suffering. The presence of what we often call natural or physical evil in our world might suggest that the Creator is himself dealing with an irrational or surd element in his creation. It is not wise to build too much upon the present postulation of sub-atomic and atomic indeterminacy by quantum physicists, but the random element is still evident at the physical level and also at the biological level, as evolution makes clear. May we not imagine that God, in creating his world, allowed for the presence of an element of the contingent and the irrational? This is understandable if we see free personal beings living in mutual commitment and love as the goal of his purpose. Such personal freedom needs latitude at the physical level in which it can operate. It also needs challenge and opposition to make personal development possible and an area in which creative vision and activity can shape and mold the physical medium. But such aspects of personal being would be impossible were there to be a perfectly ordered physical system. We may think of the Creator creating a world in which contingency and opposing physical systems are possible and in which they also play a part in his purpose. If we were to devise a Platonic myth, we might speak of the Creator devising a world in which he can produce a freedom that is consonant with discipline. Like a divine teacher, he places free personal beings in a world where they are free to exercise their creative freedom and also where they are disciplined and challenged by opposing elements in their world. This is an unfinished world, and, at the stage when free personal being emerges, God calls men into full co-operative fellowship with himself in shaping his universe, bringing its disorderly and irrational elements into line with his purpose.[30]

Just at this point, the element of natural disorder and contingency that causes pain and suffering is matched by the contingency that arises from human freedom. The process of nature, with its challenge and discipline and the attendant evils of suffering, moves into the process of history with its perverted human relationships, its selfishness and egoism, its rebellion against God and man. Man refuses to cooperate with his Creator in shaping his world and fulfilling the divine purpose. And just at this point, the persuasive and redemptive activity of the divine love becomes most evident.

If God be involved with his creation, then we cannot speak of him as impassible. He has chosen to create a world in which contingency and its attendant pain and suffering are present. His omnipotence is the omnipotence of loving restraint. He sustains his creatures and endeavors to " persuade " them, as they become increasingly conscious and " prehensive," to take the way of his purpose. But he does not coerce them. His is the way of love and its concomitant discipline. The latter is manifest, in history and at the personal level, as judgment. We may think of judgment as that divine activity in which God gives men over to their false decisions and selfish ways until they create a disorder which may turn them back in penitence to seek his way. Thus he sets guiding rails for his world, a thought that seems absent from process-thinking! Yet the very restraint of love, the sustaining of a system in which suffering and pain are constituent, the preservation of egoistical and rebellious personal beings, the movement of judgment at the personal level, are ingredient in God's experience.

If the Spirit be the divine personal presence within the created order, then the kenosis of the Spirit is also a Calvary of the Spirit. Suffering is thereby lifted up into the life of God himself. If God is involved with his world and the world is within his experience, then the consequences of natural contingency and disorder and, still more, the historical actuality of man's sinful rebellion are within that experience. God feels with his creatures. He shares their joys and their success, but he also bears their sufferings and their failures, their sin and their judgment. At the level of sin, God in his holiness can only live with sinful rebellion and sustain it in suffering. Within his all-encompassing personal presence there are centers of resistance which in mercy he sustains. As H. W. Robinson suggests: " *The actuality we call sin is existent within God only as suffering.*" [31] Alien to his purpose, God yet bears it, and in and through his suffering he redeems men from the power of their own rebellion. Even in their judgment, he suffers, as a father suffers in the punishment of his son.

As Creator and immanent Spirit, God shares such experiences in their inner intensity, for he lives within his creatures in a way that finite persons are unable to live in one another. What imagination and sympathy provide for finite man is but a glimpse of what our human experience must mean in the experience of a God of love. Once more, the insights of Hartshorne are valuable here.

At the human level, the divine " persuasion " becomes manifest in those disclosure situations in which God brings men into decisive relationship with himself. Here the processes of nature and history are drawn up in a heightened way into the divine activity. God in his revelatory and redemptive activity as Son approaches men through the media of his created order. Through the levels of inanimate and animate nature but, most of all, through persons in their historical involvement, God creates disclosure situations in which men are confronted in a new way by his presence and are challenged to the decision of faith. The fact that faith is requisite is a reminder that God remains hidden even in his revelation and comes to us through the medium of his creatures. Thereby the kenosis of the Spirit is paralleled by the kenosis of the Word. God as Son/Word accepts the limitations of the media through which he comes and yet, in so doing, he lifts them more intimately into his own life and manifests the spiritual potentiality of the physical. So he uses nature, history, and the prophetic consciousness.

This self-emptying which is the basis of divine disclosure is brought to a focus in the Incarnation. Here the Son unites himself fully with one human life in all its dimensions. In Jesus of Nazareth, God fully actualizes his purpose in one life and creates a redemptive disclosure whereby his love can act persuasively and manifestly within the process of history. By "manifestly" is meant that the Incarnation draws others into new relationship with God so that, in and through their lives also, there comes a dependent disclosure of God's love. That love which, in a hidden way, is persuasively active throughout the universe, the processes of nature and history, becomes manifestly present most of all in the Incarnation, and thereby in the lives of all those who have decisively responded to the divine disclosures which are focalized in Jesus the Christ.

Central in the Incarnation, and consequently in the Christian faith, is the Cross. For the Incarnation means the identification of God with men, in every dimension of their creaturely being. In uniting himself personally with one human life in its perfection and total commitment to himself, God draws all human life more deeply into his own experience. He knows what it is to be man, to be a creature, as only a creature can know it. This is the ultimate meaning of kenosis. A process that begins in the accepted self-limitation through creation, with its contingency and freedom, moves to its climax in the Incarnation and reaches its supreme moment in the final identification of God with his world on Calvary.

The Cross provides a window into the heart of God. It discloses that, as Bonhoeffer put it, "Only a suffering God can help." [32] Here God's identification with his world and with his rebellious creatures reaches the nadir of suffering, through which he pours into his creation a redeeming love that embraces the universe. The suffering of God's world, the consequence of both natural contingencies and human sinful decisions, is ingredient within the divine experience and borne redemptively. God's very restraint in sustaining his world means suffering. The Incarnation is the manifestation of a love that wills to transform such suffering into redemption by a consummate historical act of identification. To quote Horace Bushnell:

It is as if there were a Cross unseen, standing on its undiscovered hill, far back in the ages, out of which were sounding always, just the same deep voice of suffering love and patience, that was heard by mortal ears from the sacred hill of Calvary.[33]

From Megapolis to Incarnapolis — The Cosmic Hope

The process of history becomes, through the Incarnation, a continuing incorporation of men and their environment more intimately within the life of God. As, in Jesus of Nazareth, one human life was lifted into personal union with God so, through the Christ, men are reconciled to one another and to God. The intended relationship of God to his creatures and of his creatures to one another is being actualized in history. The phrase " in history " needs emphasis. Christian redemption is not " out of " this world but " in " this world. It covers man in his psychosomatic wholeness and in his totality of relationships. By the last phrase is meant his relationship to his fellows, his social structures, and also his relationship to his natural environment, his scientific and technological activities, and his economic planning. It is man as a whole who is redeemed, for, in the Incarnation, God potentially lifted man, in the totality of his relationships, more intimately into his life.

This redemptive process in history is brought to a focus in the Body of Christ, the community of believing and committed persons. Bonhoeffer's memorable description of the Christian as one in whom the Christ is forming himself again [34] is a reminder of the centrality of the Christian community. But this implies that the function of the Church must be that of the Christ himself. It must be the way of costly discipleship, the path of the Servant, the road of sacrificial love and the Cross. The Servant Christ is the model for his Church.

Yet the movement of God in the process of history cannot finish here, in the light of our previous discussion. The so-called secular society, the megapolis of our time, is also within the divine experience, sustained by God's presence and open to his activity. The redeeming love disclosed in the Incarnation is operative throughout God's world, and Christian men have to realize this. They cannot turn their backs on the secular world and consign it to the devil. Nor can they dream of heaven, when eternal life has to be lived here and now in this so-called secular order.

We have seen that this secular order is largely the result of the emancipating disclosure of God's nature and purpose in Christ. Its secularized values and its humanism are grounded in God's presence and activity in his world. In Jesus, God says " Yes " to his world. Sometimes, however, contemporary theologians of secularity forget that God also says " No." For the secular order is subject to demonic distortion and egoistic perversion. It is under judgment, and so also is the Church.[35] In this sense it is borne in the divine suffering and subject always to the purgative movement of the wrath of God.

God has, however, said " Yes " to our world in Christ. Bonhoeffer reminds us:

It is now essential to the real concept of the secular that it shall always be seen in the movement of being accepted and becoming accepted by God in Christ. . . . The unity of the reality of God and of the world, which has been accomplished in Christ, is repeated, or, more exactly, is realized, ever afresh in the life of men.[36]

History becomes history with God's consent. It takes on a new seriousness in Jesus Christ. So secular society, with its humanism and its secularized values, shows signs of the actualization of God's purpose. It contributes to the completion of his unfinished universe. We see this in modern science and technology, which have so much influenced the emergence of modern secular man. In them, man is learning to control his environment, to improve his own somatic and psychological structures, and to cooperate, often unconsciously, with his Creator in the movement of creation to the ultimate actualization of the divine purpose. In social reform and economic planning, again, the pressures of our time are forcing men, as Teilhard saw so prophetically, into a new understanding of community and cooperation. Man is being confronted, often unknowingly at the conscious level, by the claims and pres-

ence of God. He is related to God even though he does not acknowledge it — another aspect of the divine " persuasion."

This is indeed a sacramental universe. As God lifts it up into his
experience, so he also confronts men through it. Often scientific
insights bear the marks of divine disclosure.[37] Again, did not our
Lord indicate that to give a cup of cold water is to respond to him
without knowing it? The programs for reconstructing society and
of concern for the victims of injustice, inequality, and deprivation
are within the divine experience and responses to the divine presence and claim. We can believe that all such are gathered up in
the life of God and woven into the theme of the final consummation of his purpose.

What the Incarnation does for us is to enthrone the personal in
the heart of the universe, to make us aware that the Other who
everywhere supports and resists us is a personal presence. The
impersonal aspect of the universe is an abstraction of which science gives us increasing knowledge. Yet just as in our encounter
with another " Thou," at the level of finite personal beings, we
may treat them impersonally as objects or commit ourselves to
personal relationships with them, so with the universe. The world
becomes more than a system of physical energy, just as other persons become more than complex somatic aggregations. Actually
if I am a personal being, an agent who acts intentionally, and if I
treat the universe as impersonal, then I am concluding irrationally
that I am not a part of the world in which I act.[38] The disclosure
of the Incarnation puts this right. It enables us to see this universe
as everywhere shot through by the intention of infinite personal
being.

Yet it does more than this. It promises us that what has taken
place in the Incarnation is the manifestation of the divine intention. God discloses himself redemptively so that the Incarnation
contains the potential of a redemption in which the whole secular
order shall be gathered up and fulfilled in intimate union with
God. As God experiences this created order in suffering, so he
also transmutes that suffering through redemptive love and brings
his creatures, by the persuasion of that love, into closer relation-

ship to himself. That the demonic and sinful perversions of his world are subject to his judgment is but one aspect of this. The Cross reminds us that even God suffers under the crises of judgment and lifts them up into his redemptive purpose. Moreover, as the divine intention is actualized in the concrete existence of our universe, there is added to the divine experience the joy that is born of the actualization of purpose. Just as the artist finds self-fulfillment as his creative vision takes concrete form in paint or stone, so we may think of God as finding personal enrichment in the concrete actuality in which his creative vision finds expression. In this way, megapolis is potentially Incarnapolis, and may become so as men cooperate consciously and unconsciously with God, and as the demonic and sinful perversions are purged away.

Because of this, we may speak of the cosmic hope that ultimately God's purpose will be actualized at all levels of his creation, and he will be all in all. We can speak here only in mythical language. Men's social structures, with their actualization of personal values, and men's scientific achievements, with their increasing control over the natural order, will be gathered by God into his ultimate consummation. A transfigured universe, as Teilhard sees it, lies before humanity. It will be a transfigured universe in which man as personal being will become fully personal as God relates his creatures fully to one another and to himself in love. At the end stands the symbol of the Parousia. This is a reminder that what God has potentially achieved in the Incarnation will be consummated when the whole universe is gathered into the life of God. But it also is a reminder that the natural disorder and sinful rebellion of God's world must finally be judged and annihilated as they have been potentially already in the Incarnation.

NOTES

Chapter I. *The Problem of a Christian Philosophy*

1. *Vide* especially Frederick P. Ferré, *Language, Logic and God* (Harper & Row, Publishers, Inc., 1961); Ian T. Ramsey, *Religious Language* (London: SCM Press, Ltd., 1957); William Hordern, *Speaking of God* (The Macmillan Company, 1964); John A. Hutchison, *Language and Faith* (The Westminster Press, 1963). I have sought to deal with the issue in shorter compass in *Science and Faith: Towards a Theological Understanding of Nature* (Oxford University Press, Inc., 1967), pp. 111 ff.

2. We would mention Ian T. Ramsey, ed., *Prospect for Metaphysics* (London: George Allen & Unwin, Ltd., 1961); Michael Polanyi, *Personal Knowledge* (The University of Chicago Press, 1958); John Macquarrie, *Principles of Christian Theology* (Charles Scribner's Sons, 1966).

3. Dorothy M. Emmet, *The Nature of Metaphysical Thinking* (London: Macmillan & Co., Ltd., 1945), p. 194.

4. Cited in Herbert A. Hodges, *Wilhelm Dilthey: An Introduction* (London: Routledge & Kegan Paul, Ltd., 1944), p. 156.

5. Hodges, *op. cit.*, p. 154.

6. R. G. Collingwood, *An Essay on Metaphysics* (Oxford: At the Clarendon Press, 1940), p. 47.

7. Polanyi, *Personal Knowledge*, *passim*.

8. Emmet, *The Nature of Metaphysical Thinking*, p. 200.

9. *Ibid.*, p. 5.

10. Paul Tillich, *Systematic Theology* (3 vols., 1951, 1957, 1963, The University of Chicago Press), Vol. I, p. 58.

11. Julian Langmead Casserley, *The Christian in Philosophy* (Charles Scribner's Sons, 1951), p. 69.

12. Macquarrie, *op. cit.*, p. 15.

13. Michael Polanyi, *Science, Faith and Society* (The University of Chicago Press, 1964), p. 67.

14. Dietrich Bonhoeffer, *Letters and Papers from Prison,* ed. by Eberhard Bethge (The Macmillan Company, 1962), p. 164.

15. *Vide* especially Thomas J. J. Altizer, *The Gospel of Christian Atheism* (The Westminster Press, 1966).

16. *Vide* the volume ed. by James M. Robinson and John B. Cobb, *The Later Heidegger and Theology* (Harper & Row, Publishers, Inc., 1963).

17. *Vide* especially Tillich, *Systematic Theology,* 3 vols.

18. Tillich, *Systematic Theology,* Vol. I, p. 210.

19. Tillich, *Systematic Theology,* Vol. II, p. 14.

20. Howard Root, "Metaphysics and Religious Belief," in Ramsey, ed., *op. cit.,* p. 79.

21. Roger Mehl, *The Condition of the Christian Philosopher,* tr. by Eva Kushner (Fortress Press, 1963), pp. 23 ff.

22. *Ibid.,* p. 29.

23. *Ibid.,* p. 31.

24. *Ibid.,* pp. 29 f.

25. *Ibid.,* pp. 29, 94.

26. *Ibid.,* p. 205.

27. Casserley, *op. cit.,* p. 21.

28. Macquarrie, *op. cit.,* p. 50.

29. Casserley, *op. cit.,* p. 225.

30. Ninian Smart, "Revelation, Reason and Religions," in Ramsey, ed., *op. cit.,* p. 84.

Chapter II. *The Absolute Spirit and Process — From Being to Becoming*

1. John N. Findlay, *Hegel: A Re-examination* (Collier Books, 1962), p. 38.

2. G. W. F. Hegel, *The Phenomenology of Mind,* tr. by J. B. Baillie (The Macmillan Company, 1931), p. 80.

3. Findlay, *op. cit.,* p. 40.

4. G. W. F. Hegel, *The Philosophy of History,* tr. by J. Sibree (Dover Publications, Inc., reprint, 1956), p. 9.

5. Findlay, *op. cit.,* p. 40.

6. G. W. F. Hegel, *The Philosophy of Nature* (Dover Publications, Inc.), pp. 47–48. We note the incursion of Christian terminology. We must refer to this later.

7. Findlay, *op. cit.,* p. 42.

8. Hegel, *The Philosophy of Nature,* p. 47.

9. Hegel, *The Phenomenology of Mind,* p. 808.

10. G. W. F. Hegel, *Logic,* tr. by W. Wallace in *Encyclopaedia of the Philosophical Sciences* (Oxford: At the Clarendon Press, 1892), p. 180.

11. Cf. G. W. F. Hegel, *The Philosophy of Spirit*, tr. by W. Wallace in *Encyclopaedia of the Philosophical Sciences*, p. 163. Quoted in Findlay, *op. cit.*, p. 35.

12. Findlay, *op. cit.*, p. 36.

13. Hegel, *The Philosophy of History*, p. 10.

14. Cf. Hegel, *The Philosophy of History*, p. 457.

15. Findlay, *op. cit.*, p. 333.

16. George Boas, *Dominant Themes of Modern Philosophy* (The Ronald Press Co., 1957), p. 561.

17. Hegel, *The Philosophy of History*, pp. 17 f.

18. From *Reason in History*, II, cited from James D. Collins, *God in Modern Philosophy* (Henry Regnery Co., Publishers, 1959), p. 230.

19. Collins, *op. cit.*, p. 230.

20. Eric C. Rust, *Towards a Theological Understanding of History* (Oxford University Press, Inc., 1963), p. 56.

21. *Vide* Findlay, *op. cit.*, p. 334.

22. Findlay, *op. cit.*, p. 339.

23. Cf. G. W. F. Hegel, *Introduction to the Philosophy of Art*, Loewenberg's Selections (Charles Scribner's Sons, 1929), p. 314.

24. Findlay, *op. cit.*, p. 132.

25. G. W. F. Hegel, *Lectures in the Philosophy of Religion*, tr. by E. B. Speirs and J. Burdon Sanderson (London: Kegan Paul, Trench, Trubner & Co., 1895), Vol. I, p. 132.

26. *Ibid.*, p. 33.

27. George F. Thomas, *Religious Philosophies of the West* (Charles Scribner's Sons, 1965), p. 275.

28. Findlay, *op. cit.*, p. 142.

29. Cf. Findlay, *op. cit.*, p. 140: " But this procession to otherness is at the same time a return to self, since the conscious Son, and the Father of whom He is conscious, are one and the same reality. We have, therefore, the materials for a Trinity consisting of the Essence, of the self-conscious being that knows it, and of the knowledge of the former in the latter."

30. Hegel, *Lectures in the Philosophy of Religion*, Vol. III, p. 108, quoted in G. F. Thomas, *op. cit.*, pp. 282 f.

31. Walter T. Stace, *The Philosophy of Hegel* (Dover Publications, Inc., reprint 1955), p. 513. Remember that, for Hegel, " God " is simply a symbolic expression for the Absolute Spirit.

32. Quoted in Findlay, *op. cit.*, p. 42.

33. Findlay, *op. cit.*, p. 141.

34. Hegel, *The Phenomenology of Mind*, p. 780.

35. *Ibid.*, p. 781.

36. *Ibid.*, p. 782.

37. *Ibid.*

38. *Ibid.*, p. 783.

39. Collins, *op. cit.*, p. 234.

40. Cf. Hegel, *Lectures in the Philosophy of Religion*, p. 199.

41. Cf. *ibid.*, p. 81.

42. Hegel, *The Phenomenology of Mind*, p. 85.

43. *Ibid.*, p. 800.

44. *Vide* Findlay, *op. cit.*, pp. 145 f., where the discussion is particularly helpful.

45. *Vide* Hegel, *The Philosophy of Mind*, tr. by W. Wallace in *Encyclopaedia of the Philosophical Sciences* (London: Oxford University Press, 1964), pp. 183 ff.

46. Schmidt, tr., *Hegel's Lehre von Gott*, p. 189. Cited from G. F. Thomas, *op. cit.*, p. 280.

47. Rust, *Towards a Theological Understanding of History*, p. 57.

48. Altizer, *The Gospel of Christian Atheism*, pp. 102 f.

49. Collins, *op. cit.*, p. 236.

50. Cf. Rust, *Towards a Theological Understanding of History*, pp. 58 ff. For Benedetto Croce's own writings, consult especially *History: Its Theory and Practice*, tr. by Douglas Ainslie, 2 vols. (Russell and Russell, Inc., Publishers, 1960); *History as the Story of Liberty*, tr. by Sylvia Sprigge (London: George Allen & Unwin, Ltd., 1941).

51. Croce, *History: Its Theory and Practice*, p. 25.

52. Benedetto Croce, *Aesthetic*, tr. by Douglas Ainslie, 2d ed. reprint (Noonday Press, 1953), p. 64.

53. Rust, *Towards a Theological Understanding of History*, p. 60.

54. Cf. *ibid.*, pp. 9 f.

55. Cf. Ludwig Feuerbach, *The Essence of Christianity*, tr. by George Eliot (Harper Torchbooks, Harper & Row, Publishers, Inc., 1957), p. 5.

56. Cf. Karl Löwith, *From Hegel to Nietzsche*, tr. by David E. Green (Holt, Rinehart and Winston, Inc., 1964), pp. 78 ff.

57. Karl Barth, Introductory Essay, tr. by David E. Green, p. xiv, in *The Essence of Christianity*.

58. Löwith, *op. cit.*, p. 80.

Chapter III. *From Process and Naturalism to Creative Evolution and Emergent Deity*

1. Note especially Herbert Spencer, *First Principles* (Appleton, 1896); *Principles of Biology* (London, 1898); *Principles of Sociology* (London, 1876).

2. *The Autobiography of Charles Darwin, 1809–1882, with Original Omissions Restored*, ed. by Nora Barlow (Harcourt, Brace and World, Inc., 1959), p. 87.

3. Theodosius G. Dobzhansky, *Mankind Evolving* (Yale University Press, 1962).

4. R. A. Fisher, *Creative Aspects of Natural Law* (London: Cambridge University Press, 1950).

5. *Ibid.*, p. 18.

6. William H. Thorpe, *Biology and the Nature of Man* (London: Oxford University Press, 1962). See also L. Charles Birch, *Nature and God* (The Westminster Press, 1965).

7. Frederick Engels, *Feuerbach: The Roots of the Socialist Philosophy*, tr. by A. Lewis (Charles H. Kerr & Company, 1919), pp. 65 ff.

8. M. Shirokov and J. Lewis, *Textbook of Marxist Philosophy* (London, n.d.), p. 341. Quoted in J. Needham, *Time: The Refreshing River* (London: George Allen & Unwin, Ltd., 1943), p. 189.

9. Joseph Stalin, *Dialectical and Historical Materialism* (International Publishers, 1940), p. 11.

10. *Ibid.*, p. 7.

11. *Ibid.*

12. B. Zavadovsky, " The Physical and the Biological in the Process of Organic Evolution," in *Science at the Cross Roads* (London, 1931). Quoted in Needham, *op. cit.*, p. 244.

13. See also Frederick Engels, *Anti-Dühring*, tr. by Emile Burns (International Publishers, 1939); *Dialectics of Nature*, tr. by Clemens Dutt (International Publishers, 1940). In these books Engels does, of course, deal with the issue of history.

14. Engels, *Feuerbach*, p. 102.

15. Engels, *Anti-Dühring*, p. 54.

16. Engels, *Feuerbach*, pp. 103 f.

17. *Ibid.*, pp. 104 f.

18. Engels, *Dialectics of Nature*, p. 19.

19. *Ibid.*

20. Marx and Engels, *The Holy Family*, p. 172. Quoted in Robert C. Zaehner, *Matter and Spirit* (Harper & Row, Publishers, Inc., 1963), p. 166.

21. Engels, *Dialectics of Nature*, p. 164.

22. Zaehner, *op. cit.*, p. 177.

23. Engels, *Dialectics of Nature*, p. 21.

24. *Ibid.*, p. 25.

25. A. Lloyd Morgan, *Emergent Evolution* (London: Williams and Norgate, Ltd., 1927), pp. 2 ff.

26. C. D. Broad, *The Mind and Its Place in Nature* (London: Kegan Paul, Trench, Trubner & Co., 1925), p. 69.

27. Morgan, *op. cit.*, p. 1.

28. *Ibid.*, p. 5.

29. *Ibid.,* p. 7.

30. *Ibid.,* p. 8.

31. *Ibid.,* p. 20.

32. *Ibid.,* p. 36.

33. *Ibid.,* p. 33.

34. *Ibid.,* p. 209.

35. S. Alexander, *Space, Time and Deity* (London: Macmillan & Co., Ltd., 1920), Vol. I, pp. 38 ff.

36. Alexander, *op. cit.,* Vol. II, p. 69.

37. *Ibid.,* p. 70.

38. Errol E. Harris, *Nature, Mind and Modern Science* (London: George Allen & Unwin, Ltd., 1954), p. 401.

39. Broad, *op. cit.,* pp. 610 and 648 ff.

40. Alexander, *op. cit.,* Vol. II, p. 428.

41. *Ibid.,* p. 346.

42. *Ibid.,* p. 347.

43. *Ibid.,* p. 348.

44. *Ibid.,* p. 361.

45. Cf. *ibid.,* p. 349.

46. *Ibid.,* p. 350.

47. *Ibid.,* p. 357.

48. *Vide* Jan C. Smuts, *Holism and Evolution* (The Viking Press, Inc., 1961).

49. Harris, *op. cit.,* p. 408.

50. *Ibid.*

51. Alexander, *op. cit.,* Vol. II, p. 419.

52. A stone in flight, suddenly becoming self-conscious, might feel itself to be free, and yet actually its flight is already determined.

53. Alexander, *op. cit.,* Vol. II, p. 315.

54. Harris, *op. cit.,* p. 394.

55. Thomas M. Forsyth, *God and the World* (London: George Allen & Unwin, Ltd., 1952), p. 94.

56. Henri L. Bergson, *Creative Evolution,* tr. by A. Mitchell (Modern Library, Inc., 1944), p. 194.

57. *Ibid.,* p. 182.

58. *Ibid.,* p. 166.

59. *Ibid.*

60. *Ibid.*

61. *Ibid.,* p. 167.

62. *Ibid.,* p. 194.

63. Cf. *ibid.,* p. 195.

64. *Ibid.,* p. 332.

65. Cf. Henri L. Bergson, *The Two Sources of Morality and Re-*

ligion, tr. by R. A. Audra and C. Brereton (London: Macmillan & Co., Ltd., 1935), *passim.*

Chapter IV. *An Organismic Universe and God the Fellow Traveler*

1. Lionel S. Thornton, *The Incarnate Lord* (London: Longmans, Green & Co., 1928).
2. Dorothy M. Emmet, *Whitehead's Philosophy of Organism* (London: Macmillan & Co., Ltd., 1932).
3. *Vide* later, Ch. V.
4. Smuts, *Holism and Evolution.*
5. *Ibid.,* pp. 97 f.
6. *Ibid.,* p. 86.
7. *Ibid.,* p. 114.
8. *Ibid.,* p. 115.
9. *Ibid.,* p. 117.
10. *Ibid.,* p. 145.
11. *Ibid.,* p. 178.
12. Henri Breuil, *Beyond the Bounds of History* (London: P. R. Gawthorn, Ltd., 1949), p. 9. Cited in Charles E. Raven, *Teilhard de Chardin: Scientist and Seer* (Harper & Row, Publishers, Inc., 1962), p. 51.
13. Alfred North Whitehead, *Science and the Modern World* (London: Cambridge University Press, 1932), p. 22.
14. Cf. *ibid.,* p. 62.
15. Hume argued that the causal connection between empirical sense data, so separated into discrete entities, could not be rationally inferred or demonstrated. On the basis of this strict empiricism, causation was not a matter of logical inference but of " natural belief."
16. Whitehead, *Science and the Modern World,* pp. 68 f.
17. Cf. Rust, *Science and Faith: Towards a Theological Understanding of Nature,* Ch. II. I have developed the idea of models here in greater detail and also the criticism of current scientific naturalism or scientism. To enter into such lengthy criticism above would not contribute to the purpose of our study.
18. Whitehead, *Science and the Modern World,* pp. 134 f.
19. *Ibid.,* p. 135.
20. *Ibid.*
21. *Ibid.,* p. 140.
22. *Ibid.,* p. 141.
23. Allison H. Johnson, *Whitehead's Theory of Reality* (Beacon Press, Inc., 1952), p. 162.
24. Whitehead, *Science and the Modern World,* pp. 90 f.

25. Emmet, *Whitehead's Philosophy of Organism,* p. 87.

26. Whitehead, *Science and the Modern World,* p. 91.

27. Alfred North Whitehead, *Process and Reality* (London: Cambridge University Press, 1929), p. 35.

28. *Ibid.,* p. 34.

29. *Ibid.,* p. 91.

30. Alfred North Whitehead, *Adventures of Ideas* (Mentor Books, 1955), p. 197.

31. *Ibid.,* p. 195.

32. *Ibid.,* p. 179.

33. *Ibid.,* p. 195.

34. Forsyth, *op. cit.,* p. 109.

35. Whitehead, *Process and Reality,* p. 31.

36. *Ibid.*

37. Forsyth, *op. cit.,* p. 111.

38. I am aware that Whitehead's concept of "creativity" is by no means clear. There are those who would contend with Johnson (*op. cit.,* p. 69) that "he does not regard *creativity* as more ultimate than actual entities." Such critics would contend that references which indicate otherwise are due to Whitehead's occasional carelessness. Yet the influences of Aristotle and Spinoza are markedly present in Whitehead's thought, and I would prefer to think of "creativity" rather along the lines of Aristotle's matter or even Spinoza's substance. Indeed, Whitehead himself writes: "In the analogy with Spinoza, his one substance is for me the one underlying activity of realization individualizing itself in an interlocking plurality of modes. Thus, concrete fact is process" (*Science and the Modern World,* p. 87). Johnson points out that in *Process and Reality,* he seems to suggest that "creativity" is an eternal object which is realized in actual entities (p. 28). He also writes: "Creativity is not an external agency with its own ulterior purposes. (It is not an actual entity.) All actual entities share with God this characteristic of self-causation." (*Ibid.,* p. 339.) Now this last reference could also be understood in the way advocated in this book. Whitehead does tell us that "creativity is the ultimate behind all forms, inexplicable by form, and conditioned by *its creatures*" (*ibid.,* p. 27, italics mine). Again, he speaks of creativity as "universal throughout actuality" (*ibid.,* p. 229). The truth is that Whitehead is not clear at this point, and we must not try to make him coherent where such coherence seems lacking or, if present, is very imperfectly expressed.

39. Whitehead, *Process and Reality,* p. 487.

40. *Ibid.,* p. 363. God is also described as "the outcome of creativity" (*ibid.,* p. 122).

41. *Ibid.*, p. 488.
42. *Ibid.*, p. 487.
43. *Ibid.*, p. 486.
44. G. F. Thomas, *Religious Philosophies of the West,* pp. 366 f.
45. Whitehead, *Process and Reality,* p. 489.
46. *Ibid.*, p. 487.
47. Alfred North Whitehead, *Religion in the Making* (London: Cambridge University Press, 1927), p. 140.
48. *Ibid.*, pp. 143 f.
49. *Ibid.*, p. 140.
50. *Ibid.*, pp. 91 f.
51. Whitehead, *Process and Reality,* p. 492.
52. *Ibid.*, pp. 492 f.
53. William Temple, *Nature, Man and God* (The Macmillan Company, 1934), p. 258.
54. Whitehead, *Process and Reality,* p. 497.
55. Alfred North Whitehead. Source not identified.
56. Whitehead, *Religion in the Making,* pp. 59 f.
57. Temple, *Nature, Man and God,* p. 263.
58. *Vide* Alfred N. Whitehead, *The Function of Reason* (Beacon Press, Inc., 1958), *passim.*
59. *Ibid.*, p. 8.
60. *Ibid.*, p. 90.
61. *Ibid.*, p. 89.
62. Temple, *Nature, Man and God,* p. 260.
63. Whitehead, *Science and the Modern World,* p. 238.
64. Cf. Whitehead, *Religion in the Making,* pp. 50 ff.
65. *Ibid.*, p. 50.
66. Whitehead, *Science and the Modern World,* p. 238.
67. John B. Cobb, Jr., *A Christian Natural Theology* (The Westminster Press, 1965), p. 218.
68. *Ibid.*
69. Whitehead, *Process and Reality,* p. 47.
70. Cf. Whitehead, *Process and Reality,* pp. 46 f.
71. John B. Cobb, Jr., gives a detailed and informative analysis of this, *op. cit.*, pp. 54 f.
72. Whitehead, *Adventures of Ideas,* p. 189.
73. Cobb, *op. cit.*, pp. 71 ff.
74. Whitehead, *Process and Reality,* p. 225 (italics mine).
75. G. F. Thomas, *op. cit.*, p. 387.

Chapter V. *From Immanence to Transcendence*

1. William Temple, *Mens Creatrix* (London: Macmillan & Co., Ltd., 1917); *Christus Veritas* (London: Macmillan & Co., Ltd., 1924); *Nature, Man and God* (London: Macmillan & Co., Ltd., 1934).

2. Temple, *Nature, Man and God*, p. 130.

3. *Ibid.*, p. 129.

4. *Ibid.*, p. 219.

5. Owen C. Thomas, *William Temple's Philosophy of Religion* (London: S.P.C.K., 1961), p. 147.

6. Temple, *Nature, Man and God*, p. 87.

7. *Ibid.*, p. 88.

8. Temple, *Mens Creatrix*, p. 15. Cf. *Nature, Man and God*, p. 90.

9. Michael Foster, *Mind*, N.S. CLVII (Jan., 1931), pp. 7 ff. *Vide* Temple, *Nature, Man and God*, pp. 97 ff.

10. Foster, *op. cit.*, p. 15.

11. *Ibid.*, p. 17.

12. Temple, *Mens Creatrix*, p. 17.

13. Temple, *Nature, Man and God*, p. 100.

14. Cf. Rust, *Science and Faith: Towards a Theological Understanding of Nature*, pp. 46, 50, 60 f., 315.

15. Temple, *Mens Creatrix*, p. 154.

16. *Ibid.*, p. 155.

17. *Vide* Ch. I.

18. Temple, *Nature, Man and God*, p. 109.

19. *Ibid.*, p. 111.

20. *Ibid.*, pp. 112 and 121.

21. *Ibid.*, p. 122.

22. *Ibid.*

23. *Ibid.*, p. 129.

24. *Ibid.*

25. *Ibid.*, p. 130.

26. *Ibid.*, p. 133.

27. *Ibid.*

28. *Ibid.*, p. 153.

29. *Ibid.*, p. 155.

30. *Ibid.*, p. 156.

31. *Ibid.*, p. 161.

32. *Ibid.*, p. 196.

33. *Ibid.*, p. 265.

34. *Ibid.*, pp. 289 f.

35. *Ibid.*, p. 267.

36. *Ibid.*

37. *Ibid.*
38. *Ibid.*, p. 269.
39. *Ibid.*, p. 298.
40. *Vide ibid.*, pp. 306 f.
41. *Ibid.*, p. 306.
42. *Ibid.*, p. 315.
43. *Ibid.*, p. 314.
44. *Ibid.*
45. *Ibid.*
46. *Ibid.*, pp. 366 f.
47. *Ibid.*, p. 366.
48. *Ibid.*, p. 369.
49. *Ibid.*, pp. 435 f.
50. *Ibid.*, p. 437.
51. *Ibid.*, p. 438.
52. Temple, *Mens Creatrix*, p. 357.
53. Temple, *Nature, Man and God*, p. 447.
54. Temple, *Christus Veritas*, p. 187.
55. Temple, *Nature, Man and God*, p. 448.
56. *Ibid.*
57. *Ibid.*, pp. 479 f.
58. *Ibid.*, p. 301.
59. *Ibid.*, p. 443.
60. *Ibid.*, p. 447.
61. *Ibid.*
62. *Ibid.*
63. Cf. *ibid.*, p. 480.
64. *Ibid.*, p. 448.
65. *Ibid.*, p. 449.
66. Temple, *Christus Veritas*, p. 190.
67. Temple, *Nature, Man and God*, p. 493.
68. *Ibid.*, p. 481.
69. *Ibid.*, pp. 444 f.
70. *Ibid.*, p. 444.
71. *Ibid.*, p. 445.
72. *Ibid.*, p. 477.
73. *Ibid.*, p. 493.
74. *Ibid.*, p. 484.
75. *Ibid.*, p. 494.
76. *Ibid.*, p. 495.
77. Quoted in Frederick A. Iremonger, *William Temple, Archbishop of Canterbury: His Life and Letters* (London: Oxford University Press, 1948), p. 531.

78. *Ibid.*, pp. 531 f.

79. Owen C. Thomas, *op. cit.*, p. 139.

Chapter VI. *Beyond the Biosphere and Toward the Omega Point*

1. Pierre Teilhard de Chardin, *The Phenomenon of Man,* tr. by Bernard Wall (Harper & Row, Publishers, Inc., 1959), p. 178, n. 1.

2. Pierre Teilhard de Chardin, *The Vision of the Past,* tr. by J. M. Cohen (Harper & Row, Publishers, Inc., 1967), p. 123. This is the book in which he defends the theory of evolution.

3. *Ibid.*, p. 20.

4. Indeed, in a letter cited in Claude Cuénot, *Teilhard de Chardin,* tr. by Vincent Colimore (Helicon Press, Inc., 1965), pp. 225 f., Teilhard accuses Husserl and Merleau-Ponty of ignoring "one of the most essential dimensions of the Phenomenon; this consists not only in being perceived by an individual consciousness, but also in making it clear to that consciousness, at the same time, that it is included in a universal process of 'noogenesis.' I do not understand how anyone can call himself a 'phenomenologist' and write whole books without ever mentioning or touching on cosmogenesis and evolution." He accuses certain philosophers of still moving in "a pre-Galilean universe."

5. From *Le Phénomène humain* (1930), in *Oeuvres* III 228–229. Cited in Christopher F. Mooney, *Teilhard de Chardin and the Mystery of Christ* (Harper & Row, Publishers, Inc., 1966), p. 37.

6. Teilhard, *The Phenomenon of Man,* p. 33.

7. *Ibid.*, p. 35.

8. *Ibid.*, p. 34.

9. *Ibid.*, p. 57, n. 1.

10. Teilhard, *Oeuvres II* (1956), p. 298, n. 2. Cited in Piet F. Smulders, *The Design of Teilhard de Chardin,* tr. by Arthur Gibson (The Newman Press, 1967), p. 30.

11. Teilhard, *The Phenomenon of Man,* p. 30.

12. *Ibid.*, p. 35.

13. Pierre Teilhard de Chardin, *The Future of Man,* tr. by Norman Denney (Harper & Row, Publishers, Inc., 1964), p. 96. Cf. also Pierre Teilhard de Chardin, *The Divine Milieu* (Harper & Row, Publishers, Inc., 1960), pp. 37 f. Here he suggests that "some of the best of the Gentiles" see Christianity as not leading its followers "beyond humanity, but away from it or to one side of it."

14. Teilhard, *The Vision of the Past,* p. 23.

15. Teilhard, *The Phenomenon of Man,* p. 42.

16. *Ibid.*, p. 51.

17. *Ibid.*

18. *Ibid.*, p. 52.
19. Cf. *ibid.*, p. 56.
20. *Ibid.*
21. Cf. *ibid.*, p. 57.
22. In *ibid.*, p. 64, Teilhard states, "We shall assume that, essentially, all energy is *psychical* in nature." The translator has inadvertently rendered the French word "psychique" as physical, so our English translation needs to be corrected at this point.
23. *Ibid.*, p. 65.
24. *Ibid.*
25. *Ibid.*, p. 62.
26. *Ibid.*, p. 78.
27. *Ibid.*, p. 301.
28. *Ibid.*, pp. 72 f. Cf. Pierre Teilhard de Chardin, *Man's Place in Nature*, tr. by René Hague (Harper & Row, Publishers, Inc., 1966), pp. 17–36.
29. Teilhard, *Man's Place in Nature*, p. 32.
30. Teilhard, *The Phenomenon of Man*, p. 110.
31. Cf. *ibid.*, pp. 110 f.
32. Theodosius G. Dobzhansky, *Heredity and the Nature of Man* (Signet Book, New American Library, Inc., 1966), p. 152.
33. Teilhard, *The Phenomenon of Man*, p. 180.
34. *Ibid.*, p. 159.
35. *Ibid.*, p. 160. It is interesting how the poet in Teilhard de Chardin leads him to use physical analogies in this way. He writes that "when the anthropoid, so to speak, had been brought 'mentally' to boiling point some further calories were added. Or, when the anthropoid had almost reached the summit of the cone, a final effort took place along the axis." *Ibid.*, p. 163.
36. Teilhard, *Man's Place in Nature*, pp. 62 f.
37. Teilhard, *The Phenomenon of Man*, p. 159.
38. *Ibid.*, p. 171.
39. Teilhard, *Man's Place in Nature*, p. 94.
40. *Ibid.*, pp. 96 ff.
41. *Ibid.*, p. 98.
42. Teilhard, *The Future of Man*, pp. 113 f.
43. Teilhard, *The Phenomenon of Man*, p. 222.
44. Teilhard, *The Future of Man*, p. 40.
45. Teilhard, *The Phenomenon of Man*, p. 256.
46. Cf. Teilhard, *Man's Place in Nature*, p. 100.
47. Teilhard, *The Future of Man*, p. 54.
48. Teilhard, *The Phenomenon of Man*, p. 259.
49. *Ibid.*, p. 261.

50. *Ibid.*, p. 262.

51. Mooney, *op. cit.*, pp. 52 f.

52. Teilhard, *The Future of Man*, p. 119.

53. *Ibid.*, p. 119.

54. Mooney, *op. cit.*, p. 53.

55. Smulders, *op. cit.*, p. 112.

56. Teilhard, *The Future of Man*, p. 75.

57. Teilhard, *The Phenomenon of Man*, p. 269.

58. *Ibid.*

59. *Ibid.*, p. 270.

60. *Ibid.*

61. Teilhard, *Man's Place in Nature*, p. 121.

62. Teilhard, *The Vision of the Past*, p. 23.

63. Teilhard, "How I believe" (Peiping, 1936. Privately printed for circulation to personal friends only. Printer H. Vetch, Grand Hotel de Pekin).

64. Teilhard, *The Phenomenon of Man*, p. 294.

65. Teilhard, *The Future of Man*, p. 34.

66. Pierre Teilhard de Chardin, *Hymn of the Universe*, tr. by Simon Bartholomew (Harper & Row, Publishers, Inc., 1965), p. 76.

67. Teilhard, *The Future of Man*, p. 304, from an early writing of 1916, *La Vie Cosmique*.

68. Teilhard, *The Divine Milieu*, p. 94.

69. From "Super-humanité," quoted in Claude Tresmontant, *Pierre Teilhard de Chardin*, tr. by S. Attanasio (Helicon Press, Inc., 1959), p. 74.

70. *Ibid.*, p. 75. Also quoted from "Super-humanité."

71. Teilhard, *The Phenomenon of Man*, p. 294.

72. From *Le coeur de la matière*, cited in Tresmontant, *op. cit.*, p. 76.

73. Teilhard, *The Divine Milieu*, p. 101.

74. Teilhard, *The Future of Man*, p. 305.

75. Smulders, *op. cit.*, p. 122.

76. Teilhard, *The Divine Milieu*, p. 30.

77. *Ibid.*, p. 101.

78. Cf. *ibid.*, p. 133.

Chapter VII. *Being and Becoming — A Dipolar Deity*

1. Henry Nelson Wieman, *The Source of Human Good* (The University of Chicago Press, 1946).

2. Charles Hartshorne, *Reality as Social Process* (The Free Press of Glencoe, Inc., 1953); *Man's Vision of God* (Willett, Clark & Co.,

1964); *The Divine Relativity* (Yale University Press, paperback, 1964); *The Logic of Perfection* (The Open Court Publishing Company, 1962); Charles Hartshorne with William L. Reese, *Philosophers Speak of God* (The University of Chicago Press, 1953).

3. Daniel Day Williams, *God's Grace and Man's Hope* (Harper & Row, Publishers, Inc., 1949).

4. Cobb, *A Christian Natural Theology.*

5. Schubert M. Ogden, *Christ Without Myth* (Harper & Row, Publishers, Inc., 1961).

6. Richard H. Overman, *Evolution and the Christian Doctrine of Creation* (The Westminster Press, 1967).

7. Hartshorne, *Reality as Social Process*, p. 34.

8. *Ibid.*, p. 132.

9. *Ibid.*, p. 34.

10. *Ibid.*

11. *Ibid.*, pp. 132 f.

12. Cf. *ibid.*, p. 34.

13. *Ibid.*, p. 35.

14. Hartshorne, *The Logic of Perfection*, p. 309.

15. *Ibid.*, p. 213.

16. *Ibid.*, p. 191.

17. *Ibid.*, p. 192.

18. Hartshorne, *Reality as Social Process*, p. 133.

19. *Ibid.*, p. 134.

20. *Ibid.*, p. 36.

21. *Ibid.*, p. 35.

22. *Ibid.*, p. 36.

23. *Ibid.*, p. 134.

24. *Ibid.*, p. 135.

25. Charles Hartshorne. Source not identified.

26. Hartshorne, *The Divine Relativity*, p. 33.

27. Hartshorne, *Man's Vision of God*, p. 151.

28. *Ibid.*, p. 152.

29. Cf. Hartshorne's quotation from Plato, *ibid.*, p. 153.

30. *Ibid.*, p. 152.

31. *Ibid.*, p. 154.

32. Cf. Hartshorne, *Reality as Social Process*, pp. 54 ff.

33. Hartshorne, *Man's Vision of God*, p. 154.

34. Hartshorne, *Reality as Social Process*, p. 39.

35. *Ibid.*, pp. 38 ff.

36. *Ibid.*, p. 98.

37. *Ibid.*

38. Hartshorne, *The Divine Relativity*, p. 69.

39. Hartshorne, *Philosophers Speak of God*, p. 509.

40. *Ibid.*, p. 2b. This essay offers the clearest statement of Hartshorne's position.

41. *Ibid.*, p. 2b.

42. *Ibid.*, p. 4b.

43. Hartshorne, *Man's Vision of God*, p. 107.

44. *Ibid.*, p. 133.

45. *Ibid.*

46. *Ibid.*, p. 234.

47. *Ibid.*, p. 237.

48. Hartshorne, *Reality as Social Process*, p. 24.

49. Hartshorne, *Philosophers Speak of God*, p. 4b.

50. Hartshorne, *The Divine Relativity*, p. x.

51. Cf. Hartshorne, *Man's Vision of God*, pp. 36 f.

52. *Ibid.*, p. 234.

53. Cf. *ibid.*, p. 237.

54. Hartshorne, *The Divine Relativity*, pp. 88 f.

55. *Ibid.*, p. 89.

56. *Ibid.*, p. 90.

57. *Ibid.*, pp. 19 f.

58. Cf. Hartshorne, *Philosophers Speak of God*, p. 10b.

59. Cf. Hartshorne, *Man's Vision of God*, pp. 11 f., and *Reality as Social Process*, pp. 155 f.

60. Cf. Hartshorne, *Reality as Social Process*, p. 23.

61. *Ibid.*, p. 147.

62. Hartshorne, *Man's Vision of God*, p. 114.

63. *Ibid.*, p. 117.

64. *Ibid.*, p. 161.

65. Hartshorne, *The Divine Relativity*, p. 25.

66. *Ibid.*, p. xvii.

67. *Ibid.*, pp. xvii, 142.

68. *Ibid.*, p. 142.

69. *Ibid.*, p. 136.

70. Cf. Hartshorne, *Reality as Social Process*, p. 136.

71. Charles Hartshorne, "Omnipotence," in *An Encyclopedia of Religion*, ed. by Vergilius T. Ferm (Philosophical Library, Inc., 1945), p. 546a.

72. Cf. *ibid.*, p. 547a.

73. Hartshorne, *Philosophers Speak of God*, p. 15.

74. Cobb, *op. cit.*

75. *Ibid.*, p. 252.

76. *Ibid.*, pp. 75 ff.

77. *Ibid.*, p. 78.

78. Hartshorne, *The Logic of Perfection,* p. 261.
79. *Ibid.,* p. 262 (italics mine).
80. Cobb, *op. cit.,* p. 66, n. 49, also pp. 63 f.
81. *Ibid.,* p. 65.
82. *Ibid.,* pp. 65 ff.
83. *Ibid.,* p. 70.
84. Above, pp. 116 ff.
85. Cobb, *op. cit.,* p. 188.
86. *Ibid.*
87. *Ibid.,* pp. 188, 190 f.: God's " unity must be complete."
88. *Ibid.,* p. 245.
89. *Ibid.,* p. 243 (italics mine).
90. *Ibid.,* p. 195.
91. *Ibid.,* p. 245.

Chapter VIII. *Theistic Faith in a Secular Society*

1. Ronald Gregor Smith, *Secular Christianity* (Harper & Row, Publishers, Inc., 1966), p. 153.
2. Cf. Rust, *Science and Faith: Towards a Theological Understanding of Nature,* Ch. I.
3. H. H. Farmer, *The World and God* (London: James Nisbet & Co., Ltd., 1935).
4. Karl Heim, *God Transcendent,* tr. by Edgar P. Dickie (London: James Nisbet & Co., Ltd., 1935); *Christian Faith and Natural Science,* tr. by Neville H. Smith (London: SCM Press, 1953); *The Transformation of the Scientific World View,* tr. by W. A. Whitehouse (London: SCM Press, 1953).
5. Henry Wheeler Robinson, *The Christian Experience of the Holy Spirit* (London: James Nisbet & Co., Ltd., 1930), p. 84.
6. Julian Huxley, *Evolution in Action* (Harper & Row, Publishers, Inc., 1953).
7. Thorpe, *Biology and the Nature of Man,* p. 16.
8. *Vide* Rust, *Science and Faith: Towards a Theological Understanding of Nature,* pp. 172 ff. and *passim;* also *Towards a Theological Understanding of History, passim.*
9. *Vide* Rust, *Science and Faith: Towards a Theological Understanding of Nature,* pp. 172 ff. and 211 f.
10. John Macmurray, *The Person as Agent* (Harper & Row, Publishers, Inc., 1957); *Persons in Relation* (Harper & Row, Publishers, Inc., 1961).
11. Rust, *Science and Faith: Towards a Theological Understanding of Nature, passim.*

248   *Notes*

12. Macmurray, *Persons in Relation*, p. 209.

13. John Macmurray, *Interpreting the Universe* (London: Faber & Faber, Ltd., 1936), p. 128.

14. Macmurray, *Persons in Relation*, p. 209.

15. Macmurray, *Interpreting the Universe*, p. 134.

16. *Ibid.*, p. 136.

17. Cf. Thorpe, *op. cit.*, p. 59.

18. Cf. Rust, *Science and Faith: Towards a Theological Understanding of Nature*, pp. 272 ff.

19. Robinson, *The Christian Experience of the Holy Spirit*, p. 76.

20. Cf. Macmurray, *Interpreting the Universe*, pp. 139 f.

21. Hartshorne, *Reality as Social Process*, p. 62.

22. Macmurray, *Interpreting the Universe*, p. 140.

23. Cf. Rust, *Towards a Theological Understanding of History*, pp. 206 ff.

24. This has been developed in Robinson, *The Christian Experience of the Holy Spirit*, pp. 271–281; Rust, *Science and Faith: Towards a Theological Understanding of Nature*, pp. 188 f. and p. 189, n. 86.

25. *Vide* John N. D. Kelly, *Early Christian Doctrines* (Harper & Row, Publishers, Inc., 1959), pp. 264 f.

26. Leonard Hodgson, *Towards a Christian Philosophy* (London: James Nisbet & Co., Ltd., 1942), p. 163.

27. Cf. *ibid.*, pp. 169 f.

28. *Ibid.*, p. 170.

29. Robinson, *The Christian Experience of the Holy Spirit*, p. 87.

30. *Vide* Rust, *Science and Faith: Towards a Theological Understanding of Nature*, pp. 300 ff.; A. Farrer, *Love Almighty and Ills Unlimited* (Doubleday & Company, Inc., 1961, pp. 47 ff.); Leonard Hodgson, *For Faith and Freedom* (Charles Scribner's Sons, 1957), pp. 192–217. Hodgson's treatment is lucid and illuminating.

31. Henry Wheeler Robinson, *Suffering Human and Divine* (London: SCM Press, Ltd., 1940), p. 198.

32. Bonhoeffer, *Letters and Papers from Prison*, p. 220.

33. H. Bushnell, *The Vicarious Sacrifice* (London: Alexander Strahan, 1866), p. 31.

34. Dietrich Bonhoeffer, *Ethics*, tr. by Neville Horton Smith (The Macmillan Company, 1955), pp. 18 ff.

35. Cf. Rust, *Towards a Theological Understanding of History*, pp. 254 ff.

36. Bonhoeffer, *Ethics*, p. 65.

37. Cf. Rust, *Science and Faith: Towards a Theological Understanding of Nature*, pp. 313 ff.

38. Cf. Macmurray, *Persons in Relation*, p. 221.

Index